Praise for *Consuming Fire*

"A daily devotional featuring the words and spiritual insights of George MacDonald was a wonderful idea, and *Consuming Fire*, named after MacDonald's great sermon of the same name, may be the perfect introduction to his reflections on God and Christian living. For those who already know and love these sermons, it will provide them with an opportunity to meditate daily on the spiritual insights contained therein."
---Thomas Talbott, author of the critically acclaimed book, *The Inescapable Love of God*

"Pastors often read classic sermons when preparing their own messages. In reading some of the great preachers of the past, I've sometimes thought, 'This guy is brilliant!' But when I came to read the *Unspoken Sermons* of George MacDonald, the thought that came to me was, 'This guy knows Jesus,' and I saw my need to know Him better. This devotional, *Consuming Fire*, will give any reader fresh ways to ponder the scripture and the One toward whom the scripture points."
--John Kermott, Pastor, First Baptist Church of Sterling, IL

"At first glance, Jess Lederman's notion of a year-long series of meditations on the thought of George MacDonald seemed dubious; should not one simply be directed to read MacDonald himself? After reading the first meditations, however, I became convinced that here was a brilliant introduction to and recommendation of MacDonald. Lederman gently brings the reader under the spell of George MacDonald, and illustrates for the modern reader why we owe MacDonald for Lewis."
--Lynn E. Mitchell, Jr., Ph.D.,Clinical Professor and Director of Religious Studies, Retired, University of Houston

"C. S. Lewis once remarked that George MacDonald was his master. I think of MacDonald as a modern staretz, someone who enjoyed a profound relationship with God and intimately knew the depths of His love and mercy. The daily reflections of *Consuming Fire* are a wonderful way to enter into MacDonald's vision of the Father and the life freely given in Jesus Christ."
--Fr. Alvin Kimel, *Eclectic Orthodoxy*, a theological blog devoted to the Gospel of Jesus Christ, the Church Fathers, and the Orthodox faith

"In his lifetime, George MacDonald would often give poems or prose for publication to help raise funds for various charities. If my great-great-grandfather were here today, I am convinced that ALS is a cause to which he would have given an entire novel. Lou Gehrig's Disease is a heartbreaking affliction, and organizations such as the ALS Therapy Development Institute deserve all our support to help eradicate it. I very much hope this wonderful devotional, *Consuming Fire*, will raise both awareness and much needed funds to this end."
--Christopher Peter MacDonald, great-great grandson of George MacDonald

Consuming Fire:

The Inexorable Power of God's Love

A Devotional Version of
Unspoken Sermons by

George MacDonald

*To all who have been afflicted with ALS;
to all the caregivers;
to all those searching for a cure*

CONTENTS

FOREWORD

The writings of nineteenth century Scotsman George MacDonald have changed countless lives through the decades. MacDonald's keen insight into the human condition and the love of God's Fatherhood have given solace, comfort, and insight to many in the midst of their suffering. His writings strike so deep into the heart because MacDonald himself was well acquainted with chronic illness, disease, and the death of family members.

The human condition has not changed since MacDonald's time. Life still brings suffering in its wake. Perhaps one of the deepest forms of human anguish of all is to watch a loved one suffer. George MacDonald was acquainted with this grief as well, having to endure the death of two of his own children.

These selections compiled by Jess Lederman were chosen for the comfort they brought him and his wife as she endured the pain of ALS. Out of his acquaintance with that grief he now offers this compilation of peace-giving words from George MacDonald, hoping they will give comfort to both the sufferers and their caregivers as they walk what can be a lonely road.

I love the wisdom found in the writings of George MacDonald. This new devotional drawn from his works is a wonderful addition to the growing body of MacDonald literature, and I heartily recommend it!

Michael Phillips

PREFACE

My first wife and I came to Christ due to the transcendent writings of George MacDonald (1824-1905), the Scottish author, poet, and Christian minister whom C.S. Lewis referred to as his "master." At the time that she was diagnosed with ALS (Lou Gehrig's disease), we had read a third of his fifty or so published works, and it was an unspeakable pleasure, comfort, and inspiration during the two years of her affliction to read every word of the rest. Perhaps nowhere are MacDonald's theology and his passionate love of God and man so eloquently expressed as in the three volumes of his *Unspoken Sermons*, of which Lewis remarked that "my debt to this book is almost as much as one man can owe to another." *Consuming Fire*, a devotional version of Unspoken Sermons, contains a little over half of the text of the original, and each of the thirty-six sermons are presented in order, edited down to 365 entries. While, unlike a traditional devotional, each page is not strictly stand-alone, my objective has been to make each day's entry a complete, coherent thought. It is my fervent hope that *Consuming Fire* captures the essence of MacDonald's thinking, and will inspire readers new to his luminous prose to read the complete *Unspoken Sermons* and many more of his works. A wonderfully useful source of information on MacDonald is the George MacDonald Society's website, *The Golden Key*, at george-macdonald.com. Those of you who are old hands at MacDonald's writing already know that repeated readings yield ever new, ever thrilling insights; and I trust that this devotional will give you ample opportunity for further meditation on his words.

As of this writing, ALS is an invariably fatal, untreatable disease. Blessed with faith, my wife put her trust in God; if it were not to be his decision to cure her, but rather for her to have to patiently endure his Consuming Fire, then so be it; his will be done. But she and I knew in our bones that he wanted us to join the effort to find a cure, to end the suffering that so many tens of thousands are going through each year. To that end, we committed to giving to and raising money for the ALS Therapy Development Institute (ALSTDI) of Cambridge, MA, the world's leading nonprofit biotechnology organization dedicated to finding a cure and effective treatments for ALS. The work they are doing is beyond compare. 100% of the royalties from sales of *Consuming Fire* go to ALSTDI. I encourage you to visit their website (als.net) and support their inspired and tireless efforts.

May the grace of the Lord Jesus, and the love of God, and the fellowship of the Holy Spirit be with you.

Jess Lederman
onesimus@worksofmacdonald.com

INTRODUCTION

In his sermon entitled *The Mirrors of the Lord*, George MacDonald states that "of all writers I know, {the apostle} Paul seems to me the most plainly, the most determinedly practical in his writing. What has been called his mysticism is at one time the exercise of a power of seeing, as by spiritual refraction, truths that had not, perhaps have not yet, risen above the human horizon." Just the same could be said of MacDonald himself, and nowhere more so than in the three volumes of his *Unspoken Sermons*, in which he explores profound theological ideas—but all for the purpose of bringing even the simplest actions of our daily lives into the service of Christ.

Although volume I was published in 1867, volume II in 1885, and volume III in 1889, the thirty-six sermons form a marvelously unified whole. Even a casual reader will note that within each volume, the concluding line of every sermon but the last introduces the principal subject of the next sermon. But the deeper unity of this masterpiece of Christian thought is based on the compelling way MacDonald interweaves and develops several major themes, which are summarized briefly in the paragraphs below.

The second sermon of volume I, inspired by a verse from Hebrews, introduces the powerful motif of God as *The Consuming Fire*. God is one, and God is love; he is not sometimes a God of wrath and other times a God of love. Do we then teach that men have nothing to fear from God? By no means! "For Love loves unto purity," and is oft experienced as wrath, as the consuming fire that will not be content until our sinful nature, everything that separates us from God, is burned away. Twenty-two years after the publication of volume I, MacDonald developed these ideas at length in what may be his most influential sermon, *Justice*. "God's anger," MacDonald wrote, "is at one with his love;" so, too, God's mercy and his justice are one and the same. Mercy and punishment are not opposed; for punishment—the consuming fire—is a means to an end, that we might be the creatures he intended us to be. God's punishment, his justice, can be his most merciful act.

Many Christians think of salvation as synonymous with going to heaven and avoiding hell. But the Son has called us to be perfect, even as our Father, and in *The Hardness of the Way*, MacDonald affirms that "salvation *is* perfection." We are perfect when we are one with God. *In Abba, Father!* he writes, nothing will satisfy {God}, or do for us, but that we be one with our father." Many there are whose goal is to live forever in heaven; but in *The Way*, MacDonald writes "without oneness with God, mere existence would be but a curse." Eternal life itself *is* oneness with God, is perfection, is salvation.

And how to achieve this salvation? The consuming fire will not do all the work for us; "we must *choose* to be divine," MacDonald exhorts us in *The Creation in Christ*, "to be one with God." But a monster bars our way: the willful, prideful *self*. "The self is given to us," the Scottish seer points out in *Self-Denial*, "that we may sacrifice it." But this would be impossible, he reminds us, were it not for Christ. MacDonald rejects the notion that Christ took suffering meant for us upon himself—that would be injustice to him and to us alike, for God's punishment, his consuming fire, is essential to our salvation—rather, Christ "died that I may be like him," he writes in *Justice*, "{and} die to any ruling power in me but the will of God." Sixty years later, C.S. Lewis would lay out a similar theory of the atonement in *Mere Christianity*.

MacDonald has no patience for mere doctrine, no matter how clever, how insightful, how correct; the thing that matters is not to hold a set of beliefs about Christ, but to *live as he lived*, to "take the will of God as the very life of our being." "To follow him," he says, "is to leave one's self behind." We are not saved through beliefs *about* Christ, interpretations of why he died on the cross, or faith in what he accomplished, but through *faith in him*. And what does it mean to have faith in Christ Jesus?

In a word: *obedience.*

If we seek first to puzzle out a system of belief, a scheme of salvation, we are lost; obey first, and understanding will follow. In *The Truth in Jesus*, MacDonald writes that "it is the one terrible heresy of the church, that it has always been presenting something other than obedience as faith in Christ." The essential truth of Jesus is his absolute obedience to the Father. As disciples, as followers of Christ, we do as he did, for "the doing of the will of God is the way to oneness with God." The Lord's words to us are clear; the example of his life is clear; if we have faith in him, it means we do the things he has told us to do, live as he lived.

But shall we then despair? For who can obey what Jesus asks of us in the Sermon on the Mount? "Obedience," explains MacDonald, "is not perfection, but trying." God "knows that you can try, and that in your trying and failing he will be able to help you, until at length you shall do the will of God even as he does it himself." "Ever aiming at the perfection of God," MacDonald writes in *Righteousness*, is the very meaning of obedient faith in Christ. Put our whole heart into this, and, as MacDonald describes in *The Mirrors of the Lord*, Christ "works upon us, and will keep working till we are changed to the very likeness we have thus mirrored in us; for with his likeness he comes himself, and dwells in us."

We could never be satisfied with the legal fiction of imputed righteousness while holding on to our sins; our goal is the perfection of God. So we take the Lord at his word; we endeavor to love our neighbor, to love our enemy, to leave all behind and follow him. He has asked these things of us because they *are* possible, and the obedient faith shown by striving steadfastly after them is "called by God as righteousness in a man." Only in this way can we achieve the joy we are constantly searching for and failing to find. "Our relations with others," says MacDonald, "God first and then our neighbor, must one day become the gladness of our being."

George MacDonald is known today as a "universalist," or believer in universal reconciliation, which holds that all souls will ultimately be reconciled to God. While MacDonald never to my knowledge used those terms himself, he certainly believed that God would never abandon any of his creatures. In *The Last Farthing,* he paints a picture of what hell might be like, a grotesquely bleak vision of man alone with his own self, utterly bereft of the presence of God, which, unbeknownst to him, had been all that had ever made life bearable in the past. It is similar to the hell that C.S. Lewis imagines, in which the gates are locked from the inside; but where MacDonald differs is in his belief that such an existence would be impossible for any man to abide. At some point, the faintest glimmer of repentance would lighten the utter blackness of the prison of self. And so MacDonald imagines "a thousand steps up from the darkness, each a little less dark, a little nearer the light—but ah, the weary way! He cannot come out until he will have paid the uttermost farthing! Repentance once begun, however, may grow more and more rapid! If God once gets a willing hold, if with but one finger he touches the man's self, swift as possibility will he draw him from the darkness into the light."

I conclude this introduction by considering the theme which MacDonald chose for the very first sermon of volume I: *The Child in the Midst.* "He who receives a child in the name of Jesus," he writes, "does so perceiving wherein Jesus and the child are one." Why is this so significant? Because we must know God "as he is. To know him is to have him in us." We must understand the childlike nature of Father and Son to be one with them, and we must grasp how this nature should be manifest in us.

What is the childlike nature? "The child sees, believes, obeys— and knows he must be perfect as his father in heaven." The child who obeys is far ahead of the learned scholar, with his grand theological systems, but who does not do what the Lord has asked. MacDonald observes that the Lord's parables "are addressed to the conscience, and not to the intellect;" and so "many meaningless interpretations may be given by the wise, while work goes undone, while the child who uses them for the necessity of walking in the one path will constantly receive light from them." "And so "it is the heart of the child that alone can understand the Father."

In *The Voice of Job*, MacDonald describes Job as "bemoan{ing} himself like a child—a brave child who seems to himself to suffer wrong." Job's continual complaints "are but the form his faith takes in his trouble." As a true child of God, he trusts in the Father, "and looks to him as the source of life, the gladness of being."

Ah, dear reader, God willing, so shall we all!
Jess Lederman

THE CHILD IN THE MIDST

"And he came to Capernaum: and, being in the house, he asked them, What was it that ye disputed among yourselves by the way? But they held their peace: for by the way they had disputed among themselves who should be the greatest. And he sat down, and called the twelve, and saith unto them, If any man desire to be first, the same shall be last of all, and servant of all. And he took a child, and set him in the midst of them; and when he had taken him in his arms, he said unto them, Whosoever shall receive one of such children in my name, receiveth me; and whosoever shall receive me, receiveth not me, but him that sent me."

Mark 9:33-37

JANUARY 1ST

Nothing is required of man that is not first in God. It is because God is perfect that we are required to be perfect. And it is for the revelation of God to all, that they may be saved by knowing him, and so becoming like him, that a child is set before them in the gospel. It is the recognition of childhood as divine that will show the disciples how vain is the strife after relative place or honor in the great kingdom. He who receives a child in the name of Jesus, does so perceiving wherein Jesus and the child are one. He must not only see the *ideal* child in the child he receives—that reality of loveliness which constitutes true childhood—but must perceive that the child is like Jesus, or rather, that the Lord is like the child, and may be embraced, yea, *is* embraced, by every heart childlike enough to embrace a child for the sake of his childness. A special sense, a lofty knowledge of blessedness, belong to the act of embracing a child as the visible likeness of the Lord himself. For the blessedness is the perceiving of the truth, that the Lord has the heart of a child.

But the argument of the meaning of our Lord's words, *in my name*, is incomplete until we follow to its second and higher stage: "He that receiveth me, receiveth him that sent me." The Son is as the Father; he whose heart can perceive the essential in Christ, has the essence of the Father. To receive a child in the name of Jesus is to receive Jesus; to receive Jesus is to receive God; therefore to receive the child is to receive God himself.

JANUARY 2ND

What is the kingdom of Christ? A rule of love, of truth—a rule of service. The king is the chief servant in it. "The kings of the earth have dominion: it shall not be so among you." The great Workman is the great King, laboring for his own. So he that would be greatest among them, and come nearest to the King himself, must be the servant of all. It is *like king, like subject* in the kingdom of heaven. No rule of force, as of one kind over another kind. It is the rule of *kind*, of *nature*, of deepest nature—of *God*. If, then, to enter into this kingdom, we must become children, the spirit of children must be its pervading spirit throughout, from lowly subject to lowliest king. The lesson added by St. Luke is: "For he that is least among you all, the same shall be great." And St. Matthew says: "Whosoever shall humble himself as this little child, the same is greatest in the kingdom of heaven." Hence the sign that passes between king and subject. The subject kneels in homage to the kings of the earth: the heavenly king takes his subject in his arms. This is the sign of the kingdom between them. This is the all-pervading relation of the kingdom.

JANUARY 3RD

To receive the child because God receives it, or for its humanity, is one thing; to receive it because it is like God, or for its childhood, is another. The former will do little to destroy ambition. Alone it might argue only a wider scope to it, because it admits all men to the arena of the strife. But the latter strikes at the very root of emulation. As soon as even service is done for the honor and not for the service-sake, the doer is that moment outside the kingdom. But when we receive the child in the name of Christ, the very childhood that we receive to our arms is humanity. We love its humanity in its childhood, for childhood is the deepest heart of humanity—its divine heart; and so in the name of the child we receive all humanity.

If there is in heaven a picture of that wonderful teaching, doubtless we shall see represented in it a dim childhood shining from the faces of all the disciples, of which the center is the Son of God with a child in his arms. The childhood, dim in the faces of the men, must be shining trustfully clear in the face of the child. But in the face of the Lord himself, the childhood will be triumphant—all his wisdom, all his truth upholding that radiant serenity of faith in his father. Verily, O Lord, this childhood is life. Verily, O Lord, when thy tenderness shall have made the world great, then, children like thee, will all men smile in the face of the great God.

JANUARY 4TH

To receive a child in the name of God is to receive God himself. How to receive him? As alone he can be received— by knowing him as he is. To know him is to have him in us.

Although the true heart may at first be shocked at the truth, as Peter was shocked when he said, "That be far from thee, Lord," yet will it, after a season, receive it and rejoice in it. Let me then ask, do you believe in the Incarnation? And if you do, let me ask further, Was Jesus ever less divine than God? I answer for you, Never. He was lower, but never less divine. Was he not a child then? You answer, "Yes, but not like other children." I ask, "Did he not look like other children?" If he looked like them and was not like then, the whole was a deception, a masquerade at best. I say he was a child, whatever more he might be. God is man, and infinitely more. Our Lord is, and ever shall be, divinely childlike. He could never have been a child if he would ever have ceased to be a child, for in him the transient found nothing. Childhood belongs to the divine nature. Obedience, then, is as divine as Will, Service as divine as Rule. How? Because they are one in their nature; they are both a doing of the truth. The love in them is the same. The Fatherhood and the Sonship are one, save that the Fatherhood looks down lovingly, and the Sonship looks up lovingly. Love is all. And God is all in all. He is ever seeking to get down to us—to be the divine man to us. And we are ever saying, "that be far from thee, Lord!" We are careful, in our unbelief, over the divine dignity, of which he is too grand to think.

JANUARY 5TH

Better pleasing to God, it needs little daring to say, is the audacity of Job, who, rushing into his presence, and flinging the door of his presence-chamber to the wall, like a troubled, perhaps angry, but yet faithful child, calls aloud in the ear of him whose perfect Fatherhood he has yet to learn, "Am I a sea or a whale, that thou settest a watch over me?"

Let us dare, then, to climb the height of divine truth to which this utterance of our Lord would lead us. Does it not lead us up hither; that the devotion of God to his creatures is perfect? That he does not think about himself but about them? That he wants nothing for himself, but finds his blessedness in the outgoing of blessedness.

Ah! It is a terrible—shall it be a lonely glory this? We will draw near with our human response, our abandonment of self in the faith of Jesus. He gives himself to us—shall not we give ourselves to him? Shall we not give ourselves to each other whom he loves?

For when is the child the ideal child in our eyes and to our hearts? Is it not when, with gentle hand, he takes his father by the beard, and turns that father's face up to his brothers and sisters to kiss? When even the lovely selfishness of love-seeking has vanished, and the heart is absorbed in loving?

JANUARY 6TH

In this then, is God like the child: that he is simply and altogether our friend, our father—our more than friend, father, and mother—our infinite love-perfect God. Grand and strong beyond all that human imagination can conceive of poet-thinking and kingly action, he is delicate beyond all that human tenderness can conceive of husband or wife, homely beyond all that human heart can conceive of father or mother. He has not two thoughts about us. With him all is simplicity of purpose and meaning and effort and end—namely, that we should be as he is, think the same things, possess the same blessedness. It is so plain that anyone may see it, everyone ought to see it, everyone shall see it. It must be so. He is utterly true and good to us, nor shall anything withstand his will.

How terribly, then, have the theologians misrepresented God as a great King on a grand throne, thinking how grand he is, and making it the business of his being and the end of his universe to keep up his glory, wielding the bolts of a Jupiter against them that take his name in vain. They would not admit this, but follow what they say and it comes much to this. Brothers, have you found our king? There he is, kissing little children and saying they are like God. There he is at table, with the head of a fisherman lying on His bosom, and somewhat heavy at heart that even he, the beloved disciple, cannot yet understand him well. The simplest peasant who loves his children and his sheep were a true type of our God compared to that monstrosity of a monarch.

JANUARY 7TH

The God who is ever uttering himself in the changeful profusions of nature; who takes millions of years to form a soul that shall understand him and be blessed; who never needs to be, and never is, in haste; who welcomes the simplest thought of truth or beauty as the return for seed he has sown upon the old fallows of eternity, who rejoices in the response of a faltering moment to the age-long cry of his wisdom in the streets; the God of music, of painting , of building, the Lord of Hosts, the God of mountains and oceans; whose laws go forth from one unseen point of wisdom, and thither return without an atom of loss; the God of history working in time unto Christianity; this God is the God of little children, and he alone can be perfectly, abandonedly simple and devoted. The deepest, purest love of a woman has its well-spring in him. Our longing desires can no more exhaust the fullness of the treasures of the Godhead than our imagination can touch their measure. Of him not a thought, not a joy, not a hope of one of his creatures can pass unseen; and while one of them remains unsatisfied, he is not Lord over all.

JANUARY 8TH

Therefore, with angels and with archangels, with the spirits of the just made perfect, with the little children of the kingdom, yea, with the Lord himself, and for all them that know him not, we praise and magnify and laud his name in itself, saying *Our Father.* We do not draw back for that we are unworthy, nor even for that we are hard-hearted and care not for the good. For it is his childlikeness that makes him our God and Father. The perfection of his relation to us swallows up all our imperfections, all our defects, all our evils; for our childhood is born of his fatherhood. That man is perfect in faith who can come to God in the utter dearth of his feelings and his desires, without a glow or an aspiration, with the weight of low thoughts, failures, neglects, and wandering forgetfulness, and say to him, "Thou are my refuge, because thou art my home."

JANUARY 9TH

S uch a faith—that God is our refuge, our home—will not lead to presumption. The man who can pray such a prayer will know better than another that God is not mocked; that he is not a man that he should repent; that tears and entreaties will not work on him to the breach of one of his laws; that for God to give a man because he asked for it that which was not in harmony with his laws of truth and right, would be to damn him—to cast him into the outer darkness. And he knows that out of that prison the childlike, imperturbable God will let no man come till he has paid the uttermost farthing.

And if he should forget this, the God to whom he belongs does not forget it, does not forget him. Life is no series of chances with a few providences sprinkled between to keep up a justly failing belief, but one providence of God; and the man shall not live long before life itself shall remind him, it may be in agony of soul, of that which he has forgotten. When he prays for comfort, the answer may come in dismay and terror and the turning aside of the Father's countenance; for love itself will, for love's sake, turn the countenance away from that which is not lovely; and he will have to read, written upon the dark wall of his imprisoned conscience, the words, awful and glorious, *Our God is a consuming fire.*

THE CONSUMING FIRE

"Wherefore, we receiving a kingdom which cannot be moved, let us have grace, whereby we may serve God acceptably with reverence and godly fear, for our God is a consuming fire."

Hebrews 12:28-29

JANUARY 10TH

Nothing is inexorable but love. Love which will yield to prayer is imperfect and poor. Nor is it then the love that yields, but its alloy. For if at the voice of entreaty, love conquers displeasure, it is love asserting itself, not love yielding its claims. It is not love that grants a boon unwillingly; still less is it love that answers a prayer to the wrong and hurt of him who prays. Love is one, and love is changeless.

For love loves unto purity. Love has ever in view the absolute loveliness of that which it beholds. Where loveliness is incomplete, and love cannot love its fill of loving, it spends itself to make lovelier, that it may love more; it strives for perfection, even that itself may be perfected—not in itself, but in the object. As it was love that first created humanity, so even human love, in proportion to its divinity, will go on creating the beautiful for its own outpouring. There is nothing eternal but that which loves and can be loved, and love is ever climbing towards the consummation when such shall be the universe, imperishable, divine. Therefore all that is not beautiful in the beloved, all that comes between and is not of love's kind, must be destroyed.

And our God is a consuming fire.

JANUARY 11TH

I f this be hard to understand, it as the simple, absolute truth is hard to understand. It may be centuries of ages before a man comes to see a truth—ages of strife, of effort, of aspiration. But when once he does see it, it is so plain that he wonders he could have lived without seeing it. That he did not understand it sooner was simply and only that he did not see it. To see a truth, to know what it is, to understand it, and to love it, are all one. There is many a motion towards it, many a misery for want of it, many a cry of the conscience against the neglect of it, many a dim longing for it as an unknown need before at length the eyes come awake, and darkness of the dreamful night yields to the light of the sun of truth. But once beheld it is forever.

For this vision of truth God has been working for ages of ages. For this simple condition, this apex of life, upon which a man wonders like a child that he cannot make other men see as he sees, the whole labor of God's science, history, poetry, was evolving truth upon truth in lovely vision, in torturing law; and for this will the patience of God labors while there is yet a human soul whose eyes have not been opened, whose child-heart has not yet been born in him. For this one condition of humanity, this simple beholding, has all the outthinking of God flowed in forms innumerable from the foundation of the world; and for this, too, has the divine destruction been going forth; that his life might be our life, that in us, too, might dwell that same consuming fire which is essential love.

JANUARY 12TH

Let us look at the utterance of the apostle which is crowned with this lovely terror: "Our God is a consuming fire." Let us have grace to serve the Consuming Fire, our God, with divine fear; not with the fear that cringes and craves, but with the bowing down of all thoughts, all delights, all lives before him who is the life of them all, and will have them all pure. The kingdom he has given us cannot be moved, because it has nothing weak in it: it is of the eternal world. We, therefore, must worship him with a fear pure as the kingdom is unshakeable. He will shake heaven and earth, that only the unshakeable may remain; he is a consuming fire, that only which cannot be consumed may stand forth eternal. It is the nature of God, so terribly pure that it destroys all that is not pure as fire, which demands like purity in our worship. It is not that the fire will burn us if we do not worship thus; but that the fire will burn us *until* we worship thus; yea, will go on burning within us after all that is foreign to it has yielded to its force, no longer with pain and consuming, but as the highest consciousness of life, the presence of God. Yea, the fear of God will cause a man to flee, not from God, but from himself; not *from* God, but *to* him, the Father of himself, in terror lest he should do him or his brother wrong. And the first words which follow for the setting forth of that grace whereby we may serve God acceptably are these: "Let brotherly love continue." To love our brother is to worship the Consuming Fire.

14

JANUARY 13TH

The symbol of the consuming fire would seem to have been suggested by the fire that burned on the mountain of the old law. That fire was part of the revelation of God there made to the Israelites. Was this show upon Mount Sinai a device to move obedience, such as bad nurses employ with children? A hint of vague and false horror? Was it not a true revelation of God? If it was not a true revelation, it was none at all. God showed them what was true. He will not put on a mask. He will not speak out of flaming fire if that flaming fire is alien to him, if there is nothing in him for that flaming fire to reveal. Be his children ever so brutish, he will not terrify them with a lie. It was a revelation, but a partial one; a true symbol, not a final vision. No revelation can be other than partial. If for true revelation a man must be told all the truth, then farewell to revelation; yea, farewell to the sonship. For what revelation, other than a partial can the highest spiritual condition receive of the infinite God? But it is not therefore untrue because it is partial. Relative to a lower condition of the receiver, a more partial revelation might be truer than a fuller revelation; for the former might reveal much to him, the latter might reveal nothing. Only, whatever it might reveal, if its nature were such as to preclude development and growth, it would be but a false revelation fighting against all the divine laws of human existence. The true revelation rouses the desire to know more by the truth of its incompleteness.

JANUARY 14TH

How should the Hebrews be other than terrified at that which was opposed to all they knew of themselves, a people judging it good to honor a golden calf? They did well to be afraid. They were in a better condition, acknowledging if only a terror above them, flaming on that unknown mountain height, than stooping to worship the idol below them. Fear is better than no God, better than a god made with hands. In that fear lay, deep hidden, the sense of the infinite. The worship of fear is true, although very low; and though not acceptable to God in itself, for only the worship of spirit and of truth is acceptable to him, yet even in his sight it is precious. For he regards men not merely as they are, but as they shall be; and not merely as they shall be, but as they are now growing, or capable of growing, towards that image after which he made them that they might grow to it. Therefore a thousand stages, each in itself all but valueless, are of inestimable worth as the necessary gradations of an infinite progress. A condition which, resulting from moral decline, would indicate a devil, may of growth indicate a saint.

16

JANUARY 15TH

B ut we shall find that this very revelation of fire is itself, in a higher sense, true to the mind of the rejoicing saint as to the mind of the trembling sinner. For the former sees farther into the meaning of the fire, and knows better what it will do to him. It is a symbol which needed not to be superseded, only unfolded. While men take part *with* their sins, while they feel as if, separated from their sins, they would be no longer themselves, how can they understand that the lightning word is a Savior—that word which pierces to the dividing between the man and the evil, which will slay the sin and give life to the sinner? Can it be any comfort to them to be told that God loves them so that he will burn them clean? Can the cleansing of the fire appear to them anything beyond what it must always, more or less, be—a process of torture? They do not want to be clean, and they cannot bear to be tortured. To them Mount Sinai is crowned with the signs of vengeance. And is not God ready to do unto them even as they fear? He is against sin: in so far as, and while, they and sin are one, he is against them—against their desires, their aims, their fears, and their hopes; and thus he is altogether and always *for them*. That thunder and lighting, that blackness torn with the sound of a trumpet, was all but a faint image to the slaves of what God thinks and feels against vileness and selfishness, so that the people, fearing to do as they would, might leave a little room for that grace to grow in them, which would at length make them see that evil, and not fire, is the fearful thing.

JANUARY 16TH

Even Moses, the man of God, was not ready to receive the revelation in store; not ready, although from love to his people he prayed that God would even blot him out of his book of life. It seems the utterance of a divine despair: he would not survive the children of his people. He did not care for a love that would save him alone, and send to the dust those thousands of calf-worshipping brothers and sisters. Certainly when God told him that he that had sinned should suffer for it, Moses could not see that this was the kindest thing that God could do. How much could Moses have understood, if he had seen the face instead of the back of that form which passed the cleft of the rock amidst the thunderous vapors of Sinai? Had that form turned and that face looked upon him, the face of him who was more man than any man; the face through which the divine emotion would, in the ages to come, manifest itself to the eyes of men; bowed, it might well be, at such a moment, in anticipation of the crown with which the children of the people for whom Moses pleaded with his life, would one day crown him; the face of him who was bearing and was yet to bear their griefs and carry their sorrows, who is now bearing our griefs and carrying our sorrows; the face of the Son of God, who instead of accepting the sacrifice of one of his creatures to satisfy his justice or support his dignity, gave himself utterly unto them, and therein to the Father by doing his lovely will; who suffered unto the death, not that men might not suffer, but that their suffering might be like his, and lead them up to his perfection.

JANUARY 17TH

When we say that God is Love, do we teach men that their fear of him is groundless? No. As much as they fear, such will come upon them, possibly far more. But there is something beyond their fear, a divine fate which they cannot withstand, because it works along with the human individuality which the divine individuality has created in them. The wrath will consume what they call 'themselves;' so that the selves God made shall appear, coming out with tenfold consciousness of being, and bringing with them all that made the blessedness of the life the men tried to lead without God. They will know that now first are they fully themselves. The avaricious, weary, selfish, suspicious old man shall have passed away. The young, ever young self, will remain. That which they *thought* themselves shall have vanished: that which they *felt* themselves, though they misjudged their own feelings, shall remain—remain glorified in repentant hope. For that which cannot be shaken shall remain. That which is immortal in God shall remain in man. The death that is in them shall be consumed. It is the law of Nature, of God, that all that is destructible shall be destroyed. The destructible must be burned out of a man, or begin to be burned out of him, before he can partake of eternal life. Many a man's work must be burned, that by that very burning he may be saved "so as by fire."

The man who acquiesces in the burning is saved by the fire.

JANUARY 18TH

The man who loves God and is not yet pure, courts the burning of God. Nor is it always torture. The fire shows itself sometimes only as light—still it will be fire of purifying. The consuming fire is just the original, the active form of Purity, that which makes pure, that which is indeed Love, the creative energy of God.

The man whose deeds are evil, fears the burning. But the burning will not come the less that he fears it or denies it. Escape is hopeless, for Love is inexorable. Our God is a consuming fire. The man shall not come out till he has paid the uttermost farthing. If the man resists the burning of God, the consuming fire of Love, a terrible doom awaits him, and its day will come. He who hates the fire of God shall be cast into the outer darkness. What sick dismay shall then seize upon him! For let a man think and care ever so little about God, he does not therefore exist without God. God is here with him, upholding, warming, delighting, teaching him; making life a good thing to him. God gives him himself, though the man knows it not. But when God withdraws, when the man feels himself abandoned, then will he listen in agony for the faintest sound of life from the closed door; and if the moan of suffering humanity ever reaches the ear of the outcast of darkness, he will be ready to rush into the very heart of the Consuming Fire to know life once more.

JANUARY 19TH

I magination cannot mislead us into too much horror of being without God. For that is living death. But with this divine difference: that the outer darkness is but the most dreadful form of the consuming fire—the fire without light—the darkness visible, the black flame. God hath withdrawn himself, but not lost his hold. His face is turned away, but his hand is laid upon him still. His heart has ceased to beat into the man's heart, but he keeps him alive by his fire. And that fire will go on searching and burning in him, as in the highest saint who is not yet pure as God is pure.

But at length, O God, wilt thou not cast Death and hell into the lake of Fire—even into Thine own consuming self? Then indeed wilt thou be all in all. For then our poor brothers and sisters shall have been burnt clean and brought home. For if their moans would turn heaven for us into hell, shall a man be more merciful than God? Shall, of all his glories, God's mercy alone not be infinite? Shall a brother love a brother more than the Father loves a son? Would Christ not die yet again to save one brother more?

As for us, now will we come to thee, our Consuming Fire. And thou wilt not burn us more than we can bear. But thou wilt burn us. And although thou seem to slay us, yet will we trust in thee, even for that which thou hast not spoken, if at length we may attain unto the blessedness of those *who have not seen and yet have believed.*

THE HIGHER FAITH

"Jesus saith unto him, Thomas, because thou hast seen me, thou hast believed: blessed are they that have not seen, and yet have believed."

John 20:29

JANUARY 20TH

The aspiring child is often checked by the dull disciple who has learned his lessons so imperfectly that he has never got beyond his school-books. Full of fragmentary rules, he has perceived the principle of none of them. The child draws near to him with some outburst of unusual feeling, some wide-reaching imagination that draws into the circle of religious theory the world of nature, and the yet wider world of humanity, for to the child the doings of the Father fill the world. The answer he receives from the dull disciple is "God has said nothing about that in his word, therefore we have no right to believe anything about it. It is better not to speculate on such matters. We have nothing to do with it. It is not revealed." For such a man is incapable of suspecting that what has remained hidden from him may have been revealed to the babe.

But to the man who would live throughout the whole divine form of his being, a thousand questions will arise to which the Bible does not even allude. "Leave them," says the dull disciple. "I cannot," returns the man. "Not only for that peace of mind, without which action is impossible, depend upon the answers to these questions, but my conduct itself must correspond to these answers. Questions imply answers. He has put the questions in my heart; he holds the answers in his. I will seek them from him. I will wait, but not till I have knocked. I will be patient, but not till I have asked. I will seek until I find. He has something for me. My prayer shall go up into the God of my life."

JANUARY 21ST

Sad, indeed, would the whole matter be, if the Bible had told us *everything* God meant us to believe. But herein is the Bible itself greatly wronged. It nowhere lays claims to be regarded as *the* Word, *the* Way, and *the* Truth. The Bible leads us to Jesus, the inexhaustible, the ever unfolding Revelation of God. It is Christ "in whom are hid all the treasures of wisdom and knowledge," not the Bible, save as leading to him. And why are we told that these treasures are *hid* in him who is the *Revelation* of God? Is it that we should despair of finding them and cease to seek them? Are they not hid in him that they may be revealed to us in due time—that is, when we are in need of them?

There is more hid in Christ than we shall ever learn, but they that begin first to inquire will soonest be gladdened with revelation; and with them he will be best pleased, for the slowness of his disciples troubled him of old. The Son of God is the Teacher of men, giving to them of his Spirit, which manifests the deep things of God, being to a man the mind of Christ. The great heresy of the Church is unbelief in this Spirit. If we were once filled with the mind of Christ, we should know that the Bible had done its work, was fulfilled, and had for us passed away, that thereby the Word of our God might abide forever. The one use of the Bible is to make us look at Jesus, that through him we might know his Father and our Father, his God and our God.

JANUARY 22^(ND)

A man will please God better by believing some things that are not told him, than by confining his faith to those things that are expressly said—said to arouse in us the truth-seeing faculty, the spiritual desire, the prayer for the good things which God will give to them that ask him.

"But is this not dangerous doctrine? Will not a man be taught thus to believe the things he likes best, even to pray for that which he likes best? And will be not grow arrogant in his confidence?"

If it be true that the Spirit strives with our spirit, if it be true that God teaches men, we may safely leave those dreaded results to him. If the man is of the Lord's company, he is safer with him than with those who would secure their safety by hanging on the outskirts and daring nothing. If he is not taught of God in that which he hopes for, God will let him know it. He will receive something else than he prays for. If he can pray to God for anything not good, the answer will come in the flames of that consuming fire. These will soon bring him to some of his spiritual sense. But it will be far better for him to be thus sharply tutored, than to go on a snail's pace in the journey of the spiritual life. And for arrogance, I have seen nothing breed it faster or in more offensive forms than the worship of the letter.

JANUARY 23RD

What a man likes best *may* be God's will, may be the voice of the Spirit striving *with* his spirit, not against it; and if it be not so—if the thing he asks is not according to his will—there is that consuming fire. The danger lies, not in asking from God what is not good, nor even in hoping to receive it from him, but in not asking him, in not having him of our council. Nor will the fact that we dare not inquire his will preserve us from the necessity of acting in some such matter as we call unrevealed, and where shall we find ourselves then? The whole matter may safely be left to God.

But I doubt if a man can ask anything from God that is bad. Surely one who has begun to pray to him is child enough to know the bad from the good when it has come so near him, and dares not pray for *that*. If you refer me to David praying such fearful prayers against his enemies, I answer, you must read them by your knowledge of the man. Remember that this is he who, with the burning heart of an eastern, yet, when his greatest enemy was given into his hands, instead of taking the vengeance of an eastern, contented himself with cutting off the skirt of his garment. It was justice and right that he craved in his soul, although his prayers took a wild form of words. God heard him, and gave him what contented him. The heart's desire upon one's enemies is best met and granted when the hate is changed into love and compassion.

JANUARY 24TH

What should I think of my child if I found that he limited his faith in me and hope from me to the few promises he had heard me utter! The faith that limits itself to the promises of God may be good enough for a pagan, but for a Christian it is a miserable and wretched faith. Those who rest in such a faith try to believe in the truth of his word, but the truth of his Being they understand not. Therefore it is little wonder that they distrust those swellings of the heart which are his drawings of the man towards him, as sun and moon heave the ocean mass heavenward. Brother, sister, if such is your faith, you will not, must not stop there. You must come out of this bondage of the law to which you give the name of grace, for there is little that is gracious in it. You will yet know the dignity of your high calling, and the love of God that passeth knowledge. He is not afraid of your presumptuous approach to him. It is you who are afraid to come near him. He is not watching over his dignity. It is you who fear to be sent away as the disciples would have sent away the little children. It is you who think so much about your souls and are so afraid of losing your life that you dare not draw near to the Life of life, lest it should consume you.

Our God, we will trust thee. Shall we not find thee equal to our faith? One day, we shall laugh ourselves to scorn that we looked for so little from thee; for thy giving will not be limited by our hoping.

JANUARY 25TH

O thou of little faith! "In everything,--" I am quoting a divine soul that knew his master Christ, and in his strength opposed apostles, not to say Christians, to their faces, because they could not believe more than a little in God; could believe only for themselves and not for their fellows; could believe for the few of the chosen nation, for whom they had God's ancient *word*, but could not believe for the multitude of the nations, for the millions of hearts that God had made to search after him and find him—"In everything," says St. Paul, "by prayer and supplication, with thanksgiving, let your requests be made known unto God." For this *everything*, nothing is too small. That it should trouble us is enough. There is some principle involved in it worth the notice even of God himself, for did he not make us so that the thing does trouble us? And surely for this *everything*, nothing can be too great. When the Son of man cometh and findeth too much faith on the earth, may God in his mercy slay us. Meantime, we will hope and trust.

JANUARY 26TH

D o you count it a great faith to believe what God has said? It seems to me a little faith, and, if alone, worthy of reproach. To believe what he has *not* said is faith indeed, and blessed. For that comes of believing in him. Can you not believe in God himself? Of, confess, do you not find it so hard to believe what he has said, that even that is almost more than you can do? If I ask you why, will not the true answer be, "Because we are not quite sure that he did say it?" If you believed in God you would find it easy to believe the word. You would not even need to inquire whether he had *said* it; you would know that he meant it.

Let us then dare something. Let us not always be unbelieving children. Let us keep in mind that the Lord, not forbidding those who insist on seeing before they will believe, blesses those who have not seen and yet have believed. We know in whom we have believed, and we look for that which it hath not entered into the heart of man to conceive. Shall God's thoughts be surpassed by man's thoughts? God's giving by man's asking? God's creation by man's imagination? No. Let us climb to the height of our Alpine desires, let us ascend the spear-pointed Himalayas of our aspirations; still shall we find the depth of God's sapphire above us; still shall we find the heavens higher than the earth, and his thoughts and his ways higher than our thoughts and our ways.

JANUARY 27TH

A h Lord! Be thou in all our being; as not in the Sundays of our time alone, so not in the chambers of our hearts alone. We dare not think that thou canst not, carest not; that some things are not for Thy beholding, some questions not to be asked of thee. For are we not all thine, utterly thine? That which a man speaks not to his fellow, we speak to thee. We would not escape from our history by fleeing into the wilderness, by hiding our heads in the sands of forgetfulness, or the lethargy of hopelessness. We take it, as our very life, in our hand, and flee with it unto thee. Triumphant is the answer which thou holdest for every doubt. It may be we could not understand it yet. But thou shalt at least find faith in the earth, O Lord, if thou comest to look for it now—the faith of ignorant but hoping children, who know that they do not know, and believe that thou knowest.

And for our brothers and sisters, who cleave to what they call Thy word, thinking to please thee so, they are in Thy holy safe hands, who hast taught us that *whosoever shall speak a word against the Son of man, it shall be forgiven him; though unto him that blasphemes against the Holy Ghost, it shall not be forgiven.*

IT SHALL NOT BE FORGIVEN

"And whosever shall speak a word against the Son of man, it shall be forgiven him; but unto him that blasphemeth against the Holy Ghost, it shall not be forgiven."

Luke 12:10

JANUARY 28TH

Our Lord had no design of constructing a system of truth in intellectual forms. The truth of the moment in its relation to him, The Truth, was what he spoke. He spoke out of a region of realities which he knew could only be suggested, not represented, in the forms of intellect and speech. His words invade our darkness with vivid flashes of life and truth, rousing us with sharp stings of light to will our awaking, to arise from the dead and cry for the light which he can give, not in the lightning of words only, but in indwelling presence and power.

How, then, must the truth fare with those who, having neither glow nor insight, will build intellectual systems upon the words of our Lord, or of his disciples? A little child could understand Plato better than such as they could understand St. Paul. The sense they find in the words must be a sense small enough to pass through their narrow doors. And if mere words, without the interpreting sympathy, may mean almost anything, how shall the man, bent at best on the salvation of his own soul, understand, for instance, the meaning of that apostle who was ready to encounter banishment itself from the presence of Christ, that the beloved brethren of his nation might enter in? To men who are not simple, simple words are the most inexplicable of riddles.

JANUARY 29TH

I f we are bound to search after what our Lord means—and he speaks that we may understand—we are at least equally bound to refuse any interpretation which seems to us unlike him, unworthy of him. He himself says, "Why do ye not of your own selves judge what is right?" Some misapprehension may cause us to refuse the true interpretation, but we are none the less bound to refuse and wait for more light. To accept anything as the will of our Lord which to us is inconsistent with what we have learned to worship in him already, is to introduce discord into that harmony whose end is to unite our hearts and make them whole.

He requires of us that we should do him no injustice. He would come and dwell with us, if we would but open our chambers to receive him. How shall we receive him if, avoiding the judging of what is right, we hold this or that daub of authority or tradition hanging up on our walls to be the real likeness of our Lord? We may close our doors against the Master himself as an impostor, not finding him like the picture that hangs in our oratory. Better to refuse even the truth for a time, than, by accepting into our intellectual creed that which our heart cannot receive, not seeing its real form, to introduce hesitation into our prayers and a misery into our love. If it be the truth, we shall one day see it other than it appears now, and love it because we see it lovely; for *all* truth is lovely.

JANUARY 30TH

To mistake the meaning of the Son of man may well fill a man with sadness. But to care so little for him as to receive as his what the noblest part of our nature rejects as low and poor, or selfish and wrong, that surely is more like the sin against the Holy Ghost that can never be forgiven, for it is a sin against the truth itself, not the embodiment of it in him.

Words for their full meaning depend upon their source, the person who speaks them. An utterance may even seem commonplace till you are told that thus spoke one whom you know to be always thinking, always feeling, always acting. Recognizing the mind whence the words proceed, you know the scale by which they are to be understood. So the words of God cannot mean just the same as the words of men. "Can we not, then, understand them?" Yes—we can understand them *more* than the words of men. Whatever a good word means, as used by a good man, it means just infinitely more as used by God. And the feeling or thought expressed by that word takes higher and higher forms in us as we become capable of understanding him; that is, as we become like him.

JANUARY 31ST

To understand our Lord's words as quoted by Luke, I begin by asking what human forgiveness means; for it is through the human that we must climb up to the divine. So let us look at the feelings associated with the exercise of what is called forgiveness.

One man will say, "I forgive, but I cannot forget. Let the fellow never come in my sight again!" This is a sending away of the penalties which the wronged believes he can claim from the wrong-doer. *But there is no sending away of the wrong itself from between them.* Another man will say, "I suppose I must forgive him; for if I do not forgive him, God will not forgive me." This man is a *little* nearer the truth. A third will say, "He has wronged me grievously. It is a dreadful thing to me, and more dreadful still to him, for he has hurt me, but has nearly killed himself. I cannot feel the same toward him yet, but I would destroy this evil deed that has come between us. I send it away. And I would have him destroy it from between us, too, by abjuring it utterly." Which comes nearest to the divine idea of forgiveness? For the Divine creates the Human; the Divine forgiveness creates our forgiveness and therefore can do so much more. It can take up all our wrongs, small and great, and carry them away from between our God and us.

Christ is God's Forgiveness.

FEBRUARY 1ST

L et us consider human forgiveness as between a father and a son. For although God is so much more to us, yet fatherhood is the last height of the human stair whence our understanding can see him afar off. There are various kinds and degrees of wrongdoing, which need varying kinds and degrees of forgiveness. An outburst of anger in a child, for instance, scarcely wants forgiveness. One child, the moment the fault was committed, the father would clasp to his bosom; the father's hatred of the sin would burst forth in his pitiful tenderness towards the child who was so wretched as to have done the sin, and so destroy it. But suppose a father discovers in his child a habit of sly cruelty towards his younger brothers, or the animals of the house—of meanness, deceit, and evil. He might say to himself, "I cannot forgive him. This is beyond forgiveness." He might *say* so while all the time he was striving to let forgiveness find its way; his love might grow yet greater because of the wandering and loss of his son. For love is divine, and then most divine when it loves according to *needs* and not according to *merits*.

But the forgiveness would be but in the process of making, as it were, or of drawing nigh to the sinner. Not till the son's opening heart received the divine flood of destroying affection, and his own affection burst forth to meet it and sweep the evil away, could it be said to be finished, to have arrived. Not till then could the son be said to be forgiven.

FEBRUARY 2ND

God is forgiving us every day, sending from between him and us our sins and their fogs and darkness. Witness the shining of his sun and the falling of his rain, the filling of their hearts with food and gladness, that he loves them that love him not. When some sin that we have committed has clouded all our horizon and hidden him from our eyes, he sweeps away a path for his forgiveness to reach our hearts, that it may by causing our repentance destroy the wrong, and make us able even to forgive ourselves. For some are too proud to forgive themselves, till the forgiveness of God has had its way with them, has drowned their pride in the tears of repentance and made their hearts come again like the heart of a little child.

Looking upon forgiveness, then, as the perfecting of a work ever going on, as the contact of God's heart and ours, in spite and in destruction of the intervening wrong, we may say that God's love is ever in front of his forgiveness. God's love is perfect, working out the forgiveness. God loves where he cannot yet forgive—where forgiveness in the full sense is as yet simply impossible, because no contact of hearts is possible, because that which lies between has not even begun to yield to his holy destruction.

FEBRUARY 3RD

Some things between the Father and his children, as between a father and his child, may comparatively, and in a sense, be made light of—I do not mean made light of in themselves: away they must go—inasmuch as, evils or sins though they be, they yet leave room for the dwelling of God's Spirit in the heart, forgiving and cleansing away the evil. When a man's evil is fading out of him, and he is growing better and better, that is the forgiveness coming into him more and more. Perfect in God's will, it is having its perfect work in the mind of the man. When the man hath, with his whole nature, cast away his sin, there is no room for forgiveness any more, for God dwells in him, and he in God. When Nathan uttered "Thou art the man," the forgiveness of God laid hold of David, the heart of the king was humbled to the dust; and when he thus awoke from the moral lethargy that had fallen upon him, he found that he was still with God. "When I awake," he sang to his Lord, "I am still with thee."

FEBRUARY 4TH

There are two sins, both of spiritual condition, which *cannot be forgiven*; that is, which cannot be excused, passed by, made little of by the tenderness even of God, inasmuch as they will allow no forgiveness to come into the soul, they will permit no good influence to go on working alongside of them; they shut God out altogether. Therefore the man can never receive into himself the holy renewing saving influences of God's forgiveness. The one of these sins is against man; the other against God.

The former is unforgiveness to our neighbor, the shutting of him out from our mercies, from our love. It may be infinitely less evil to murder a man than to refuse to forgive him; the former may be the act of a moment of passion, the latter is the heart's choice. We quench the relations of life between us; we close up the passages of possible return. This is to shut out God, the Life, the One. For how are we to receive the forgiving presence while we shut out our brother? Tenfold the forgiveness lies in the words, "If ye forgive not men their trespasses, neither will your heavenly Father forgive your trespasses." Those words are kindness indeed. God holds the unforgiving man with his hand, but turns his face away from him. If, in his desire to see the face of his Father, he turns his own towards his brother, then the face of God turns round. God loves the sinner so much that he cannot forgive him in any other way than by lifting him out of the mire of his iniquity.

FEBRUARY 5TH

To return to Luke 12:10: is the refusal of forgiveness contained in it a condemnation to irrecoverable impenitence? Strange righteousness would be the decree that because a man has done wrong, he shall forever remain wrong! Do not tell me the condemnation is merely a leaving of the man to the consequences of his own will. God will not take shelter behind such a jugglery of logic or metaphysics. He is neither schoolman nor theologian, but our Father in heaven. He knows that that in him would be the same unforgiveness for which he refuses to forgive man. This would be to say that Satan has overcome, and that Jesus has been less strong than the adversary, the destroyer. What then shall I say of such a doctrine of devils as that even if a man did repent, God would not or could not forgive him?

All sin is unpardonable. There is no compromise to be made with it. We shall not come out except clean, except having paid the uttermost farthing. But the special unpardonableness of the sins we are considering lies in their shutting out God. The man who denies truth, who resists duty, who says that which is good is of Satan, or that which is bad is of God, denies the Spirit, shuts out the Spirit; and without the Spirit to witness with his spirit, no man could know himself forgiven, even if God appeared to him and said so. The full forgiveness is when a man feels that God is forgiving him, and this cannot be while he opposes himself to the very essence of God's will.

FEBRUARY 6TH

The men of whom our Lord spoke refused the truth, knowing that it was true; not carried away by passion, but by cold self-love, and envy, avarice, and ambition. Not merely doing wrong knowingly, but setting their whole natures knowingly against the light. Of this nature must the sin against the Holy Ghost surely be. "This is the condemnation, that light is come into the world, and men loved darkness rather than light, because their deeds were evil." Was not their *condition* unpardonable? How, through all this mass of falsehood, could the pardon of God reach the essential humanity within them? Forgiveness while they were such was impossible. Out of this they must come, else there was no word of God for them. But the very word that told them of the unpardonable state in which they were, was just the one form the voice of mercy could take in calling on them to repent.

If the Spirit of God is shut out from a man's heart, how is he to become better? God who has made us can never be far from any man who draws the breath of life. May not then one day some terrible convulsion from the center of his being shake such a man so that through all the deafness of his death, the voice of the Spirit may be faintly heard, the still small voice that comes after the tempest and the earthquake? May there not be a fire that even such can feel? Who shall set bounds to the consuming of the fire of our God, and the purifying that dwells therein?

FEBRUARY 7TH

"Father, forgive them, for they know not what they do," said the Divine, making excuses for his murderers, not after it was all over, but at the very moment when he was dying by their hands. When the Father succeeded in answering his prayer, then his forgiveness in the hearts of the murderers broke out in sorrow, repentance, and faith. Here was a sin dreadful enough surely—but easy for our Lord to forgive. But must we believe that Judas—who repented even to agony, who repented so that his high-prized life, self, and soul, became worthless in his eyes and met with no mercy at his own hand—could find no mercy in such a God? I think, when Judas fled from his hanged and fallen body, he fled to the tender help of Jesus, and found it—I say not how. I believe Jesus loved Judas even when he was kissing him with the traitor's kiss, and I believe that he was his Savior still. I cannot believe O my Lord, that thou wouldst not forgive thy enemy, even when he repented. Nor will I believe that thy holy death was powerless to save thy foe—that it could not reach to Judas. Have we not heard of those, thine own, taught of thee, who could easily forgive their betrayers in thy name? And if thou forgive, will not thy forgiveness find its way at least in redemption and purification?

FEBRUARY 8TH

B ut for him that speaketh against the spirit of Truth, against the Son of God revealed within him, he is beyond the teaching of that Spirit now. Let him know what it is to be without the God he hath denied. Away with him to the Outer Darkness! Perhaps that will make him repent.

My friends, I offer this as only a contribution towards the understanding of our Lord's words. But if we ask him, he will lead us into all truth. And let us not be afraid to think, for he will not take it ill. Beyond all discoveries in his words and being, there lie depths within depths of truth that we cannot understand, and yet shall be ever going on to understand. The fact that some things have become to us so much simpler than they were, and that great truths have come out of what once looked common, is ground enough for hope that such will go on to be our experience through the ages to come. Our advance from our former ignorance can measure but a small portion of the distance that lies between our childishness and his manhood, between our love and his love, between our dimness and his mighty vision. To him ere long may we all come, still children, more children than ever, to receive from his hand the *white stone, and in the stone a new name written, which no man knowest saving he that receiveth it.*

THE NEW NAME

"To him that overcometh, I will give a white stone, and in the stone a new name written, which no man knoweth saving he that receiveth it."

Revelation 2:17

FEBRUARY 9TH

In the passage about the gift of the white stone, we find the essence of religion. What the mystic[1] meaning may be must be taken differently by different minds. I think the writer of Revelation sees in its whiteness, purity, and in its substance, indestructibility; but I care chiefly to regard the stone as the form whereby the name is represented as passing from God to man. The giving of the white stone with the new name is the communication of what God thinks about the man to the man. It is the divine judgment. The true name is one which expresses the character, the nature, the meaning of the person who bears it. It is the man's own symbol, the sign which belongs to him and to no one else. Who can give a man this, his own name? God alone. To whom is this name given? To him that overcometh. When is it given? When he has overcome. Why does God wait till then? Just as repentance comes because God pardons, yet the man becomes aware of the pardon only in the repentance, so it is only when the man has *become* his name that God gives him the stone with the name upon it, for then first can he understand what his name signifies. God's name for a man must then be the expression in a mystical word—a word of that language which all who have overcome understand—of his own idea of the man, that being whom he had in his thought when he began to make the child. To tell the name is to seal the success—to say, "In thee also I am well pleased."

---

[1] I use the word *mysticism* as representing a mode of embodying truth, common, in various degrees, to almost all, if not all, the writers of the New Testament. A mystical mind perceives that the highest expression of which the truth admits lies in the symbolism of nature, and the human customs that result from human necessities, and so prosecutes thought about truth by dealing with the symbols themselves after logical forms. This is the highest mode of conveying the deepest truth, and the Lord himself often employed it.

FEBRUARY 10TH

The mystic symbol of the white rock has for its center of significance the personal relation of every man to his God. To him who offers unto God his own self as sacrifice, to him that overcometh, him who has brought his individual life back to its source, who knows that he is one of God's children, he giveth the white stone. The name is one "which no man knoweth saving he that receiveth it." He is to God a peculiar being, made after his own fashion and that of no one else; for when he is perfected he shall receive the new name which no one else can understand. Hence he can worship God as no man else can worship him, can understand God as no man else can understand him. God give me grace to be humble before thee, brother, and look up to thee for what revelation of God thou and no one else canst give. Each man lifts up a different humanity to the common Father. And for each God has a different response. With every man he has a secret—the secret of the new name. In every man there is a loneliness, an inner chamber of peculiar life into which God only can enter. I say not it is the *innermost* chamber, but a chamber into which no brother, no sister can come. From this it follows that there is a chamber in God himself into which none can enter but the one, the individual man, out of which chamber that man has to bring revelation and strength for his brethren. This is that for which he was made—to reveal the secret things of the Father.

FEBRUARY 11TH

Each of us is a distinct flower in the spiritual garden of God, each of us watered and shone upon and filled with life, for the sake of his completed being, which will blossom out of him at last to the glory and pleasure of the great gardener. For each has within him a secret of the Divinity; each is growing towards the revelation of that secret to himself, and so to the full reception of the divine. Every moment that he is true to his true self, some new shine of the white stone breaks on his inward eye, some fresh channel opens up for the coming glory of the flower, the conscious offering of his whole being in beauty to the Maker.

What an end lies before us! To have a consciousness of our own ideal being flashed into us from the thought of God! Surely for this we may well give away all our paltry self-consciousness, our self-admiration and self-worship! Surely to know what he thinks about us will pale out of our souls all our thoughts about ourselves! And we may well hold them loosely now, and be ready to let them go.

FEBRUARY 12TH

"But is there not the worst of all dangers involved in such teaching—the danger of spiritual pride?" If there be, are we to refuse the spirit for fear of the pride? Here there is no possibility of comparison with one's neighbor, for no one knows what the white stone contains except the man who receives it. Here is room for endless aspiration towards the unseen ideal; none for ambition. Relative worth is not only unknown; to the children of the kingdom it is unknowable. Each esteems the other better than himself. How shall the rose, the glowing heart of the summer heat, rejoice against the snowdrop risen with hanging head from the white bosom of the snow? Both are God's thoughts, both are dear to him, both are needful to the completeness of his earth and the revelation of himself.

"God has cared to make me for himself," says the victor with the white stone. "What matter whether I be called a grass of the field, or an eagle of the air? A stone to build into his temple, or a Boanerges to wield his thunder? I am his, his idea, his making; perfect in my kind, yea, perfect in his sight; full of him, revealing him, alone with him. Let him call me what he will. The name shall be precious as my life. I seek no more."

FEBRUARY 13TH

G one will be all anxiety as to what a man's neighbors may think about him. It is enough that God thinks about him. To be something to God, is that not praise enough? To be a thing God cares for and would have complete, is that not life itself?

Neither will he thus be isolated from his fellows. Each will feel the sacredness and awe of his neighbor's dark and silent speech with his God. Each will regard the other as a prophet, and look to him for what the Lord hath spoken, some gospel of truth which, when spoken, his neighbors shall receive and understand. In God each will draw nigh to each. Yes, there will be danger, as everywhere; but he giveth more grace. And if the man who has striven up the heights should yet fall from them into the deeps, is there not that fire of God, the consuming fire, which burneth and destroyeth not?

To one who has not already had some speech with God, or at least felt some aspiration towards the fount of his being, all this will appear foolishness. So be it. But Lord, help them and us, and make our being grow into thy likeness. If through ages of strife and ages of growth, yet let us at last see thy face and receive the white stone from thy hand. That we may grow, give us day by day our daily bread. Fill us with the words that proceed out of thy mouth. Help us to lay up *treasures in heaven, where neither moth nor rust doth corrupt.*

THE HEART WITH THE TREASURE

"Lay not up for yourselves treasures upon the earth, where moth and rust doth corrupt, and where thieves break though and steal. But lay up for yourselves treasures in heaven, where neither moth nor rust doth corrupt, and where thieves do not break through nor steal. For where your treasure is, there will your heart be also."

Mathew 6:19-21

FEBRUARY 14TH

To understand the words of our Lord is the business of life. For it is the main road to the understanding of The Word himself. And to receive him is to receive the Father, and so to have Life in ourselves. And Life, the higher, the deeper, the simpler, the original, is the business of life.

The Word is that by which we live, namely, Jesus himself; and his words represent, in part, in shadow, in suggestion, himself. Any utterance worthy of being called *a truth*, is human food; how much more *The Word*, presenting no abstract laws of our being, but the vital relation of soul and body, heart and will, strength and rejoicing, beauty and light, to Him who first gave birth to them all! The Son came forth *to be*, before our eyes and in our hearts, that which he had made us for, that we might behold *the truth* in him, and cry out for the loving God, who, in the highest sense of all is The Truth, not as understood, but as understanding, living, and being, doing and creating the truth.

FEBRUARY 15TH

"I am the truth," said our Lord, and by those who are in some measure like him in being the truth, the Word can be understood. Let us try to understand him.

What is the power of his word, *For. For where your treasure is, there will your heart be also?* The meaning of the reason thus added is not obvious upon its surface. It has to be sought for because of its depth and its simplicity. But it is so complete, so immediately operative on the conscience through its poetic suggestiveness, that when it is understood, there is nothing more to be said, but everything to be done. What is with the treasure must fare as the treasure; the heart which haunts the treasure-house where the moth and rust corrupt will be exposed to the same ravages as the treasure. Many a man, many a woman, fair and flourishing to see, is going about with a rusty, moth-eaten heart within that form of strength or beauty. If God sees your heart corroded with the rust of cares, riddled into caverns by the worms of ambition and greed, then your heart is as God sees it, for God sees things as they are. And one day you will be compelled to see, nay, to *feel* your heart as God sees it, and to know that the cankered thing is indeed the center of your being.

FEBRUARY 16TH

Nor does the lesson apply to those only who worship Mammon; it applies equally to those who in any way worship the transitory, who seek the praise of men more than the praise of God, who would make a show in the world by taste, intellect, power, art, or genius of any kind. Nor to such only, but surely to those as well whose pleasures are of a more transitory nature still, such as the pleasures of the senses. The hurt lies not in that these pleasures pass away and leave a fierce disappointment behind, for that is only so much the better; the hurt lies in that the immortal, created in the image of the everlasting God, is housed with the fading and the corrupting, and clings to them till it is infected with their disease, which assume in it a form more terrible in proportion to the superiority of its kind. That which is mere decay in the one becomes moral vileness in the other, that which fits the one for the dunghill casts the other into the outer darkness. It creeps into a burrow in the earth, where its budded wings wither and damp and drop away from its shoulders, instead of haunting the open plains, spreading abroad its young pinions to the sun and the air, and strengthening them in further and further flights, till at last they should become strong enough to bear the God-born into the presence of its Father in heaven.

He whose heart is sound because it haunts the treasure-house of heaven may *be tempted of the devil, but will be first led up of the Spirit into the wilderness.*

THE TEMPTATION IN THE WILDERNESS

"Then was Jesus led up of the Spirit into the wilderness, to be tempted of the devil. And when he had fasted forty days and forty nights, he was afterward an hungered. And when the tempter came to him, he said, if thou be the Son of God, command that these stones be made bread. But he answered and said, It is written, Man shall not live by bread alone, but by every word that proceedeth out of the mouth of God. Then the devil taketh him up into the holy city, and setteth him on a pinnacle of the temple, and saith unto him, If thou be the Son of God, cast thyself down; for it is written he shall give his angels charge concerning thee, and in their hands they shall bear thee up, lest at any time thou dash thy foot against a stone. Jesus said unto him, It is written again, thou shall not tempt the Lord thy God. Again, the devil taketh him up into an exceeding high mountain, and showeth him all the kingdoms of the world, and the glory of them; and saith unto him, All these things will I give thee, if thou wilt fall down and worship me. Then saith Jesus unto him, Get thee hence, Satan; for it is written, Thou shalt worship the Lord thy God, and him only shalt thou serve. Then the devil leaveth him; and behold, angels came and ministered unto him.

Matthew 4:1-11

FEBRUARY 17TH

T hink of our Lord's understanding, imagination, and heart, in which lay the treasures of wisdom and knowledge. Must he not have known, felt, imagined, and rejoiced in things that could not be told in human words, nor understood by human hearts? There is no attempt made to convey to us even the substance of the battle of those forty days. Such a conflict of spirit as absorbed all the human necessities of *The Man* in the cares of the Godhead could not be intelligible to us. It is not till the end of those forty days that the divine event begins to become human enough to be capable of being spoken in human forms to the ears of men.

Emerging from the storms of the ocean of divine thought and feeling, bearing with him the treasures won in the strife, our Lord is an hungered; and from this moment the temptation is human, and can be in some measure understood by us. But the inward experiences of our Lord could be conveyed to the disciples only in a parable. For far plainer things than these, our Lord chose this form, for it is the fullest form in which truth can be embodied, and to the parable will the teacher of the truth ever return. He who asserts that the passage contains a simple narrative of actual events must explain how Satan could be so foolish as to think that the temptation he presented could have tempted our Lord. But told as a parable, the story is as full of meaning as it would be bare if received as a narrative.

FEBRUARY 18TH

N ow arises the question crucial to the elucidation of the story: *How could the Son of God be tempted?* If anyone says that he was not moved by those temptations, that he was not tempted, then for human need, struggle, and hope, it bears no meaning. But asserting that these were real temptations, then how could the Son of God be tempted with evil? In the answer to this lies the center of the whole interpretation: he was not tempted with Evil, but with Good; with inferior forms of good, while the higher forms of good held were biding their time, God's time. The Son of God could not be tempted with evil, but I believe that he could be tempted with good—to yield to which temptation would have been evil in him, and ruin to the universe.

One may ask, Does not all evil come from good? Yes; but it has come *from* it. A good corrupted is no longer a good. Such could not tempt our Lord. Revenge may originate in a sense of justice, but it is revenge, not justice; an evil thing, fearfully unjust. The Lord could not have felt tempted to take vengeance upon his enemies, but he might have felt tempted to destroy the wicked from the face of the earth—to destroy them from the face of the earth, I say, not to destroy them forever. To that I do not think he could have felt tempted.

We shall see how the devil tempted him *to* evil, but not *with* evil.

FEBRUARY 19TH

L et us look at the individual temptations represented in the parable. First, he was hungry, and the devil said, *Make bread of this stone.* Let no one think to glorify the Lord's fast by calling it miraculous. Wonderful such fasts are on record on the part of holy men; and inasmuch as the Lord was more of a man than his brethren, insomuch might he be farther withdrawn in the depths of his spiritual humanity from the outer region of his physical nature. At the end of forty days, it was not hunger alone that made food tempting to him, but that exhaustion of the whole system, wasting itself all the time it was forgotten, which, reacting on the mind when the mind was already worn out with its own tension, must have deadened it so, that (speaking after the experiences of his brethren, which alone will explain his) it could for a time see or feel nothing of the spiritual, and could only *believe in* the unfelt, the unseen. What a temptation was here, knowing that to eat would restore the lost vision of the eternal! But it was God's business to take care of him, his to do what the Father told him to do. In nothing was he to be beyond his brethren, save in faith. No refuge for him, any more than for them, save in the love and care of the Father. "Man shall not live by bread alone, but by every word that proceedeth out of the mouth of God." Yea, even by the word which made that stone a stone. Everything is all right. It was life indeed for him to leave alone that which the Father had made, rather than alter one word that he had spoken.

FEBRUARY 20TH

Without bread a man will die; but he will not find that he dies. He will only find that the tent which hid the stars from him is gone, and that he can see the heavens. Our Lord says, "I can do without the life that comes of bread; without the life that comes of the word of my Father, I die indeed." In the higher aspect of the first temptation, arising from the fact that a man cannot feel the things be believes except under certain conditions of physical well-being dependent upon food, the answer is the same: A man does not live by his *feelings* any more than by bread, but by the Truth, that is, the Word, the Will of God.

No word is fully a Word of God until the man therein recognizes God. Even Christ himself is not The Word of God in the deepest sense *to a man* until he is the Revelation of God to the man, until the Spirit that is the meaning in the Word has come to him. The words of God are as the sands and the stars, but the end of all and each is to reveal God. When we receive the word of God, his will becomes our will, and so we live by God. But the word of God once understood, a man must live by the faith of what God is, and not by his own feelings even in regard to God. And when he can no longer *feel* the truth, he shall not therefore die. He lives because God is true; and he is able to know that he lives because he knows, having once understood the word, that God is truth. He believes in the God of former vision, lives by that word therefore, when all is dark and there is no vision.

FEBRUARY 21ST

We now come to the second attempt of the Enemy. "Then if God is to be so trusted, try him. Here is the word itself for it: he shall give his angels charge concerning thee; take him at his word. Throw thyself down, and strike the conviction in to me that thou art the Son of God. For thou knowest thou dost not look like what thou sayest thou art." Satan quotes Scripture as a verbal authority; our Lord meets him with a Scripture by the truth which governs his conduct. His answer contains the same principle as before, namely, that to the Son of God the will of God is Life. It was a temptation to show the powers of the world that he was the Son of God, above the laws of Nature, and thus stop the raging of the heathen and the vain imaginations of the people. It would be but to show them the truth. But he was the *Son* of God: what was his *Father's* will? Such was not the divine way of convincing the world of sin, of righteousness, of judgment. If the Father told him to cast himself down, that moment the pinnacle pointed naked to the sky. If the devil threw him down, let God send his angels; or, if better, allow him to be dashed to pieces in the valley below. But never will he forestall the divine will. The Father shall order what comes next. The Son will obey. In the path of his work he will turn aside for no stone. There let the angels bear him in their hands if need be. But he will not choose the path because there is a stone in it. He will not choose at all. He will go where the Spirit leads him.

FEBRUARY 22ND

The story of the temptation in the wilderness throws some light upon the words of our Lord, "If ye have faith and doubt not, if ye shall say unto this mountain, Be thou removed, and be thou cast into the sea; it shall be done." Good people have been tempted to tempt the Lord their God upon the strength of this saying, just as Satan sought to tempt our Lord on the strength of the passage he quoted from the Psalms. Happily for such, the assurance to which they would give the name of faith generally fails them in time. Faith is that which, knowing the Lord's will, goes and does it; or, not knowing it, stands and waits, content in ignorance as in knowledge. It is the noblest exercise to act with uncertainty of the result, when the duty itself is certain, or even when a course seems with strong probability to be duty. But to put God to the question in any other way than by saying, What wilt thou have me to do? is an attempt to compel God to declare himself, or to hasten his work. It is presumption of a kind similar to the making of a stone into bread. The faith which will move mountains is that confidence in God which comes from seeking nothing but his will. A man who was thus faithful would die of hunger sooner than say to the stone, *Be bread;* would meet the scoffs of the unbelieving without reply and with apparent defeat, sooner than say to the mountain, *Be thou cast into the sea,* even if he know that it would be torn from its foundations at the word, except he knew first that God would have it so.

FEBRUARY 23RD

The temptation in the wilderness was an epitome and type of the temptations to come. And as Jesus refused to make stones bread, so throughout his life he never wrought a miracle to help himself; as he refused to cast himself from the temple to convince Satan or glory visibly in his Sonship, so he steadily refused to give the sign which the human Satans demanded. How easy it seems to have confounded them, and strengthened his followers! But such conviction would stand in the way of a better conviction in his disciples. For neither adversary nor disciple could in any true sense be convinced by such a show, which would but prove his power. It might prove the presence of a god, but would it prove God himself? Would it bring him nearer to them, who could not see him in the face of his Son? To say, *Thou art God*, without knowing what *"Thou"* means, is of no use. God is a name only, except we know *God*. Our Lord did not care to be so acknowledged.

On the same principle, he would not do miracles where unbelief predominated. I do not think he cared much about them. A mere marvel is soon forgotten, and long before it is forgotten, many minds have begun to doubt the senses, their own even, which communicated it. Inward sight alone can convince of truth, signs and wonders never. But the vision of the truth itself, something altogether beyond the region of signs and wonders, is the power of God; it is salvation.

61

FEBRUARY 24TH

We shall now look at the third temptation. The first was to help himself in his need; the second to assert the Father; the third to deliver his brethren. To deliver them, that is, after the fashion of men, from the outside. Indeed, the whole Temptation may be regarded as the contest of the seen and the unseen, of the outer and inner. And as in the others, the evil in this last lay in that it was a temptation to save his brethren, instead of doing the Will of his Father.

Could it not be other than a temptation to think that he might, if he would, lay a righteous grasp upon the reins of government? Glad visions arose before him of the prisoner breaking jubilant from the cell of injustice, of the widow lifting up the bowed head before the devouring Pharisee. Could he not mold the people at his will? Could he not, transfigured in his snowy garments, call aloud in the streets of Jerusalem, "Behold your King?" The fierce warriors of his nation would beat their ploughshares into swords to fight a grand holy war against the tyrants of the race. Ah! But when were his garments white as snow? When, through them, did the light stream from his glorified body? Not when he looked to such a conquest, but when, on a mount like this, he "spake of the decease that he should *accomplish* at Jerusalem." Not even thine own visions of love and truth, O Savior of the world, shall be thy guides to thy goal, but the will of thy Father in heaven.

FEBRUARY 25TH

A nd how would our Lord, in thus conquering, be a servant of Satan? Wherein would this be a falling-down and a worshipping of him who was the lord of misrule and its pain?

I will not inquire whether such an enterprise could be accomplished without the worship of Satan, whether men could be managed for such an end without more of less of the trickery practiced by every ambitious leader, every self-serving conqueror--- without double-dealing, tact, flattery, and finesse. If these were necessary, such a career for our Lord refuses to be for a moment imagined. But I will ask whether to know better and do not so well, is not a serving of Satan; whether to lead men on in the name of God as towards the best when the end is not the best, is not a serving of Satan; whether to flatter their pride by making them conquerors of the enemies of their nation instead of their own evils, is not a serving of Satan; in a word, whether, to desert the mission of God, who knew that men could not be set free in that way, and sent him to be a man, a true man, the one man, among them, that his life might become their life, and that so they might be as free in prison or on the cross as upon a hillside or on a throne; whether to give men over to the lie of believing other than spirit and truth to be the worship of the Father, other than love the fulfilling of the law, other than the offering of their best selves the service of God; whether to desert God thus, and give men over thus, would not have been to fall down and worship the devil.

FEBRUARY 26TH

Nothing but the obedience of the Son, the obedience unto death, the absolute *doing* of the will of God because it was the truth, could redeem the prisoner, the widow, the orphan. But it would redeem them by redeeming also the conquest-ridden ruler, the stripe-giving jailer, the unjust judge. The earth should be free because Love was stronger than Death. He would not pluck the spreading branches of the tree; he would lay the axe to its root. It would take time, but the tree would be dead at last. It would take time, but his Father had time enough. It would take courage and strength and self-denial and endurance, but his Father could give him all. It would cost pain of body and mind, yea, agony and torture; but those he was ready to take on himself. It would cost him the vision of many sad and, to all but him, hopeless sights: he must see tears without wiping them, hear sighs without changing them into laughter, see the dead lie, and let them lie, see Rachel weeping for her children and refusing to be comforted; he must go to his grave and they not know that thus he was setting all things right for them. His work must be one with and completing God's Creation and God's history. The disappointment and sorrow and fear he could, he would bear. The will of God should be done. Man should be free, not merely as man thinks of himself, but as God thinks of him. Man shall grow into the likeness of the divine thought, free not in his own fancy, but in absolute divine fact of being. The great and beautiful and perfect will of God *must* be done.

FEBRUARY 27TH

"Get thee hence, Satan: for it is written, Thou shalt worship the Lord Thy God, and him only shalt thou serve."

It was when Peter would have withstood him as he set his face steadfastly to meet this death at Jerusalem, that he gave Peter the same kind of answer that he gave to Satan in the wilderness. "Then the devil leaveth him, and behold angels came and ministered unto him," saith St. Matthew. They brought him the food he had waited for, walking in the strength of the word. He would have died if it had not come now.

"And when the devil had ended all the temptation, he departed from him for a season." So saith St. Luke. Then Satan ventured once more. When? Was it when, in the agony of the last faint, the Lord cried out, "Why hast thou forsaken me?" When, having done the great work, having laid it aside clean and pure as the linen cloth that was ready now to enfold him, another cloud than that on the mount overshadowed his soul, and out of it came a voiceless persuasion that, after all was done, God did not care for his work or for him?

Even in those words, the adversary was foiled—and forever. For when he seemed to be forsaken, his cry was still, *"My God! My God!"*

THE ELOI

"My God, my God, why hast thou forsaken me?"

Matthew 27:46

FEBRUARY 28TH

The Lord hides nothing that can be revealed, and will not warn away the foot that treads in naked humility even upon the ground of that terrible conflict between him and Evil, when the smoke of the battle rose up between him and his Father, and for one terrible moment ere he broke the bonds of life and walked weary and triumphant into his arms, hid God from the eyes of his Son. He will give us even to meditate the one thought that slew him at last, when he could bear no more, and fled to the Father to know that he loved him, and was well-pleased with him. The Lord hides not his sacred sufferings, for truth is light, and would be light in the minds of men. Let us then put off our shoes, and draw near, and bow the head, and kiss those feet that bear forever the scars of our victory.

It is with the holiest fear that we should approach the terrible fact of the sufferings of our Lord. Let no one think that those were less because he was more. These sufferings were awful indeed when they began to invade the region about the will; when the struggle to keep consciously trusting in God began to sink in darkness; when his will put forth its last determined effort in that cry after the vanishing vision of the Father: My God, my God, why hast thou forsaken me? Never before had he been unable to see God beside him. Yet never was God nearer to him than now. He could not see, could not feel him near, and yet it is "*My* God" that he cries.

FEBRUARY 29TH

Thus the Will of Jesus, in the very moment when his faith seems about to yield, is finally triumphant. It has no *feeling* now to support it, no beatific vision to absorb it. It stands naked in his soul and tortured, as he stood naked and scourged before Pilate. Pure and simple and surrounded by fire, it declares for God. The sacrifice ascends in the cry, *My God.* The cry comes not out of happiness, out of peace, out of hope. It was a cry *in* desolation, but it came out of Faith. It is the last voice of Truth, speaking when it can but cry. The divine horror of that moment is unfathomable by human soul. It was blackness out of darkness. And yet he would believe. Yet he would hold fast. God was his God yet. *My God--* and in the cry came forth the Victory, and all was over soon. Of the peace that followed that cry, the peace of a perfect soul, large as the universe, pure as light, ardent as life, victorious for God and his brethren, he himself alone can ever know the breadth and length and depth and height.

MARCH 1ST

Without this last trial of all, the temptations of our Master had not been so full as the human cup could hold; there would have been one region through which we had to pass wherein we might call aloud upon our Captain-brother, and there would be no voice or hearing: he had avoided the fatal spot! The temptations of the desert came to the young, strong man with his road before him and the presence of his God around him; nay, gathered their very force from the exuberance of his conscious faith. "Dare and do, for God is with thee," said the devil. "I know it, and therefore I will wait," returned the King. And now, after three years of divine action, when his course is run, when the giving up of the ghost is at hand, when friends have forsaken him and fled, comes the voice of the enemy again at his ear: "Despair and die, for God is not with thee. All is in vain. Death, not life, is Thy refuge." "My God, my God, why hast thou forsaken me?" the Master cries.

The foreseen horror has come; he is drinking the dread cup, and the Will has vanished from his eyes. In agony, the Will of Jesus arises, perfect, and of itself, unsupported, declares—a naked consciousness of misery hung in the waste darkness of the universe—declares for God, in defiance of pain, of death, of the blackness within and around it; calls aloud upon the vanished God. This is the Faith of the Son of God. God withdrew that the perfect Will of the Son might arise and go forth to find the Will of the Father.

MARCH 2ND

B ut what can this Alpine apex of faith have to do with the creatures who call themselves Christians, creeping about in the valleys, hardly knowing that there are mountains above them? We are and remain such creeping Christians because we look at ourselves and not at Christ. When the inward sun is shining, and the wind of thought, blowing where it lists amid the flowers and leaves of fancy and imagination, rouses glad forms and feelings, it is easy to look upwards and say '*My God.*' It is even easy in pain, so long as it does not pass certain bounds, to hope in God for deliverance, or pray for strength to endure. But what is to be done when all feeling is gone? When a man does not know whether he believes or not, whether he loves or not? When art, poetry, religion are nothing to him, so swallowed up is he in pain, or mental depression, or temptation, or he knows not what. It seems to him then that God does not care for him, and certainly he does not care for God. If he is still humble, he thinks that he is so bad that God cannot care for him. And he then believes that God loves us only because and while we love him, instead of believing that God loves us always, that we live only by his love. Or he does not believe in God at all, which is better.

So long as we have nothing to say to God, nothing to do with him, save in the sunshine of the mind when we feel him near us, we are poor creatures, willed upon, not willing; reeds blown about of the wind; not bad, but poor creatures.

MARCH 3RD

How do we act when our feelings for God are gone? Do we not sit mourning over their loss? Or worse, make frantic efforts to rouse them? Or, ten times worse, relapse into a state of temporary atheism, and yield to the pressing temptation? Are we conscious of evil thoughts, but too lazy to rouse ourselves against them? We know we must get rid of them someday, but meantime—never mind. No impulse comes to arouse us, and so we remain as we are.

God does not, by the instant gift of his Spirit, make us always desire good, love purity, and aspire after him and his will. He wants to make us in his own image, *choosing* the good, *refusing* the evil. How should he effect this if he were *always* moving us from within, as he does at divine intervals, towards the beauty of holiness? God gives us room *to be*, that we may act of ourselves, that we may exercise the pure will for good. Do not, therefore, imagine me to mean that we can do anything of ourselves without God. If we choose the right at last, it is all God's doing, and only the more his that it is ours, only in a far more marvelous way his than if he had kept us filled with holy impulses precluding the need for choice.

MARCH 4TH

For this very point God has been educating us, leading us, pushing us: that we may choose him and his will, and so be tenfold more his children, of his own best making, in the freedom of the will that we find for the first time to be our own when we make it a loving sacrifice to him, for which he has been working from the foundations of the earth, than we could be in the most ecstatic worship flowing from the divinest impulse, without this *willing* sacrifice. For God made our individuality as well as, and a greater marvel than, our dependence; made our *apartness* from himself, that freedom should bind us divinely dearer to himself, with a new and inscrutable marvel of love; for the Godhead is still at the root, is the making root of our individuality, and the freer the man, the stronger the bond that binds him to him who made his freedom. He made our wills, and is striving to make them free; for only in the perfection of our individuality and the freedom of our wills can we be altogether his children.

This is full of mystery, but can we not see enough in it to make us very glad and very peaceful?

MARCH 5TH

See, then, what lies within our reach every time that we are thus lapt in the folds of night. Troubled soul, thou art not bound to feel, but art bound to arise. God loves thee whether thou feelest or not. Thou canst not love when thou wilt, but thou art bound to fight the hatred in thee to the last. He changes not because thou changest. Nay, he has a special tenderness of love towards thee for that thou art in the dark and hast no light, and his heart is glad when thou dost arise and say, "Thou art my God. I am thy child. Forsake me not." Then fold the arms of thy faith, and wait in quietness until light goes up in thy darkness. Fold the arms of thy faith, but not of thy Action: think of something that thou ought to do, and go and do it, if it be but the sweeping of a room, the preparing of a meal, or a visit to a friend. Heed not thy feelings; do thy work.

As God lives by his own will, and we live in him, so has he given us the power to will in ourselves. Then, if ever the time should come, as perhaps it must come to each of us, when the earth shall be but a sterile promontory, when God himself shall be but a name, and Jesus an old story, then, even then, we shall be able to cry out with our Lord, "My God, my God, why hast thou forsaken me?" Nor shall we die then, without being able to take up his last words as well, and say, "*Father, into Thy hands I commend my spirit.*"

THE HANDS OF THE FATHER

"Father, into Thy hand I commend my spirit."

Luke 23:46

MARCH 6TH

S t. Matthew, St. Mark and St. Luke tell us of a cry with a loud voice, and the giving up of the ghost, between which St. Luke records the words, "Father, into Thy hands I commend my spirit." Surely never in all books, in all the words of men, can there be so much expressed as lay unarticulated in that cry of the Son of God. Now had he made his Father Lord no longer in the might of making and loving alone, but Lord in right of devotion and deed of love. Now should inward sonship and the spirit of glad sacrifice be born in the hearts of men; for the divine obedience was perfected by suffering. He had been amongst his brethren what he would have his brethren be. He had done for them what he would have them do for God and for each other. God was henceforth inside and beneath them, as well as around and above them, suffering with them and for them, giving them all he had, his very life-being, his essence of existence, what best he loved, what best he was. He had been among them, their God-brother. And the mighty story ends with a cry.

Then the cry meant, *It is finished*; the cry meant, *Father into thy hands I commend my spirit*. Every highest human act is just a giving back to God of that which he first gave to us. Every act of worship is a holding up to God of what God hath made us. "Lord, I am thy child, and know not how to thank thee save by uplifting the offering of the overflowing of thy life, and calling aloud, 'It is thine; it is mine. I am thine, and therefore I am mine.'"

75

MARCH 7TH

The last act of our Lord in thus commending his spirit at the close of his life, was only a summing up of what he had been doing all his life. He had been offering this sacrifice, the sacrifice of himself, all those years, and in thus sacrificing he had lived the divine life. Every morning when he went out ere it was day, every evening when he lingered on the night-lapt mountain after his friends were gone, he was offering himself to his Father in the communion of loving words, of speechless feeling, of healing deeds. For the way to worship God while the daylight lasts is to work; the service of God is the helping of our fellows.

This commending of our spirits to the Father is not a grievous burden, but the highest privilege we possess, the simplest, most blessed thing in the world. For a man may say, I am going out into the business and turmoil of the day, where so many temptations may come to do less faithfully, less kindly, less diligently than the Lord would have me do. Father, into thy hands. Am I going to do a good deed? Then, of all times, Father, into thy hands, lest the enemy should have me now. Am I going to do a hard duty, from which I would gladly be turned aside? To refuse a friend's request? Am I in pain? Take my spirit, Lord, and see, as thou art wont, that it has no more than it can bear. Am I going to die? Father, into thy hands I commend my spirit. For it is thy business, not mine. Thou wilt know every shade of my suffering, Thou wilt care for me with thy perfect fatherhood.

MARCH 8TH

Think, brothers and sisters, we walk in the air of an eternal fatherhood. Graciousness and truth are around, above, beneath us, yea, in us. When we are least worthy, then, most tempted, hardest, unkindest, let us yet commend our spirits into his hands. Whither else dare we send them? And shall we dare to think if we, being evil, know how to give good gifts to our children, God will not give us his own spirit when we come to ask him? Will not some heavenly dew descend cool upon the hot anger? Some genial rain-drop on the dry selfishness, some glance of sunlight on the cloudy hopelessness?

Nor is there anything we can ask for ourselves that we may not ask for another. We may commend any brother, any sister, to the common fatherhood. Indeed, we shall never be able to rest in the bosom of the Father till the fatherhood is fully revealed to us in the love of the brothers. He cannot be our father save as he is their father; and if we do not see him and feel him as their father, we cannot know him as ours. Never shall we know him aright until we rejoice and exult that he is the Father of all. He that loveth not his brother whom he hath seen, how can he love God whom he hath not seen? For to rest at last in those hands into which the Lord commended his spirit, we must have learned already *to love our neighbor as ourselves.*

LOVE THY NEIGHBOR

"Thou shalt love thy neighbor as thyself."

Matthew 22:39

MARCH 9TH

Our Lord quoted from the words of God to Moses, "*Thou shalt not avenge, nor bear any grudge against the children of thy people, but thou shalt love thy neighbor as thyself: I am the Lord.* Leviticus 19:18

Our Lord never thought of being original. The older the saying, the better, if it utters the truth. In him it becomes fact: the *Word* was made *flesh*.

The same words are twice quoted by St. Paul, and once by St. James, always in a similar mode: they represent love as the fulfilling of the law. And will the law fulfil love? No, verily. A man is not a lover because he keeps the law, he keeps the law because he is a lover. It is impossible to keep the law towards one's neighbor except one loves him. The man who tries most to keep the law will be the man most aware of defeat. We are not made for law, but for love. Love is infinitely more than law—it is the creator of the law. Had it not been for love, not one of the shall-nots of the law would have been uttered. Were there no love in us, what sense of justice could we have? For that is not justice which consists only in a sense of our own rights.

MARCH 10TH

Of what use then is the law? To lead us to Christ, the Truth. To waken in our minds a sense of what our deepest nature, the presence, namely, of God *in* us, requires of us—to let us know, in part by failure, that the purest effort of will of which we are capable cannot lift us up even to the abstaining from wrong to our neighbor. What man, for instance, who loves not his neighbor and yet wishes to keep the law, will dare be confident that never by word, look, tone, gesture, or silence, will he bear false witness against that neighbor? What man can judge his neighbor aright save him whose love makes him refuse to judge him? Therefore are we told to love, and not judge. It is the sole justice of which we are capable, and that perfected will comprise all justice. In order to fulfil the commonest law, we must rise into a loftier region altogether, a region that is above law, because it is spirit and life and makes the law: in order to keep the law towards our neighbor, we must love our neighbor. We are not made for law, but for grace—or for faith, to use another word so much misused. We are made on too large a scale altogether to have any pure relation to mere justice, if indeed we can say there is such a thing. It is but an abstract idea which, in reality, will not be abstracted. The law comes to make us long for the needful grace— that is, for the divine condition, in which love is all, for God is Love.

MARCH 11TH

T hough the fulfilling of the law is the practical form love will take, and the neglect of it is the conviction of lovelessness; though it is the mode in which a man's *will* must begin at once to be love to his neighbor, yet, that our Lord meant by the love of our neighbor, not the fulfilling of the law towards him, but that condition of being which results in the fulfilling of the law and more, is clear from his story of the good Samaritan. "Who is my neighbor?" asked the lawyer. And the Lord taught him that everyone for whom he could do anything was his neighbor. Which of the inhibitions of the law is illustrated in the tale? Not one. The love that is more than law, and renders its breach impossible, lives in the endless story, coming out in tenderness and active loving-kindness.

A man, beginning to try to love his neighbor, finds that this can no more be reached in itself, by the man's will, than the law could be so reached. As a man cannot keep the law without first rising into the love of his neighbor, so he cannot love his neighbor without first rising higher still. It is the man fulfilled of God from whom he came and by whom he is, who alone can as himself love his neighbor who came from God too and is by God too. In God alone can man meet man. When the mind and life of Christ course through the man who has become a part of his body, then the love of his brothers is there as conscious life. From Christ through our neighbors comes the life that makes us a part of his body.

MARCH 12TH

I t *is* possible to love our neighbor as ourselves. Our Lord *never* spoke hyperbolically, although that is the supposition on which many unconsciously interpret his words, in order to persuade themselves that they believe them. Let us suppose a man endeavors obedience; he begins to think about his neighbors and tries to feel love towards them. He finds at once they begin to classify themselves. Some he loves already, and he remembers the words of our Lord, "If ye love them which love you, what reward have ye?" So his mind fixes upon a second class, a man who is no enemy, but who is dull and uninteresting. With all his effort, he finds the goal as far off as ever. Naturally, the question arises, "Is it my duty to love him who is unlovable?" Certainly not, if he is unlovable. But that is begging the question. Thereupon the man asks, "How, then, is the man to be loved by me? Why should I love my neighbor as myself?"

We must not answer, "Because the Lord says so." No man can love his neighbor *merely* because the Lord says so. A man cannot obey any command in the way the Lord loves until he sees the reasonableness of it. I do not say to put off obeying *until* he sees the command's reasonableness; that is quite another thing. It is beautiful to obey the Lord; it is more beautiful yet to worship the radiant source of our light, and it is for the sake of obedient vision that our Lord commands us. For then our heart meets his: we see God.

MARCH 13TH

I magine a conversation which might pass in a man's mind on each side of the question, Why should I love my neighbor? "He is the same as I, therefore I ought to love him." *"Why? I am I. He is he."* "But he has the same thoughts, feelings, hopes, sorrows, joys, as I." *"And why should I love him for that? He must mind his, I can only do with mine. I cannot get into his consciousness, nor he into mine. I wish I could love him, but I do not see why. I am an individual, as is he. My self must be closer to me that he can be. Two bodies keep me apart from his self. I am isolated with myself."*

Now, here lies the mistake at last. The thinker falsely judges the individuality of each man a separation between them. On the contrary, it is the sole possibility and very bond of love. 'Otherness' is the essential ground of affection. Whenever anything does not exist that ought to be there, the space it ought to occupy assumes the appearance of a separating gulf. The negative appears to be a positive. Where a man does not love, the not-loving must seem rational. For no one loves because he sees why, but because he loves. No human reason can be given for the highest necessity of divinely created existence. For reasons are always from above. Love cannot be argued about in its absence, it cannot be dealt with by the algebra of the reason or imagination. Indeed, the very talking about it raises a mist between the mind and the vision of it. But let a man once love, and all the difficulties which appeared opposed to love will just be so many arguments for loving.

MARCH 14TH

Let a man once find another who has fallen among thieves; let him be a neighbor to him, pouring oil and wine into his wounds, and binding them, and setting him on his own beast, and paying for him at the inn; let him do all this merely from a sense of duty; let him abate no jot of his Jewish superiority; let him condescend to the very baseness of his own lowest nature; yet such will be the virtue of obeying an eternal truth even to his poor measure, of putting in actuality what he has not even seen in theory, of doing the truth even without believing it, that even if the truth does not after the deed give the faintest glimmer as truth in the man, he will yet be ages nearer the truth than before, for he will go on his way loving that Samaritan neighbor a little more than his Jewish dignity will justify. How much more if he be a man who would love his neighbor if he could, will the higher condition unsought have been found in the action! For man is a whole; and so soon as he *unites himself* by obedient action, the truth that is in him makes itself known to him. For his action is his response to his maker's design, his individual part in the creation of himself, his yielding to the All in all. When will once begins to aspire, it will soon find that action must precede feeling, that the man may know the foundation itself of feeling.

With those who recognize no authority as the ground for tentative action, a doubt, a suspicion of truth ought to be ground enough for putting it to the test.

MARCH 15TH

The two truths by which man lives are Love to God and Love to Man. And the whole system of divine education as regards the relation of man and man has for its end that a man should love his neighbor as himself. It is not a lesson that he can learn by itself, or a duty the obligation of which can be shown by argument, any more than the difference between right and wrong can be defined in other terms than their own. "But that difference," it may be objected, "is self-evident to everyone, whereas the loving of one's neighbor is not seen to be a primary truth; so far from it, that far the greater number of those who hope for an eternity of blessedness through him who taught it, do not really believe it to be a truth; believe, on the contrary, that the paramount obligation is to take care of one's self at much risk of forgetting one's neighbor."

The human race generally has got as far as the recognition of right and wrong, and most men are born capable of making the distinction. But the race has not yet lived long enough for its latest offspring to be born with the perception of the truth of love to the neighbor. It is to be seen by the present individual only after a long reception of, and submission to, the education of life. And once seen, it is believed.

MARCH 16TH

Consider the relation of brotherhood and sisterhood. Why does my brother come of the same father and mother? Why do I behold the helplessness and confidence of his infancy? Why do we behold the wonder of the sunset and the mystery of the growing moon together? Why do we quarrel, vow revenge and silence and endless enmity, and unable to resist the brotherhood within us, wind arm in arm and forget all within the hour? Is it not that Love may grow lord of all between us? Is it not that I may feel towards him what there are no words to express—a love in which the divine self rushes forth in utter self-forgetfulness, a love stronger than death?

But if we stop there, what will be the result? He who loves not his brother for deeper reasons than those of common parentage will cease to love him at all. The love that enlarges not its borders, that is not ever spreading into universal brotherhood, will contract, shrivel, decay, and die. There is a bond between me and the most wretched liar that ever died for the murder he would not even confess, closer infinitely than that which springs only from having the same mother and father. My brother in the flesh is my first neighbor, that I may learn brotherhood. My second neighbor is anyone with whom I have human dealings: the man who mends my clothes; the man who drives me in his cab, the man who begs from me in the street, and to whom, it may be, for his own sake, I must not give.

MARCH 17TH

A man must not choose his neighbor; he must take the neighbor that God sends him. In him, whoever he be, lies, hidden or revealed, a beautiful brother. The neighbor is just the man who is next to you at the moment, the man with whom any business has brought you in contact. Thus will love spread in wider and stronger pulses till the whole human race will be to the man sacredly lovely. Drink-debased, vice-defeatured, pride-puffed, they will yet be brothers, yet be sisters, yet be God-born neighbors. Any rough-hewn semblance of humanity will at length be enough to move the man to reverence and affection. It is harder for some to learn this than for others. There are whose first impulse is ever to repel and not to receive. But learn they must. Even these may grow in this grace until a countenance unknown will awake in them a yearning of affection rising to pain, because there is for it no expression, and they can only give the man to God and be still.

And now will come in all the arguments out of which the man tried in vain before to build a stair up to the sunny heights of love. "Ah brother! Thou hast a soul like mine," he will say. "Thou art oppressed with thy sorrows, uplifted with thy joys. Perhaps thou knowest not so well as I, that a region of gladness surrounds all thy grief, of light all thy darkness. Oh, my brother! I will love thee. I cannot come very near thee: I will love thee the more! Thou art not me; thou art another life—a second self; therefore I can, and will love thee."

MARCH 18TH

W hen once to a man the human face is the human face divine, and the hand of his neighbor is the hand of a brother, then will he understand what St. Paul meant when he said, "I could wish that myself were accursed from Christ for my brethren." But he will no longer understand those who, so far from feeling the love of their neighbor an essential of their being, expect to be set free from its law in the world to come. There, on the battlements of safety in the narrow circle of their heaven, they will regard hell from afar and say to each other, "Listen to their moans. But do not weep, for they are our neighbors no more." St. Paul would be wretched before the throne of God, if he thought there was one man beyond the pale of his mercy, and that as much for God's glory as for the man's sake. Who that loves his brother would not, upheld by the love of Christ, arise from the company of the blessed and walk down into the dismal regions of despair to sit with the last of the unredeemed, and be himself more blessed in the pains of hell than in the glories of heaven? Who, I mean, that had the mind of Christ, that had the love of the Father?

But it is a wild question. God is, and shall be, All in all. Father of our brothers and sisters, thou wilt not be less glorious than we, taught of Christ, are able to think thee. It is because we hope not for them in thee, not knowing thee, not knowing thy love, that we are so hard and heartless to the brothers and sisters whom thou hast given us.

MARCH 19TH

The love of our neighbor is the only door out of the dungeon of self. A man may think his consciousness is himself, whereas his life consists in the inbreathing of God, and the consciousness of the universe of truth. To have himself, to know himself, to enjoy himself, he calls life; whereas, if he would forget himself, tenfold would be his life in God and his neighbors. The region of man's life is a spiritual region. God, his friends, his neighbors, his brothers all, are the wide world in which alone his spirit can find room. 'Himself' is his dungeon. If he feels it not now, he will yet feel it one day—feel it as a living soul would feel being prisoned in a dead body and buried in a stone-ribbed vault within the last ripple of the sound of the chanting people in the church above. His life is in loving all forms of life, his health is in the body of which the Son of Man is the head. The whole region of life is open to him; he must live in it or perish.

But he may have begun to love his neighbor, with the hope of ere long loving him as himself, and, notwithstanding, start back affrighted at yet another word of our Lord, seeming to be another law yet harder than the first, although in truth it is not another, for without obedience to it the former cannot be attained. A man has not yet learned to love his neighbor as himself if his heart sinks within him at the words, *"I say unto you, Love your enemies."*

LOVE THINE ENEMY

"Ye have heard that it hath been said, Thou shalt love thy neighbor, and hate thine enemy; but I say unto you, Love your enemies, bless them that curse you, do good to them that hate you, and pray for them which despitefully use you, and persecute you; that ye may be the children of your Father, which is in heaven; for he maketh his sun to rise on the evil and on the good, and sendeth rain on the just and on the unjust. For if ye love them which love you, what reward have ye? Do not even the publicans the same? And if ye salute your brethren only, what do ye more than others? do not even the publicans so? Be ye therefore perfect, even as your Father which is in heaven is perfect."

Matthew 5:43-48

MARCH 20TH

I s this not at length too much to expect? Will a man ever love his enemies? He may come to do good to them that hate him; but when will he pray for them that despitefully use him and persecute him? When?

When he is the child of his Father in heaven. Then shall he love his neighbor as himself, even if that neighbor is his enemy. In the passage in Leviticus 19:18, quoted by our Lord and his apostles, we find the neighbor and the enemy are one: "Thou shalt not avenge, nor bear any grudge against the children of thy people, but thou shalt love thy neighbor as thyself: I am the Lord."

Look at the glorious way in which Jesus interprets the scripture that went before him. "I am the Lord" –"That ye may be perfect, as your Father in heaven is perfect." Is it then reasonable to love our enemies? God does; therefore it must be the highest reason. But is it reasonable to expect that man should become capable of doing so? Yes, on one ground: that the divine energy is at work in man, to render at length man's doing divine as his nature is. For this our Lord prayed when he said: "That they all may be one, as thou Father, art in me, and I in thee, that they also may be one in us." Nothing could be less likely to human judgment; yet our Lord knows that one day it will come.

MARCH 21ST

Why should we love our enemies? "Are our enemies men like ourselves?" let me begin by asking. Yes. "Upon what ground? The ground of their enmity?" No. "In virtue of cruelty, heartlessness, injustice?" Certainly not. We do not call the offering of human sacrifices, the torturing of captives, and cannibalism, 'humanity.' The humanity of men who do such deeds lies in something deeper. It is in virtue of the divine essence which is in them that that we call our enemies men and women. It is this humanity that we are to love—something deeper altogether than, and independent of, the region of hate. "Is this humanity in every one of our enemies?" Yes, else there were nothing to love. Then we *must* love it, come between us and it what may.

But how can we love a man or a woman who is cruel and unjust to us? Who sears with contempt, who is self-righteous, self-seeking, self-admiring? Who can even sneer, the most inhuman of human faults, far worse in its essence than mere murder? These things cannot be loved. But are these the man? Lies there not within him a divine element of brotherhood, something which, once awakened to be its own holy self in the man, will loathe these unlovely things tenfold more than we loathe them now? Shall this divine thing have no recognition from us? Say rather, "My love shall come as near thee as it may; and when thine comes forth to meet mine, we shall be one in the indwelling God."

MARCH 22ND

I f anyone say, "Do not make such vague distinctions. Look at *that* person. Can you deny he is unlovely? How then can you love him?" I answer, "That person, with the evil thing cast out of him, will be his real self. The thing that now makes you dislike him is separable from him, is therefore not he; it makes himself so much less himself, for it is working death in him. Now he is in danger of ceasing to be a person at all. Begin to love him now and help him into the loveliness which is his."

But those who will not acknowledge the claim of love, may yet acknowledge the claim of justice. There are those who would shrink with horror from the idea of doing injustice to some of their neighbors, yet would shrink with equal horror from the idea of loving them. But it is impossible to be just without love, and much more cannot justice co-exist with hate. It is hard enough to be just to our friends; how shall our enemies fare with us? For man is not made for justice from his fellows, but for love, which is greater than justice. *Mere* justice is an impossibility, a fiction of analysis. It does not exist between man and man, save relative to human *law*. Love is the law of our condition, without which we can no more render justice than a man can keep a straight line walking in the dark. The eye is not single, and the body is not full of light. No man who is even indifferent to his brother can recognize the claim which the man's humanity has upon him. Nay, the very indifference itself is an injustice.

MARCH 23RD

ach man must ask, "Is my neighbor indeed my enemy, or am I my neighbor's enemy, and so take him to be mine? Awful thought! Or, if he be mine, am I not his? Am I not refusing to acknowledge the child of the kingdom within his bosom, so killing the child of the kingdom within my own?" We are accountable for the ill in ourselves and have to kill it, and for seeing the good in our neighbor, that we might cherish it. He only, in the name and power of God, can kill the bad in him; we can cherish the good in him by being good to it across all the evil fog that comes between our love and his good. Nor ought it to be forgotten that this fog is often the result of misapprehension and mistake. O brother, sister, across this weary fog, I call to the divine in thee, not to say, "Why hatest thou me?" but to say, "In God's name, I love thee." And I will wait until the true self looks out of thine eyes, and knows the true self in me.

And again I ask, what if we are in the wrong and do the wrong, and hate because we have injured? What then? Why, then, let us cry to God as from the throat of hell; struggle as if possessed of an evil spirit; call out, as one buried alive, from the sepulcher of our evil consciousness, that God would take pity upon us, the chief of sinners. Nothing will help but the Spirit proceeding from the Father and the Son, casting out and revealing. It will be with a terrible cry and a lying as one dead, that such a demon will go out. But what a vision will then arise in the depths of the purified soul!

94

MARCH 24TH

"Be ye therefore perfect, even as your father which is in heaven is perfect." "Love your enemies, and ye shall be the children of the highest." It is the divine glory to forgive. Yet will a time come when the Unchangeable will cease to forgive; when it will not more belong to his perfection to love his enemies; when he will look calmly, and his children look calmly too, upon the everlasting torments of our brothers and sisters?

O brother, believe it not, lest it quench forgiveness in thee, and thou be not forgiven, but go down with those thy brothers to the torment; whence, if God were not better than that phantom some callest God, thou shouldst never come out; but whence assuredly thou shalt come out when thou hast paid the uttermost farthing; when thou hast learned of God in hell what thou didst refuse to learn of him upon the gentle-toned earth: the story of him who was mighty to save, because he was perfect in love.

O Father, thou art All-in-all, perfect beyond the longing of thy children, and we are all and altogether thine. Thou wilt make us pure and loving and free. We shall stand fearless in thy presence, infinite in the love of each other, because perfect in thy love. Lord Jesus, let the heart of a child be given to us, that so we may arise from the grave of our dead selves and die no more, but see face to face the God of the Living.

THE GOD OF THE LIVING

"He is not a God of the dead, but of the living; for all live unto him."

St. Luke 20:38

MARCH 25TH

S hall God call himself the God of the dead, of those who were alive once, but whom he either could not or would not keep alive? Is that the Godhood, and its relation to those who worship it? "Trust in me, for I took care of your fathers once upon a time, though they are gone now. Worship and obey me, for I will be good to you for threescore years and ten, or thereabouts; and after that, when you are not, and the world goes on all the same without you, I will call myself your God still." Nay, God changes not. If he has once said to a man, "I am thy God," and that man has died the death of the Sadducee's creed, then we have a right to say God is the God of the dead.

What Godlike relation can the ever-living, life-giving, changeless God hold to creatures who partake not of his life, who have death at the very core of their being? If they are not worth keeping alive, then God's creating is a poor thing, and he is not so divine as even the poor thoughts of those his dying creatures have been able to imagine him. This that we call death is but a form in the eyes of men. It looks final, an awful cessation, an utter change; it seems not probable that there is anything beyond. But our Lord says, "All live unto him." With him death is not. The beloved pass from our sight, but they pass not from thine. Thy life sees our life, O Lord. All are present to thee. Thou thinkest about us eternally more than we think about thee. The little life that burns within the body of this death, glows unquenchable in thy true-seeing eyes.

MARCH 26TH

L et us inquire what is meant by the resurrection of the body. With what body do the resurrected come? Surely we are not required to believe that the same body is raised again; that is against science, common sense, and Scripture. St. Paul represents the matter quite otherwise. A man's material body will be to his consciousness at death no more than the old garment he throws aside at night, intending to put on a new and a better in the morning. Yet not the less is the doctrine of the Resurrection needful as the very breath of life to our longing souls. Let us know what it means, and we shall see that it is precious.

What is the use of this body of ours? It is the means of Revelation to us. It is by the body that we come into contact with Nature, with our fellow-men, with all their revelations of God to us. It is through the body that we receive all the lessons of passion, of suffering, of love, of beauty, of science. It is through the body that we are both trained outwards from ourselves, and driven inwards into our deepest selves to find God. It is no less of God's making than the spirit that is clothed therein. We cannot yet have learned all that we are meant to learn through the body. How much of the teaching even of this world can the most diligent and most favored man have exhausted before he is called to leave it! Is all that remains to be lost? Who that has loved this earth can but believe that the spiritual body of which St. Paul speaks will be a yet higher channel of such revelation?

MARCH 27TH

We need not only a body to convey revelation to us, but to reveal us to others. Therefore the new body must be like the old. Nay, it must be the same body, glorified as we are glorified, with all that was distinctive of each from his fellows more visible than ever before. The accidental, the nonessential, the incomplete will have vanished. That which made the body what it was in the eyes of those who loved us will be tenfold there. Every eye shall see the beloved, every heart will cry, "My own again! More mine because more himself than ever I beheld him!" Do we not say on earth, "He is not himself today," or "She is more like herself than I have seen her for long?" For we carry a better likeness of our friends in our hearts than their countenances, save at precious seasons, manifest to us.

Shall a man love his neighbor as himself, and must he be content not to know him in heaven? Shall the love that God has created towards father and mother, brother and sister, wife and child, go moaning and longing to all eternity; or worse, far worse, die out of our bosoms? No, God will not take you, has not taken you from me to bury you out of my sight in the abyss of his own unfathomable being, where I cannot follow and find you, myself lost in the same awful gulf. Our God is an unveiling, a revealing God. He will raise you from the dead, that I may behold you; that that which vanished from the earth may again stand forth, looking out of the same eyes of eternal love and truth.

MARCH 28TH

In the changes which, thank God, must take place when the mortal puts on immortality, shall we not feel that the nobler our friends are, the more they are like themselves; that the more the idea of each is carried out in the perfection of beauty, the more like they are to what we thought them in our most exalted moods, to that which we saw in them in the rarest moments of profoundest communion, to that which we beheld through the veil of all their imperfections when we loved them the truest?

Lord, evermore give us this Resurrection, like thine own in the body of thy Transfiguration. Let us see and hear, and know, and be seen, and heard, and known, as thou seest, hearest, and knowest. Give us glorified bodies through which to reveal the glorified thoughts which shall then inhabit us, when not only shalt thou reveal God, but each of us shall reveal thee.

And for this, Lord Jesus, come thou, the child, the obedient God, that we may be one with thee, and with every man and woman whom thou hast made, in the Father.

THE WAY

"If thou wouldst be perfect."

St. Matthew 19:21

MARCH 29TH

Let us consider the story of the rich youth who came to our Lord. We find in St. Matthew the commencement of the conversation very different from that given in the Gospels of St. Mark and St. Luke. Yet they blend perfectly.

As Jesus went out of a house, the young man came running to him, and kneeling down in the way, addressed him as "Good Master." The words with which the Lord interrupts his address reveal the whole attitude of his being. At that moment, just as much as when in the garden of Gethsemane, his whole thought, his whole delight, was in the thought, the will, the being of his Father. To its home in the heart of the Father his heart ever turned. That was the mystery of his gladness; his life was hid with God. Every truth and grandeur of life passed before him as it was; neither ambition nor disappointment could distort them to his eternal childlike gaze; he beheld and loved them from the bosom of the Father. It was not for himself he came to the world; he came that men might know the Father who was his joy, his life. The sons of men were his Father's children like himself: that the Father should have them all in his bosom was the one thought of his heart; that should be his doing for his Father, cost him what it might! He did not care to hear himself called good. He was there to let men see the goodness of the Father. For that he entered the weary dream of the world, in which the glory was so dulled and clouded. "You call me good! You should know my Father!'

MARCH 30TH

The Lord's greatness consisted in his Father being greater than he: who calls into being is greater than who is called. The Father was always the Father, the Son always the Son; yet the Son is not of himself, but by the Father. All that is the Lord's is the Father's, and all that is the Father's he has given to the Son. The Lord's goodness is of the Father's goodness; because the Father is good, the Son is good. When the word *good* enters the ears of the Son, his heart lifts it at once to his Father. His words contain no denial of goodness in himself; in his grand self-regard he was not the original of his goodness, neither did he care for his own goodness, except to be good. But for his Father's goodness, he would spend life, suffering, and death to make that known! His other children must learn to give him his due, and love him as did the primal Son! The Father was all in all to the Son, and the Son no more thought of his own goodness than an honest man thinks of his honesty. When the good man sees goodness, he thinks of his own evil: Jesus had no evil to think of, but neither does he think of his goodness; he delights in his Father's.

'Why do you call me good? None is good except God alone."

MARCH 31ST

hecked thus, the youth turns to the question which, working in his heart, had brought him running, and made him kneel: what good thing shall he do that he may have eternal life? He thought to gain his objective by a doing, when the very thing desired was *a being*: he would have that as a possession which must possess him. But the Lord cared neither for isolated truth nor for orphaned deed. It was truth in the inward parts, it was the good heart, the mother of good deeds, he cherished. It was good men he cared about, not notions of good things, or even good actions, save as the outcome of life, of love and will in the soul taking shape and coming forth. He would die to make men good and true. His whole heart would respond to the cry of sad publican or despairing Pharisee, "How am I to be good?'

When the Lord says, "Why askest thou me concerning that which is good?' we must not put emphasis on the *me*: he was the proper person to ask, only the question was not the right one. The good thing was a small matter; the good Being was all in all. 'Why ask me about the good thing? There is one living good, in whom the good thing, and all good, is alive. Ask me rather about the good person, the good being—the origin of all good. It is not with this or that good thing we have to do, but with that power whence comes our power even to speak the word *good*. To know God is to be good. It is not to make us do all things right he cares, but to make us hunger and thirst after righteousness.

APRIL 1ST

The youth is looking for some unknown good thing to do, and the Lord sends him back to the doing of what he knows, and that in answer to his question concerning the way to eternal life. He has already more than hinted where the answer lies, namely, in God himself, but that the youth is not yet capable of receiving; he must begin with him farther back: "If thou wouldst enter into life, keep the commandments." For verily, if the commandments have nothing to do with entering into life, why were they ever given to men? They are the beginning of the way. If a man had kept all those commandments, yet would he not therefore have in him the life eternal; nevertheless, without keeping of the commandments there is no entering into life; the keeping of them is the path to the gate of life. It is not life, but it is the way to it.

The Lord says nothing about the first table of the law: why does he not tell this youth as he did the lawyer, that to love God is everything? He had given him a glimpse of the essence of his own life, had pointed the youth to the heart of all, for him to think of afterwards: he was not ready for it yet. To love God with all our heart, and soul, and strength, and mind, is to know God, and to know him *is* eternal life. But to begin with that would be as sensible as to say to one asking how to reach the top of some mountain, "Just set your foot on that shining snow-clad peak, high there in the blue, and you will at once be where you wish to go."

APRIL 2ND

The young man was not yet capable of seeing or believing that to love God is eternal life. How many Christians are? How many care that they are not? The Lord tells him he must keep the commandments, and when the young man asks, "Which?" specifies only those that have to do with his neighbor, ending with the highest and most difficult. If I am told, 'But no man can perfectly keep a single commandment of the second table any more than of the first,' I respond, surely not—else why should they have been given? Is there no meaning in the word *keep* except it be qualified by *perfectly*? That no keeping but a perfect one will *satisfy* God, I hold with all my heart; but that there is none else he *cares* for, is one of the lies of the enemy. What father is not pleased with the first tottering attempt of his little one to walk? What father would be satisfied with anything but the manly step of the full-grown son?

The youth responds at once that he *has* observed the commandments; there must be a keeping of them which, although anything but perfect, is yet acceptable to the heart of him from whom nothing is hid. The immediate end of the commandments never was that men should succeed in obeying them, but that, finding they could not do that which yet must be done, they should be driven to the source of life and law. This had been wrought in the youth; he desired eternal life, of which there was no word in the law: the keeping of the law had served to develop a hunger which no keeping of the law could fill.

APRIL 3RD

Having kept the commandments, the youth needed and was ready for a further lesson. The Lord saw in him sore need of perfection—the thing the commonplace Christian thinks he can best do without—the thing the elect hungers after with an eternal hunger. Perfection, the perfection of the Father, is eternal life. 'If thou wouldst be perfect,' said the Lord. What an honor for the youth to be by him supposed desirous of perfection! And what an enormous demand does he make of him! To gain the perfection he desired, the one thing lacking was that he should sell all that he had, give it to the poor, and follow the Lord! Much, much more would be necessary before perfection was reached, but certainly the next step, to sell and follow, would have been the step into life: had he taken it, in the very act would have been born in him that whose essence is eternal life, needing but process to develop it into the glorious consciousness of oneness with The Life.

Was it not hard? Hard to let earth go, and take heaven instead? For eternal life, to let dead things drop? Let him say it was hard who does not know the Lord! The youth was so pleasing in the eyes of the Master, that he would take him to be with him—to walk with him, and rest with him, and go with him only to do for him what he did for his Father in heaven—to plead with men, be a mediator between God and men. He would set him free at once, a child of the kingdom, an heir of the life eternal.

APRIL 4TH

I do not suppose that the youth was one whom ordinary people would call a lover of money; I imagine he was just like most good men of property: he valued his possessions—looked on them as a good. I suspect that in the case of another, he would value a man more who had *means*, value a man less who had none—like most who are reading these words. They have not a notion how entirely they will one day have to alter their judgment, or have it altered for them, in this respect: well for them if they alter it themselves! From this false way of thinking, the Lord would deliver the young man. As the thing was, he was a slave, for a man is in bondage to whatever he cannot part with that is less than himself. The young man would enter into freedom and life, delivered from the bondage of mammon by the lovely will of the Lord in him, one with his own. By the putting forth of the divine energy in him, he would escape the corruption that is in the world through lust—that is, the desire or pleasure of *having*. But the young man would not.

Was the Lord then premature in his demand? Was the youth not ready for it? I do not believe it. He gave him the very next lesson in the divine education for which he was ready; it was time the demand should be made upon him. It was time that he should refuse, so that he would know what manner of spirit he was of, and meet the confusions of soul, the sad searchings of heart that must follow. A time comes to every man when he must obey, or make such refusal—*and know it.*

APRIL 5TH

Was the refusal of the young man of necessity final? Because he declined to enter into life, was the door of life closed against him? Verily, I have not so learned Christ. And that the lesson was not lost, I see in this, that he went away sorrowful. Was such sorrow, in the mind of an earnest youth, likely to grow less or more? Could the nature of one who had kept the commandments be so slight that, after having sought and talked with Jesus, he would care less about eternal life than before? Many, alas! have looked upon his face, yet have never seen him, and have turned back; some have kept company with him for years, and denied him; but their weakness is not the measure of the patience or the resources of God. Perhaps this youth was never one of the Lord's so long as he was on the earth, but perhaps, when he saw that the Master himself cared nothing for the wealth he had told him to cast away, he became one of those who sold all they had, and came and laid the money at the apostles' feet. In the meantime he had that in his soul which made it heavy: by the gravity of his riches the world held him, and would not let him rise. He counted his weight his strength, and it was his weakness. And how now would he go on with his keeping of the commandments? Would he not begin to see more plainly his shortcomings, the larger scope of their requirements? Might be not feel the keeping of them more imperative than ever, yet impossible without something he had not? It needs all the power of a live soul to keep the law—a power of life, not of struggle; the strength of love, not the effort of duty.

APRIL 6TH

The youth had begun early to climb the eternal stair. He had kept the commandments, and by every keeping had climbed. But because he was *well-to-do,* he felt *well-to-be;* quite, but for that lack of eternal life! His possessions gave him a standing in the world. He knew himself looked up to; he liked to be looked up to; he looked up to himself because of his means, forgetting that *means* are but tools, and poor tools, too. To part with his wealth would be to sink to the level of his inferiors! Why should he not keep it? Why not use it in the service of the Master? What wisdom could there be in throwing away such a grand advantage? He could devote it, but he could not cast it from him! He could devote it, but he could not devote himself! He could not make himself naked as a little child and let his Father take him! To him it was not the word of wisdom the "Good Master" spoke. How could a rich man believe he would be of more value without his money, that the battle of God could be better fought without its impediment? But the Master had repudiated money that he might do the will of his Father; and the disciple must be as his master. Had he done as the Master told him, he would soon have come to understand.

Obedience is the opener of eyes.

APRIL 7TH

There is this danger to every good youth in keeping the commandments, that he will probably think of himself more highly than he ought to think. Doubtless such a youth is exceptional; but the number of fools not yet acknowledging the first condition of manhood nowise alters the fact that he who has begun to recognize duty is but a tottering child on the path of life. The Father's arms are stretched out to receive him; but he is not at all the admirable creature that he thinks himself. I do not know what share this besetting sin of *the good young man* may have had in the miserable failure of the rich youth; but it may well be that he thought the Master under-valued his work as well as his wealth, and was less than fair to him.

The eternal life he sought was likely but the poor idea of living forever, all that commonplace minds grasp at for eternal life. When a man has eternal life, that is, when he is one with God, what should he do but live forever? But without oneness with God, mere existence would be but a curse. How miserable his precious things, his golden vessels, his stately house, must have seemed when he went back to them from the face of the Lord! Surely it cannot have been long before in shame and misery he cast all from him, even as Judas cast away the thirty pieces of silver. For, although never can man be saved without being freed from his possessions, it is yet only *hard*, not impossible, *for a rich man to enter into the kingdom of God.*

THE HARDNESS OF THE WAY

"Children, how hard is it!"

St. Mark 10:24

APRIL 8TH

I suspect there is scarcely a young man rich and thoughtful who is not ready to feel our Lord's treatment of this young man hard. He is apt to ask, "Why should it be difficult for a rich man to enter into the kingdom of heaven?" He is ready to look upon this as an arbitrary decree, arising from some prejudice in the divine mind. Why should the rich fare differently? They do not perceive that the law is they *shall* fare like other people, whereas they want to fare as rich people. The rich man does not by any necessity belong to the kingdom of Satan, but into that kingdom he is especially welcome, whereas into the kingdom of heaven he will be just as welcome as any other man.

I suspect that many a rich man turns from this story with a resentful feeling. To the man born to riches they seem not merely a natural, but an essential condition of well-being; and the man who has *made* his money feels it by the labor of his soul, the travail of the day, and the care of the night. Each feels a right to have and to hold. Why should he not "make the best of both worlds?" He would compromise, and serve Mammon a little and God much. He would not put the lower in utter subservience to the higher by casting away the treasure of this world and taking the treasure of heaven instead. He would gain as little as may be of heaven—but something, with the loss of as little as possible of the world. That which he desires of heaven is not its best; that which he would not yield of the world is its most worthless.

APRIL 9TH

I can well imagine an honest youth thus reasoning with himself: "If I make up my mind to be a Christian, shall I be required to part with all I possess? It must have been comparatively easy in those times to give up the kind of things they had! If I had been he, I am sure I should have done it—at the demand of the Savior in person. But I do not love money as he was in danger of doing. I try to do good with my money! If everyone with a conscience had to give up all, the world would go to the devil! Besides, he said, 'If thou wouldst be perfect, go, sell that thou hast.' I cannot be perfect; it is hopeless; and he does not expect it."

It would be more honest if the youth said, "I do not want to be perfect; I am content to be saved." Such as he little think that perfection *is* salvation. I will suppose myself in conversation with such a youth. I should little care to set forth anything called truth, except in siege for surrender to the law of liberty. If I cannot persuade, I would be silent. I would not labor to instruct the keenest intellect; I would rather learn for myself. To persuade the heart, the will, the action, is alone worth the full energy of a man. His strength is first for his own, then for his neighbor's manhood. He must first pluck out the beam from his own eye, then the mote out of his brother's—if indeed it be more than the projection of the beam in his own. To make a man happy as a lark might be to do him grievous wrong; to make a man wake, rise, look up, and turn, is worth the life and death of the Son of the Eternal.

APRIL 10TH

I ask the youth, "Have you been keeping the commandments?" "I will not dare to say that," I suppose him to answer. "But," I ask, "Does your answer imply that, counting the Lord a hard master, you have taken the less pains to do as he would have you? Or that, bending your energies to the absolute perfection he requires, you have the more perceived the impossibility of fulfilling the law? Have you, filled with desire to be perfect, gone kneeling to the Master to learn more of the way to eternal life? Or are you so well satisfied with what you are, that you have never hungered and thirsted after the righteousness of God, the perfection of your being? If so, then be comforted; the Master does not require of you to sell what you have and give to the poor. *You* follow him! Bring him a true heart, an obedient hand: he has given his life-blood for that; but your money—he neither needs it nor cares for it. *Go and keep the commandments.* They are enough for you. When in keeping them you have found the great reward of loving righteousness, and that with all the energy you can put forth you are but an unprofitable servant; when you are aware of a something beyond all that your mind can think, yet not beyond what your heart can desire—a something that seems as if it never could be yours, which yet your life is worthless without; when you have come therefore to the Master with the cry, "What shall I do that I may inherit eternal life?" it may be he will then say to you, "Sell all that you have and give to the poor, and come follow me."

APRIL 11TH

"For the rich young man to have sold all and followed our Lord," I tell the inquiring youth, "would have been to accept God's patent of peerage: to you it is not offered. Were one of the disobedient, in the hope of the honor, to part with all he possessed, he would but be sent back to keep the commandments in the new and easier circumstances of his poverty. And does this comfort you? Then alas for you! Your relief is to know that the Lord has no need of you—does not require you to part with your money, does not offer you himself instead!"

"But I do not trust in my riches," this youth might reply. "I trust in the merits of my Lord and Savior. I trust in his finished work, in the sacrifice he has offered."

"Yes!" I respond. "You will trust in anything but the Man himself who tells you it is hard to be saved! Not all the merits of God and his Christ can give you eternal life; only God and his Christ can; and they cannot, would not if they could, without your keeping the commandments. The knowledge of the living God *is* eternal life. What have you to do with his merits? You have to know his being, himself."

Many there are who think *they can do without eternal life, if only they may live forever!* Those who know what eternal life means count it the one terror to live on without it.

APRIL 12TH

Take then the Lord's words: "Children, how hard is it to enter into the kingdom of God!" It is quite like his way of putting things. Calling them first to reflect on the difficulty for every man of entering into the kingdom of God, he reasserts in yet stronger phrase the difficulty of the rich man: "It is easier for a camel to go through a needle's eye, than for a rich man to enter into the kingdom of God." It always will be hard to enter into the kingdom of heaven. It is hard even to believe that one must be born from above—must pass into a new and unknown consciousness. The ceremonial Christian and the law-faithful Jew both shrink from the self-annihilation, the life of grace and truth, the all-embracing love that fills the law full and sets it aside. They cannot accept a condition of *being* as in itself eternal life. And hard to believe in, this life, this kingdom of God, this simplicity of absolute existence, is hard to enter. How hard? As hard as the Master could find words to express: "If any man cometh unto me, and hateth not…his own life also, he cannot be my disciple." And the rich man must find it harder than another to hate his own life. None can know how difficult it is to enter into the kingdom of heaven, but those who have tried—tried hard, and have not ceased to try. Let any tell me of peace, of joy unspeakable as the instant result of the new birth; I deny no such statement. All I care to say is, that, if by salvation they mean less than absolute oneness with God, I count it no salvation, neither would be content with it if it included every joy in the heaven of their best imagining.

APRIL 13TH

D emands previously unknown are continually being made upon the Christian: it is the ever fresh rousing and calling, asking and sending of the Spirit that worketh in the children of obedience. When he thinks he has attained, then is he in danger; when he finds the mountain he has so long been climbing show suddenly a distant peak, whose glory-crowned apex it seems as if no human foot could ever reach—then is there hope for him; proof there is then that he has been climbing, for he beholds the yet unclimbed; he sees what he could not see before; if he knows little of what he is, he knows something of what he is not. He learns ever afresh that he is not in the world as Jesus was in the world; but the very wind that breathes courage as he climbs is the hope that one day he shall be like him, seeing him as he is.

The man who, for consciousness of well-being, depends upon anything but the life essential, is a slave. He is not perfect who, deprived of every *thing*, would not be calmly content; for none the less would he be possessor of all things, the child of the Eternal. *Things* are given us, this body first, that through them we may be trained both to independence and true possession of them. We must possess them; they must not possess us. No man who has not the Father so as to be eternally content in him alone, can possess a sunset or a mine of gold or the love of a fellow-creature according to its nature, as God would have him possess it. But he who has God, has all things.

APRIL 14TH

It is imperative to get rid of the tyranny of *things*. If you ask, "Will not Death ransom us from this tyranny? Therefore why hasten the hour?" I answer, only when a man begins to abstain, then first he recognizes the strength of his passion. When the fetters of gold are gone, on which the man delighted to gaze, though they held him fast to his dungeon wall, when the truth begins to dawn upon him that those fetters were a horror and a disgrace, then will the good of saving death appear, and the man begin to understand that *having* never could be well-being; that it is not by possessing we live, but by life we possess. In this way is the loss of the things he thought he had, a motioning, hardly *towards*, yet in favor of deliverance. It may seem to the man the first of his slavery when it is in truth the beginning of his freedom. Never soul was set free without being made to feel its slavery; nothing but itself can enslave a soul, nothing without itself can free it.

When the drunkard--free of his body, but, retaining his desire, unable to indulge it--has time at length to think, surely there dawns for him then at last a fearful hope! Not until, by the power of God and his own obedient effort, he is raised into such a condition that, be the temptation what it might, he would not yield for an immortality of unrequited drunkenness—all its delights and not one of its penalties—is he saved.

APRIL 15TH

Thus death may give a new opportunity—with some hope for the multitude counting themselves Christians, who are possessed by *things* as by a legion of devils; who stand well in their church; whose lives are regarded as stainless; who are kind, friendly, give largely, believe in the redemption of Jesus, talk of the world and the church; yet whose care all the time is to heap up, to make much into more, to add house to house and field to field, burying themselves deeper and deeper in the ash-heap of *Things*.

But it is not the rich man only who is under the dominion of things; they too are slaves who, having no money, are unhappy from the lack of it. The man who is ever digging his grave is little better than he who already lies moldering in it. The money the one has, the money the other would have, is in each the cause of an eternal stupidity. To the one as to the other comes the word, *"How is it that ye do not understand?"*

THE CAUSE OF SPIRITUAL STUPIDITY

"How is it that ye do not understand?"

St. Mark. 8:21

APRIL 16TH

After feeding the four thousand with seven loaves and a few small fishes, Jesus, having crossed the lake, was met on the other side by certain Pharisees, whose attitude towards him was such that he betook himself again to the boat. On the way back across, the disciples realized that they had but a single loaf. Jesus, still thinking of the Pharisees, and desirous of destroying their influence on his disciples, began to warn them against them. In so doing he made use of a figure they had heard him use before—that of leaven as representing a hidden but potent and pervading energy: the kingdom of heaven, he had told them, was like leaven hid in meal, gradually leavening the whole of it. He now tells them to beware of the leaven of the Pharisees. The disciples, occupied with their lack of provision, the moment they heard the word *leaven*, thought of bread, and imagined perhaps a warning against some danger of defilement from Pharisaical cookery. The leaven like that of the Pharisees was even then at work in their hearts; for the sign the Pharisees sought, they had had a few hours before, and had already, in respect of all that made it of value, forgotten.

It is to the man who is obedient to the word of the Master, that the word of the Master unfolds itself. For life, that is, action, is alone the human condition into which the light of the Living can penetrate; life alone can assimilate life, can change food into growth. See how the disciples here fooled themselves!

APRIL 17TH

See how the Lord calls the disciples to their senses. He does not tell them in so many words where they are wrong; he attacks instead the cause in themselves which led to their mistake—a matter always of infinitely more consequence than any mistake itself, for the one is an untruth in the soul, the other a mere dead blunder born of it. The word-connection between their blunder and our Lord's exhortation is not to be found; the logic of what the Lord said is not on the surface. Often he speaks not to the words but to the thought; here he speaks not even to the thought, but to the whole mode of thinking, to the inward condition of the men.

Our Lord sought to rouse in the disciples a sense of their lack of confidence in God, which was the cause of their blunder as to his meaning. He makes them go over the particulars of the miracles of the loaves, not to refresh their memories—they well enough remembered the marvel—but to make their hearts dwell on them; for they had failed to see their central revelation: the eternal fact of God's love and care and compassion. They knew the number of men, the number of loaves, but they had forgotten the Love that had so broken the bread that its remnants twenty times outweighed its loaves. Having thus questioned them like children, he turns the light of their thoughts upon themselves, and demands, "How is it that ye do not understand?" Then they did understand. He who trusts can understand; he whose mind is set at ease can discover a reason.

APRIL 18TH

The lesson our Lord would have his disciples understand, the only one worthy of the miracle, was that God cared for his children and would provide for their necessities. This lesson they had not learned. No doubt the power of the miracle was some proof of his mission, but the love of it proved it better, for it made it worth proving; it was a throb of the Father's heart. The ground of the Master's upbraiding is not that they did not understand him, but that they did not trust God; that after all they had seen, they yet troubled themselves about bread. The miracles of Jesus were the ordinary works of his Father, wrought small and swift that we might take them in. The lesson of them was that help is always within God's reach when his children want it. The Son's mission was not to show himself as having all power in heaven and earth, but to reveal his Father, to show him to men such as he is, that men may know him, and knowing, trust him. It were a small boon indeed that God should forgive men, and not give himself. It would be but to give them back themselves. Only God, just as he is, God the gift, can turn the sorrow of men's existence into joy. Jesus came to give them God, who is eternal life.

APRIL 19TH

The answer to the Lord's reproach, "How is that ye do not understand?" is plainly this: their minds were so full of care about the day's bread, that they could not think with simplicity about anything else. When the Lord reminded them of what their eyes had seen, and so of what he was and what God was, and of the foolishness of their care, the moment their fear was taught to look up, that moment they began to see what the former words of the Lord must have meant.

The next hour, the next moment, is as much beyond our grasp and as much in God's care, as that a hundred years away. Care for the next minute is just as foolish as care for the morrow. Those claims only of the morrow which have to be prepared today are of the duty of today; the moment which coincides with work to be done, is the moment to be minded; the next is nowhere till God has made it.

It was not this and that fault the Lord had come to set right, but the primary evil of life without God, the root of all evils. If a man forget a thing, God will see to that; man is not lord of his memory or his intellect. But man is lord of his will, his action. That forethought only is right which has to determine duty, and pass into action. To the foundations of yesterday's work well done, the work of the morrow will be sure to fit. Work done is of more consequence for the future than the foresight of an archangel.

APRIL 20TH

With the disciples as with the rich young man, it was *Things* that prevented the Lord from being understood. The disciples were a little further on than he, for they had left all and followed the Lord; but neither had they yet got rid of *Things*. The paltry solitariness of a loaf was enough to hide the Lord from them, to make them unable to understand him. Why, having forgotten, could they not trust? Surely if he had told them that for his sake they must go all day without food, they would not have minded! But they lost sight of God, and were as if either he did not see, or did not care for them.

In the former case it was the possession of wealth, in the latter the not having more than a loaf, that rendered them incapable of receiving the word of the Lord: the evil principle was precisely the same. If it be *Things* that slay you, what matter whether things you have, or things you have not? The youth, not trusting in God, the source of his riches, cannot brook the word of his Son, offering him better riches, more direct from the heart of the Father. The disciples, forgetting who is lord of the harvests of the earth, cannot understand his word, because filled with the fear of a day's hunger. He did not trust in God as having given; they did not trust in God as ready to give.

We are like them when, in *any* trouble, we do not trust him.

APRIL 21ST

D istrust is atheism, and the barrier to all growth. Lord, we do not understand thee, because we do not trust thy Father—whole-hearted to us, as never yet was mother to her first-born! Full of care, as if God had none, we think this and that escapes his notice, or for this and that he does not think! While we who are evil would die to give our children bread to eat, we are not certain the only Good will give us anything of what we desire! The things of thy world so crowded our hearts, that there is no room in them for the things of thy heart, which would raise ours above all fear, and make us merry children in our Father's house! Tomorrow makes today's whole head sick, its whole heart faint. When we should be still, sleeping or dreaming, we are fretting about an hour that lies a half sun's journey away! Not so doest thou, Lord! Thou doest the work of thy Father! But thou knowest it is difficult, *things* pressing upon every sense, to believe that the informing power of them is in the unseen; that out of it they come; that, where we can see no hand directing, a will, nearer than any hand, is moving them from within, causing them to fulfil his word!

Lord, help us to obey, to resist, to trust.

APRIL 22ND

The care that is filling your mind at this moment, or but waiting till you lay the book aside to leap upon you—that need which is no need, is a demon sucking the spring of your life. If you say that yours is a reasonable and unavoidable care, I ask if there is something about it which you must do at this very moment. If not, then you are allowing it to usurp the place of something that *is* at this moment required—the greatest thing that can be required: to trust in the living God, whose will is your life. If God chooses not to give you what you think you need, it is because you only *think* you need it; he will give you something else, something which, though you do not think you want it, you are none the less miserable just because you do not have it. Instead of his great possessions, the young man was to have the company of Jesus, and treasure in heaven. When God refused to deliver a certain man from a sore evil, concerning which he three times besought him, unaccustomed to be denied, God gave him instead his own graciousness, consoled him in person for his pain.

I speak of course of St. Paul; but God deals with all his children after his own father-nature. No scripture is of private interpretation even for a St. Paul. It sets forth God's way with man. If thou art not willing that God should have his way with thee, then, in the name of God, be miserable—till thy misery drive thee to the arms of the Father.

APRIL 23RD

There will be this difference between the rich that loves his riches and the poor that hates his poverty—that, when they die, the heart of the one will be still crowded with things and their pleasures, while the heart of the other will be relieved of their lack; the one has had his good things, the other his evil things. But the rich man who held his things lightly, and did not let them nestle in his heart; who was a flowing stream and not a stagnant pool; who was ever and always forsaking his money—starts, in the new world, side by side with the man who accepted, not hated, his poverty. Each will say, "I am free!"

For the only air of the soul, in which it can breathe and live, is the present God and the spirits of the just; that is our heaven, our home, our all-right place. Cleansed of greed, jealousy, vanity, pride, possession, all the thousand forms of the evil self, we shall be God's children, not one desiring to be before another, any more than to cast that other out; for ambition and hatred will then be seen to be one and the same spirit. "What thou hast, I have; what thou desirest, I will; I give to myself ten times in giving once to thee. My lack, that thou mightest have, would be rich possession."

APRIL 24TH

D ost thou not believe God good enough to care for thee? I would reason with thee to help rid thee of thy troubles, for they hide from thee the thoughts of thy God. The things readiest to be done are not merely in general the most neglected, but, even by the thoughtful man, the oftenest postponed. But may a man become strong in righteousness without first learning to speak truth to his neighbor? Shall a man climb the last flight of the stair who has never set foot on the lowest step? He who does the truth in the small thing is of the truth; he who will do it only in a great thing, who postpones the small thing near him to the great things farther from him, is not. We are like the disciples in the boat, anxious over their one loaf, yet with the Bread of Life at their side. We too dull our understandings with trifles, waste the heavenly time with hurry. To those who possess their souls in patience come the heavenly visions. When a book has been borrowed from me and not returned, and I have forgotten the borrower but fret over the missing volume, while there are countless on my shelves from which the moments thus lost might gather treasure; am I not like the disciples?

Is it not time I lost a few things when I care for them so unreasonably? This losing of things is of the mercy of God; it comes to teach us to let them go.

APRIL 25TH

With every trouble, great or small, go to God, and appeal to him, the God of your life. If your trouble is such that you cannot appeal to him, the more need you should appeal to him! Where one cannot go to God, there is something especially wrong. If you let thought for the morrow, or the next year, or the next month, distress you; if you let the chatter of what is called the public, annoy you; if you seek or greatly heed the judgment of men, you set open your windows to the mosquitoes of care, to drown with their buzzing the voice of the Eternal!

If you tell me that but for care, the needful work of the world would be ill done, I ask you what work will be better done by the greedy or anxious than by the free, fearless soul? Can care be a better inspirer than God? Is he worthy the name of man who, for the fear of starvation, will do better work than for the joy that his labor is not in vain in the Lord? I know as well as you that you are not likely to get rich that way; but neither will you block up the gate of the kingdom of heaven against yourself.

APRIL 26TH

A mbition in every shape has to do with *Things*, with outward advantages for the satisfaction of self-worship; it is that form of pride, foul shadow of Satan, which usurps the place of aspiration. The sole ambition that is of God is the ambition to rise above oneself; all other is of the devil. Yet it is nursed and cherished in many a soul that thinks itself devout, filling it with petty cares and disappointments that swarm like bats and shut out the glory of God. The love of the praise of men, the desire of fame, the pride that takes offence, the puffing-up of knowledge, these and every other form of self-worship—we must get rid of them all. We must be free. The man whom another enslaves may be free as God; to him who is a slave in himself, God will not enter in; he will not sup with him, for he cannot be his friend. He will sit by the humblest hearth where the daily food is prepared; he will not eat in a storage room, let the things stored be thrones and crowns. *Will not*, did I say? *Cannot*, I say. Men full of things would not once partake with God were he by them all day long.

APRIL 27TH

G od will not force any door to enter in. He may send a tempest about the house; yea, shake the house to its foundations. The door must be opened by the willing hand, ere the foot of Love will cross the threshold. Every tempest is but an assault in the siege of love. The terror of God is but the other side of his love; it is love outside the house, that would be inside—love that knows the house is no home, is but a tent, until the Eternal dwells there. Things must be cast out to make room for their souls—the eternal truths which in things find shape and show.

But who is sufficient to cast them out? If a man take courage and encounter the army of bats and demon-snakes that infests the place of the Holy, it is but to find the task too great for him; that the temple of God will not be cleansed by him; that the very dust he raises in sweeping is full of corruptive forces. Let such as would do what they must yet cannot, be what they must yet cannot, remember, with hope and courage, that he who knows all about our being, once *spake a parable to the end that they ought always to pray, and not to faint.*

THE WORD OF JESUS ON PRAYER

"They ought always to pray."

St. Mark. 18:1

APRIL 28TH

The impossibility of doing what we would, as we would, drives us to look for help. Everything difficult indicates something more than our theory of life yet embraces, checks some tendency to abandon the narrow path, leaving open only the way ahead. There is a reality of being in which all things are easy and plain—oneness, that is, with the Lord of Life, and to the point of this prayer every difficulty directs us. But remember: if prayer be anything at all, it is a thing to be done; what matter whether you agree with me or not, if you do not pray?

In the Parable of the Unrighteous Judge, we can take comfort that the Lord recognizes difficulty in the matter of prayer—sees that we need encouragement to go on praying, that it looks as if we were not heard, that it is no wonder we should be ready to faint and leave off. The widow has to go often to the judge who can help her, gaining her end only at long last. The Lord recognizes how things must look to those whom he would have go on praying. Here as elsewhere, he teaches us that we must not go by the look of things, but by the reality behind the look. A truth, a necessity of God's own willed nature, is enough to set up against a whole army of appearances. It looks as if he did not hear you: never mind, he does. The unrighteous judge cared nothing for the woman; those who cry to God are his own chosen. He has made them to cry: they do cry: will he not hear them? For God and those who seek his help are closer than two hands clasped hard in love.

APRIL 29TH

The Lord has made a bold assertion in the face of what seems great delay on the part of God. Having made it, why does he seem to check himself with a sigh, adding, "Nevertheless, when the Son of Man cometh, shall he find faith on the earth?" After all he had said and done, when he came again, after time given for the holy leaven to work would he find men trusting the Father? Would he find them believing, despite the tyranny of appearances? Would they be children enough to know God was hearing them and working for them, though they could not hear him or see him work? That it was because the goal God had in view for them was so high and far, that they could detect no movement of approach thereto? The Lord's sigh meant that the Father would have a dreary time to wait ere his children would know, that is, trust in, him. If men would but make haste, and stir themselves up to take hold on God!

The Lord seems here to refer to his second coming—concerning the time of which, he refused information; concerning the mode of which, he said it would be unexpected; but concerning the duty of which, he insisted it was to be ready: we must be faithful, and at our work. Do those who say, lo here are the signs of his coming, think to be too keen for him, and spy his approach? If, instead of speculation, we gave ourselves to obedience, what a difference would soon be seen in the world! Many eat and drink and talk and teach in his presence; few do the things he says to them! *Obedience* is the one key of life.

APRIL 30TH

I f there be a God, and I am his creature, there may be, there should be, there must be some communication open between him and me. If anyone say there is a God, but one scarce good enough to care about his creatures, I will grant him that it were foolish to pray to such a God; but the notion that, with all the good impulses in us, we are the offspring of a cold-hearted devil, is so horrible in its inconsistency, that I would ask that man what hideous disregard of the truth makes him capable of the supposition!

If I find my position, my consciousness, that of one far from home, nay, that of one in some sort of prison; if I find that I can neither rule the world in which I love, nor my own thoughts or desires; that I cannot quiet my passions, order my likings, determine my ends, will my growth, forget when I would, or recall what I forget; that I cannot love where I would, or hate where I would; that I am no king over myself; that I cannot supply my own needs, do not even always know which of my seeming needs are to be supplied, and which treated as impostors; if, in a word, my own being is in every way too much for me; if I can neither understand it, be satisfied with it, not better it—may it not well give me pause—the pause that ends in prayer?

MAY 1ˢᵀ

He that is made in the image of God must know him or be desolate: the child must have the Father! Witness the dissatisfaction of my soul without him! It cannot act from itself, save in God; acting from what seems itself without God, is a mere yielding to impulse. Instincts of betterment tell me I must rise above my present self—perhaps even above all my possible selves: I see not how to obey, how to carry them out! Surely this world of my unwilled, unchosen, compelled existence, cannot be shut out from him, cannot be unknown to him, unpresent to him from whom I am! Nay, is it not his thinking in which I think? Whatever passes in me must be as naturally known to him as to me. My thought must lie open to him: if he makes me think, how can I elude him in thinking? *"If I should spread my wings toward the dawn, and sojourn at the last of the sea, even there thy hand would lead me, and thy right hand would hold me!"* If I speak to him, if I utter words ever so low; if I but think words to him, nay, if I only think to him, surely he hears, and knows, and acknowledges! Then shall I not think to him? Shall I not tell him my troubles—how he, even he, has troubled me by making me? How unfit I am to be that which I am? That my being is not to me a good thing yet? Shall I not tell him that I need him to comfort me? Shall I not cry to him to be in me rest and strength? Every need of God, lifting up the heart, is a seeking of God, is a begging for himself, is profoundest prayer, and the root and inspirer of all other prayer.

MAY 2ND

The skeptic may scoff, "We *know* that the wind blows: why should we not *know* that God answers prayer?" I reply, What if God does not care to have you know it at second hand? What if there would be no good in that? The sole assurance worth a man's having, even if the most incontestable evidence were open to him from a thousand other quarters, is that to be gained only from personal experience—that assurance in himself which he can least readily receive from another, and which is least capable of being transmuted into evidence for another. The evidence of Jesus Christ could not take the place of that. A truth is of enormous import in relation to the heart, and conscience, and will; it is of little consequence merely as a fact having relation to the understanding. God may hear all prayers that ever were offered to him, and a man may believe that he does, nor be one whit the better for it, so long as God has no prayers of his to hear, he no answers to receive from God. Reader, if you are in any trouble, try whether God will not help you; and if you are in no need, why should you ask questions about prayer? True, he knows little of himself who does not know that he is wretched, and miserable, and poor, and blind, and naked; but until he begins at least to suspect a need, how can he pray? And for one who does not want to pray, I would not lift a straw to defeat such a one in the argument whether God hears or does not hear prayer: for me, let him think what he will—it matters nothing in heaven or earth; whether in hell I do not know.

MAY 3RD

erhaps a man has once believed in God, and prayed to him in great trouble of heart and mind, and at last decides that God did not hear him, and has not prayed since. How, I ask, do you know that he did not hear you? "He did not give me what I asked, though my very soul depended on it." In your judgment. Perhaps he knew better. "I would have believed in him if he had heard me." Till the next desire came which he would not grant, and then you would have turned your God away. A desirable believer you would have made! A worthy brother to him who thought nothing fit to give the Father less than his all! You would accept of him no decision against your desire! God has not to consider his children only at the moment of their prayer. If a man be not fit to be refused, if he be not ready to be treated with love's severity, what he wishes may perhaps be given him in order that he may wish it had not been given him; but barely to give a man what he wants because he wants it, and without further purpose of his good, would be to let a poor ignorant child take his fate into his own hands. Yet is every prayer heard; and the real soul of the prayer may require, for its real answer, that it should not be granted in the form in which it was requested. God knows you better than you know yourself. You shall be satisfied, if you will but let him have his way with the creature he has made. That God should as a loving Father listen, hear, consider, and deal with the request after the perfect tenderness of his heart, is to me enough; it is little that I should go without what I pray for.

MAY 4TH

C oncerning this thing," says St. Paul, "I besought the Lord thrice, that it might depart from me. And he hath said unto me, My grace is sufficient for thee; power is made perfect in weakness." God had a better thing for Paul than granting his prayer and removing his complaint: he would make him strong; the power of Christ should descend and remain upon him; he would make him stronger than his suffering, make him a sharer in the energy of God. Verily, if we have God, we can do without the answer to any prayer.

"But if God is so good, and if he knows all that we need, and better far than we do ourselves, why should it be necessary to ask him for anything?" I answer, What if he knows prayer to be the thing we need first and most? What if the main object in God's idea of prayer be the supplying of our great, our endless need—the need of himself? What if the good of all our smaller and lower needs lies in this, that they help to drive us to God? Hunger may drive the runaway child home, and he may or may not be fed at once, but he needs his mother more than his dinner. Communion with God is the one need of the soul beyond all other need; prayer is the beginning of that communion, and need is the motive of that prayer.

MAY 5TH

Our wants are for the sake of coming into communion with God, our eternal need. If gratitude and love immediately followed the supply of our needs, if God our Savior was the one thought of our hearts, then it might be unnecessary that we should ask for anything we need. But seeing we take our supplies as a matter of course, feeling as if they came out of nothing, or from the earth, or own thoughts, instead of out of a heart of love and a will which alone is force, it is needful that we should be made to feel some at least of our wants, that we may seek him who alone supplies all of them, and find his every gift a window to his heart of truth. So begins a communion, a talking with God, which is the sole end of prayer; yea, of existence itself. To bring his child to his knee, God withholds that man may ask.

For how can God give into the soul of a man what it needs, while that soul cannot receive it? The ripeness for receiving is the asking. When the soul is hungry for the light, for the truth—when its hunger has waked its higher energies, thoroughly roused the will, and brought fitness for receiving the things of God, that action is prayer. Then God can give; then he can be as he would towards the man, for the glory of God is to give himself. We thank thee, Lord Christ, for by thy pain alone do we rise towards the knowledge of this glory of thy Father and our Father.

MAY 6TH

Every gift of God is but a harbinger of his greatest and only sufficing gift—that of himself. No gift unrecognized as coming from God is at its own best; therefore many things that God would gladly give us, things even that we need because we are, must wait until we ask for them, that we may know whence they come; when in all gifts we find him, then in him we shall find all things.

Sometimes to one praying will come the feeling rather than the question, "Would he not be better pleased if I left matters altogether to him?" It comes, I think, of a lack of faith and childlikeness. Such thoughts have no place with St. Paul; he says, "Casting all your care upon him, for he careth for you;" "In everything making your request known unto him." It may even come of ambition after spiritual distinction. In every request, heart and soul and mind ought to supply, "Thy will be done;" but the making of any request brings us near to him, into communion with our Life. Does it not also help us to think of him in all our affairs, and learn in everything to give thanks? Anything large enough for a wish to light upon, is large enough to hang a prayer upon: the thought of him to whom that prayer goes will purify and correct the desire. To say, "Father, I should like this or that," would be enough at once, if the wish were bad, to make us know it and turn from it. Surely it is better to tell him all without fear or anxiety. Was it not thus the Lord carried himself towards his Father when he said, "If it be possible, let this cup pass from me?"

MAY 7TH

The Lord cared more for his Father's will than his own fear: "Nevertheless, not my will, but thine be done." There is no apprehension that God might be displeased with him for saying what he would like, and not leaving it all to his Father. Neither did he regard his Father's plans as necessarily so fixed that they could not be altered by his prayer. The true son-faith is that which comes with boldness, fearless of the Father doing anything but what is right, fatherly, patient, and full of loving-kindness. We must not think to please him by any asceticism even of the spirit; we must speak straight out to him. The true child will not fear, but lay bare his wishes to the perfect Father. The Father may will otherwise, but his grace will be enough for the child.

As to any notion of prevailing by entreaty over an unwilling God, that is heathenish, and belongs to such as think him a hard master, or one like the unjust judge. What so quenching to prayer as the notion of unwillingness in the ear that hears! And when prayer is dull, what makes it flow like the thought that God is waiting to give, wants to give us everything! "Let us therefore come boldly to the throne of grace, that we may obtain mercy, and find grace to help in time of need." We shall be refused our prayer if that be better; but what is good, our Father will give us with divine good will. The Lord spoke his parable "to the end that they ought always to pray, *and not to faint.*"

MAN'S DIFFICULTY CONCERNING PRAYER

"—and not to faint."

St. Luke 18:1

MAY 8TH

How should any design of the All-wise be altered in response to prayer of ours? Because he is the All-wise, who sees before him, and will not block his path. Such objection springs from poorest idea of God in relation to us. It supposes him to have cares and plan and intentions concerning our part of creation, irrespective of us. What is the whole system of things for, but our education? Does God care for suns and planets, for divine mathematics and ordered harmonies, more than for his children? He lays no plans irrespective of his children; and, his design being that they shall be free, active, live things, he sees that space be kept for them: they need room to struggle out of their chrysalis, to undergo the change that comes with the waking will. Surely he may keep his plans in a measure unfixed, waiting the free desire of the individual soul! Is not the design of the first course of his children's education just to bring them to the point where they shall pray? And shall his system be then found hard and fast, as if informed of no live, causing soul, so that he cannot answer the prayer because of the system which has its existence for the sake of the prayer? How could he be Father, who creating, would not make provision, would not keep room for the babbled prayers of his children? Is his perfection a mechanical one? Has he himself no room for choice? What stupidity of perfection would that be which left no margin about God's work, no room for change of plan upon change of fact—yea, even the mighty change that, behold now at length, his child is praying!

MAY 9TH

A divine perfection that were indeed, where was no liberty! If but for himself, God might well desire no change, but he is God for the sake of his growing creatures; all his making and doing is for them, and change is the necessity of their very existence. They need a mighty law of liberty, into which shall never intrude one atom of chance. Is the one idea of creation the begetting of a free, grand, divine will in us? And shall that will, praying with the will of the Father, find itself manacled by foregone laws? No man is so tied by divine law that he can nowise modify his work: shall God not modify his? Law is the slave of Life. If you say, he has made things to go, set them going, and left them—then I say, If his machine interfered with his answering the prayer of a single child, he would sweep it from him—not to bring back chaos, but to make room for his child. If you say, There can be but one perfect way, I answer, Yet the perfect way to bring a thing so far, to a certain crisis, can ill be the perfect way to carry it on after that crisis: the plan will have to change then. God is not occupied with a grand toy of worlds and suns, of forces and waves; these but constitute a portion of his workshops and tools, for the bringing out of righteous men and women to fill his house of love. Would he have let his Son die for a law of nature, as we call it? These doubtless are the outcome of willed laws of his own being; but they take their relations in matter only for the sake of the birth of sons and daughters, that they may yet again be born from above.

MAY 10TH

In all his miracles, Jesus did only in miniature what his Father does ever in the great—in far wider, more elaborate, and beautiful ways; and I will adduce from them an instance of answer to prayer from which we can learn much.

Poor, indeed, was the making of the wine in earthen pots of stone, compared with its making in the lovely growth of the vine, the live roots gathering water from the earth; but what makes it precious to me is the regard of our Lord to a wish of his mother. She had suggested to him that here was an opportunity for appearing in his own greatness, the potent purveyor of wine for the failing feast. It was not in his plan, as we gather from his words: "What to me and thee, woman?" he said: "my hour is not yet come;" but from his look and tone she knew that her desire, scarce half-fashioned into request, was granted. What am I thence to conclude, but that, at the prayer of his mother, he made room in his plans for the things she desired? It was not his wish then to work a miracle, but if his mother wished it, he would! This was a case in which he could do so, for it would interfere nowise with the will of his Father. Was the perfect son to be the only son of man who needed do nothing to please his mother—nothing but what fell in with his plan for the hour? Not so could he be the root, the living heart of the great response of the children to the Father of all! The Son then could change his intent, and spoil nothing: so can the Father; for the Son does nothing but what he sees the Father do.

MAY 11TH

What are we to think concerning prayer for others? If the fitness of answering prayer lies in the praying of him who prays, the attitude necessary to reception does not belong to those *for* whom prayer is made, but *to* him by whom it is made. What fitness then can there be in praying for others? Will God give to another for our asking what he would not give without it? If we believe that God knows every man's needs, and will, for love's sake, not spare one pang that may serve to purify the soul of one of his children, then how can we think he will in any sort alter his way with one because another prays for him? The prayer would arise from nothing in the person prayed for—why should it influence God?

The argument I know not how to answer. I can only, feeling all the difficulty, say "Yet I believe I may pray for my friend—for my enemy—for anybody! There must be some genuine, essential good and power in the prayer of one man for another to the maker of both." The Lord himself prayed to his Father for those the Father loves because they have received his Son. Those who believe in Jesus will be satisfied, in the face of the incomprehensible, that in what he does, reason and right must lie; but not therefore do we understand. At the same time, though I cannot explain, I can show some ground upon which, even had he not been taught to do so, but left alone with his heart, a man might yet pray for another.

MAY 12TH

If God has made us to love like himself, and like himself long to help; if there are those for whom we, like him, would give our lives; if the love in us would, for the very easing of the love he kindled, gift another—like himself who chooses and cherishes even the love that pains him; if, in the midst of a sore need to bless, to give, to help, we are aware of an utter impotence; and if all our hope for ourselves lies in God—what is there for us, what can we think of, what do, but go to God? And where is the natural refuge, there must be the help. There can be no need for which he has no supply. I think God will help my friend that I may be helped—perhaps help me to help him. You see, in praying for another, we pray for ourselves—for the relief of the needs of our love. Would God give us love, and leave that love altogether helpless in us?

God is ever seeking to lift us up into the sharing of his divine nature. See the grandeur of the creative love of the Holy! Nothing less will serve it than to have his children, through his and their suffering, share the throne of his glory! If he would have his children fellow-workers with him; if he has desired and willed that not only by the help of his eternal Son, but by the help also of the children who through him have been born from above, other children shall be brought to his knee, to the plenty of his house, why should he not have kept some margin of room wherein their prayers may work for those whom they have to help?

MAY 13TH

A prayer for another will react upon the mind that prays, its light will grow, will shine the brighter. And, prayer in its perfect idea being a rising up into the will of the Eternal, may not the help of the Father become one with the prayer of the child, and for the prayer of him he holds in his arms, go forth for him who does not yet will to be lifted to his embrace? To his bosom God himself cannot bring his children at once, and not at all except through his own suffering and theirs. But will not any good parent find some way of granting the prayer of the child who comes to him, saying, "Papa, this is my brother's birthday; I have nothing to give him, and I do love him so! Could you give me something to give him, or give him something for me?"

It may be asked: Could not God have given the gift without the prayer? Why should the good of anyone depend on the prayer of another? I can only answer with the return question, why should my love be powerless to help another? If *in* God we live and move and have our being; if the very possibility of loving lies in this, that we exist in and by God himself, we must then be nearer to each other, we must by prayer come closer to each other, than by any bodily proximity or interchange of help. Surely, in the Eternal, hearts are never parted! Surely, through the Eternal, a heart that loves and seeks the good of another, must hold that other within reach!

MAY 14TH

Surely the system of things would not be complete in relation to the best thing in it—love itself—if love had not help in prayer. If I love and cannot help, does not my heart move me to ask him to help who loves and can? Will he answer, "Child, do not trouble me; I am already doing all I can"? If such answer came, who that loved would not be content? But what if the eternal, limitless Love, which, demanding all, gives all, should say, "Pray on, my child; I am hearing you; it goes through me in help to him. We are of one mind about it; I help and you help. I shall have you all safe home with me by and by! There is no fear, only we must work, and not lose heart. Go, and let your light so shine before men that they may see your good things, and glorify me by knowing that I am light and no darkness."

But it may be that the answer to prayer will come in a shape that seems a refusal. It may come even in an increase of that from which we seek deliverance. I know of one who prayed to love better: a sore division came between—out of which at length rose a dawn of tenderness. Our vision is so limited, our theories so small; our faith so continually fashions itself to the fit of our dwarf intellect, that there is endless room for rebellion against ourselves: we must not let our poor knowledge limit our not-so-poor intellect, our intellect limit our faith, our faith limit our divine hope; and reason must humbly watch over all—reason, the candle of the Lord.

MAY 15TH

There are moods of such satisfaction in God that a man may feel as if nothing were left to pray for, as if he had but to wait with patience for what the Lord would work; there are moods of such hungering desire, that petition is crushed into an inarticulate crying; and there is a communion with God that asks for nothing, yet asks for everything. This last is the very essence of prayer, though not petition. It is possible for a man, not indeed to believe *in* God, but to believe there is a God, and yet not desire to enter into communion with him; but he that prays and does not faint will come to recognize that to talk with God is more than to have all prayers granted—that it is the need of all prayer, granted or refused. And he who seeks the Father more than anything he can give, is likely to have what he asks, for he is not likely to ask amiss.

Even such as ask amiss may sometimes have their prayers answered. The Father will never give the child a stone that asks for bread; but I am not sure that he will never give the child a stone that asks for a stone. If the Father say, "My child, that is a stone; it is not bread;" and the child answer, "I am sure it is bread; I want it," may it not be well he should try his bread?

MAY 16TH

In the very structure of the Lord's parable of the unrighteous judge, he seems to take delay in the answering of prayer for granted, and says notwithstanding, "He will avenge them speedily!" The reconciling conclusion is that God loses no time, though the answer may not be immediate. He may delay because it would not be safe to give us at once what we ask: we are not ready for it. Time may be necessary for the working out of the answer. And perhaps, indeed, the better the gift we pray for, the more time is necessary for its arrival. To give us the *spiritual* gift we desire, God may have to begin far back in our spirit, in regions unknown to us, and do much work that we can be aware of only in the results. With his own presence, the one thing for which most earnestly we cry, he may be approaching our consciousness from behind, coming forward through regions of our darkness into our light, long before we begin to be aware that he is answering our request—has answered it and is visiting his child. To *avenge speedily* must mean to make no delay beyond what is absolutely necessary. Because the Son of Man did not appear for thousands of years after men began to cry out for a Savior, shall we imagine he did not come the first moment it was well he should come? Can we doubt that to come a moment sooner would have been to delay, not to expedite, his kingdom? For anything that needs a process, to begin to act at once is to be speedy. God does not put off like the unrighteous judge; he does not delay until irritated by the prayers of the needy: he will hear while they are yet speaking; yea, before they call he will answer.

MAY 17TH

No prayer for any revenge that would gratify the selfishness of our nature, a thing to be burned out of us by the fire of God, needs think to be heard. Be sure, when the Lord prayed his Father to forgive those who crucified him, he uttered his own wish and his Father's will at once: God will never punish according to the abstract abomination of sin, as if men knew what they were doing. "Vengeance is mine," he says: with a right understanding of it, we might as well pray for God's vengeance as for his forgiveness, for that vengeance is to destroy the sin—to make the sinner abjure and hate it; nor is there any satisfaction in a vengeance that seeks or effects less. If nothing else will do, then hell-fire; if less will do, whatever brings repentance. Friends, if any prayers are offered against us because of some wrong you or I have done, God grant us his vengeance! Let us not think that we shall get off!

But perhaps, in saying "He will avenge them speedily," the Lord was thinking of what most troubles his true disciples; and the suggestion is comforting to those whose foes are *within* them; for, if so, he recognizes the evils of self, against which we fight, not as parts of ourselves, but as our foes, on which he will avenge the true self that is at strife with them. And certainly no evil is, or ever could be, of the essential nature of the creature God made! The thing that is not good in us, however associated with our being, is against that being, not of it—is its enemy, on which we need to be avenged. When we fight, he will avenge.

MAY 18TH

Until we fight, evil shall have dominion over us, a dominion to make us miserable; other than miserable can no one be, under the yoke of a nature contrary to his own. Comfort thyself then, who findest thine own heart and soul, or rather the things that move therein, too much for thee: God will avenge his own elect. He is not delaying: he is at work for thee. Only thou must pray, and not faint. Ask, ask; it shall be given you. Seek most the best things; to ask for the best things is to have them; the seed of them is in you, or you could not ask for them.

But from whatever quarter come our troubles, whether from the world outside or the world inside, still let us pray. In his own right way, the only way that could satisfy us, for we are of his kind, will God answer our prayers with help. He will avenge us of our adversaries, and that speedily. Only let us take heed that *we* be adversaries to no man, but fountains of love and forgiving tenderness to all. And from no adversary, either on the way with us, or haunting the secret chamber of our hearts, let us hope to be delivered till we *have paid the last farthing.*

THE LAST FARTHING

"—Verily I say unto thee, thou shalt by no means come out thence, till thou have paid the last farthing."

St. Matthew 5:26

MAY 19TH

There is a thing wonderful and admirable in the parables, not readily grasped, but specially indicated by the Lord himself—their unintelligibility to the mere intellect. They are addressed to the conscience and not to the intellect, to the will and not to the imagination. They are strong and direct but not definite. They are not meant to explain anything, but to rouse a man to the feeling, "I am not what I ought to be, I do not the thing I ought to do!" Many meaningless interpretations may be given by the wise, while work goes undone, while the child who uses them for the necessity of walking in the one path will constantly receive light from them. The greatest obscuring of the words of the Lord comes from those who give themselves to *interpret* rather than *do* them. It was not for our understanding, but for our will, that Christ came. He who does that which he sees, shall understand; he who is set upon understanding rather than doing, shall go on stumbling and speaking foolishness. The gospel itself, and in it the parables of the Truth, are to be understood only by those who walk by what they find. The Lord did not intend that any should know what, known but intellectually, he would imagine he had grasped. When the pilgrim of the truth comes on his journey to the region of the parable, he finds its interpretation. It is not a jewel to be stored, but a well springing by the wayside.

MAY 20TH

L et us try to understand what the Lord himself said about his parables, taking St. Matthew 13:14-15. The purport is, that those who by insincerity and falsehood close their deeper eyes, shall not be capable of using the more superficial eyes of their understanding. They shall not see what is not for such as they. It is the punishment of the true Love, and is continually illustrated and fulfilled. This will help to remove the difficulty that the parables are plainly for the teaching of the truth, and yet the Lord speaks of them as for the concealing of it. They are for the understanding of that man only who is practical—who does the thing he knows, who seeks to understand vitally. They reveal to the live conscience, otherwise not to the keenest intellect---though at the same time they may help to rouse the conscience with glimpses of the truth, where the man is on the borders of waking. Ignorance may be at once a punishment and a kindness: all punishment is kindness, and the best of which the man at the time is capable: To say to them certain things so that they could understand, would but harden them more, because they would not do them; they should have but parables—lanterns of the truth, clear to those who will walk in the light, dark to those who will not. "You choose the dark; you shall stay in the dark till the terrors that dwell in the dark frighten you, and cause you to cry out." God puts a seal upon the will of man; that seal is either his great punishment, or his mighty favor: "Ye love the darkness, abide in the darkness." "O woman, great is thy faith; be it done unto thee even as thou wilt!"

MAY 21ST

The parable in Matthew 5:21-26 is an appeal to the common sense of those that hear it, in regard to every affair of righteousness. With respect to what claims lie against you, do at once what you must do one day. As there is no escape from payment, escape at least the prison that will enforce it. It is useless to think to escape the eternal law of things. To the honest man and to the man who would be honest, the word is of truly gracious import. To the untrue, it is a terrible threat. "Thou shalt render the right, cost you what it may," is a dread sound in the ears of those whose life is a falsehood; but for those who love righteousness, it is a joy profound as peace to know that God is determined upon such payment, is determined to have his children clean, clear, pure as very snow; is determined that not only shall they with his help make up for whatever wrong they have done, but at length be incapable, under any temptation, of doing the thing that is not divine.

There is no escape from strict justice, from doing *all* that is required of us. A way to avoid any demand of righteousness would be an infinitely worse way than the road to the everlasting fire, for its end would be eternal death. No, there is no escape. There is no heaven with a little of hell in it. Out Satan must go, every hair and feather!

MAY 22ND

Neither shalt thou be delivered from the necessity of *being* good by being made good. Neither death nor any admittance into good company will make thee good; though, doubtless, if thou be willing and try, these and all other best helps will be given thee. There is no clothing in a robe of imputed righteousness, that poorest of legal cobwebs spun by spiritual spiders. Christ is our righteousness, not that we should escape punishment, still less escape being righteous, but as the live potent creator of righteousness in us, so that we, with our wills receiving his spirit, shall like him resist unto blood, striving against sin; shall know in ourselves, as he knows, what a lovely thing is righteousness, what a mean, ugly, unnatural thing is unrighteousness. He is our righteousness, and that righteousness is no fiction, no pretense, no imputation.

Righteousness is just fairness—from God to man, from man to God and to man; it is giving everyone his due. He is righteous, and no one else, who does this. And any system that claims there is any salvation but that of becoming righteous even as Jesus is righteous; that a man can be made good, without his own willed share in the making; that a man is saved by having his sins hidden under a robe of imputed righteousness—that system is of the devil and not of God. Thank God, not even error shall injure the true of heart; it is not wickedness. They grow in the truth, and as love casts out fear, so truth casts our falsehood.

MAY 23RD

I read in this parable that a man had better make up his mind to be righteous, to be fair, to do what he can to pay what he owes, in any and all the relations of life. Arrange your matters with those who have anything against you; you will have to do it, and that under less easy circumstances than now. Putting it off is of no use. The thing has to be done, and there are means of compelling you.

Consider a dispute wherein a man considers himself in the right. He wants nothing but his rights! I respond to him, it is a very small matter *to you* whether or not the man gives you your rights; it is life or death to you whether or not you give him his. Whether he pay you what you count his debt or no, you will be compelled to pay him all you owe him. If you owe him a dollar and he owes you a million, you must pay him whether he pays you the million or not. If, owing you love, he gives you hate, you, owing him love, have still to pay it. Love unpaid, a justice not done, a praise withheld, a false judgment passed: these uttermost farthings you must pay him, whether he pays you or not. The same holds with every demand of God: by refusing to pay, the man makes an adversary who will compel him—and that for the man's own sake. There is a prison, and its doors do not open until entire satisfaction is rendered, the last farthing paid.

MAY 24TH

The main debts whose payment God demands are those which lie at the root of all right, those we owe in mind, and soul, and being. Whatever in us can be or make an adversary, whatever could prevent us from doing the will of God, or from agreeing with our fellow—all must be yielded. Our every relation, both to God and our fellow, must be acknowledged heartily. Smaller debts, if any debt can be small, follow as a matter of course.

If the man acknowledge, and would pay if he could, but cannot, the universe will be taxed to help him. If the man accepts the will of God, he is the child of the Father, the whole power and wealth of the Father is for him, and the uttermost farthing will easily be paid. If the man denies the debt, or, acknowledging, does nothing toward paying it, then—at last—the prison! God in the dark can make a man thirst for the light, who never in the light sought but the dark. The cells of the prison may differ in degree of darkness; but they are all alike in this, that not a door opens but to payment. There is no day but the will of God, and he who is of the night cannot be forever allowed to roam the day; unprized, the light must be taken from him, that he may know what the darkness is. When the darkness is perfect, when he is totally without the light he has spent the light in slaying, then will he know darkness.

MAY 25TH

I think I have seen from afar something of the final prison of all, and I will endeavor to convey what I think it may be. It is the ghastly dark beyond the gates of the city of which God is the light—where the evil dogs go ranging, silent as the dark, for there is no sound any more than sight. The man wakes from the final struggle of death in absolute loneliness. Not a hint, not a shadow of anything outside his consciousness reaches him. All is dark and dumb; no motion—not the breath of a wind, nothing to suggest being or thing besides the man himself, no sign of God anywhere. In the midst of the live world he cared for nothing but himself; now in the dead world he is in God's prison, his own separated self. He would not believe in God because he never saw God; now he doubts if there be such a thing as the face of a man. Next after doubt comes reasoning on the doubt: "The only one must be God! I know no one but myself: I must myself be God!" Soon, misery will beget on imagination a thousand shapes of woe, which he will not be able to rule—a whole world of miserable contradictions and cold-fever dreams. In such evil case, I believe the man would be glad to come in contact with the worst-loathed insect; his enemy, could he but be aware of him, he would be ready to worship. For the misery would be not merely the absence of all other beings, but the fearful, endless, unavoidable presence of his own self. It is the lovely creatures God has made all around us, in them giving us himself, that, until we know him, save us from the frenzy of aloneness. The man who minds only himself must at last go mad if God did not interfere.

MAY 26TH

Can there be any way out of the misery of such a hell? Will the soul that could not believe in God, with all his lovely world around testifying of him, believe when shut in the prison of its own, lonely self? It would for a time try to believe that it was indeed nothing, a mere glow of the setting sun on a cloud of dust, a paltry dream that dreamed itself—then, ah, if only the dream might dream it was no more! Self-loathing, and that for no sin, from no repentance, would begin and grow and grow; and if a being be capable of self-disgust, is there not some room for hope—as much as a pinch of earth in the cleft of a rock might yield for the growth of a pine? All his years in the world he had received the endless gifts of sun and air, earth and sea and human face divine; now the poorest thinning of the darkness he would hail as men of old the glow of a descending angel; it would be as a messenger from God. Not that he would think of God! It takes long to think of God; but hope, not yet seeming hope, would begin to dawn in his bosom, and the thinner darkness would be as a cave of light, a refuge from the horrid self of which he used to be so proud. And the light would grow and grow across the awful gulf between the soul and its haven—its repentance—for repentance is the first pressure of the bosom of God; and in the twilight, struggling and faint, the man would feel another thought beside his, another thinking Something nigh his dreary self—perhaps the man he had most wronged, most hated—and would be glad that someone was near him: the man he had most injured and was most ashamed to meet, would be a refuge from himself—oh, how welcome!

MAY 27TH

So might I imagine a thousand steps up from the darkness, each a little less dark, a little nearer the light—but, ah, the weary way! He cannot come out until he will have paid the uttermost farthing! Repentance once begun, however, may grow more and more rapid! If God once gets a willing hold, if with but one finger he touches the man's self, swift as possibility will he draw him from the darkness into the light. For that for which the forlorn, self-ruined wretch was made, was to be a child of God, a partaker of the divine nature, an heir of God and joint heir with Christ. Out of the abyss into which he cast himself, refusing to be the heir of God, he must rise and be raised. To the heart of God, the one and only goal of the human race—the refuge and home of all and each, he must set out and go, or that last glimmer of humanity will die from him. Whoever will live must cease to be a slave and become a child of God. There is no half-way house of rest, where ungodliness may be dallied with, nor prove quite fatal. Be they few or many cast into such a prison as I have endeavored to imagine, there can be no deliverance for the human soul, whether in that prison or out of it, but in paying the last farthing, in becoming lowly, penitent, self-refusing—so receiving the sonship and learning to cry, *Father!*

ABBA, FATHER!

"—the spirit of adoption, whereby we cry, Abba, Father."

Romans 8:15

MAY 28TH

The hardest, gladdest thing in the world is to cry *Father!* from a full heart. I would help whom I may to call thus upon the Father, for there are things in all forms of the systematic teaching of Christianity to check this outgoing of the heart—with some to render it simply impossible. Such a cold wind blowing at the very gate of heaven—thank God, *outside* the gate!—is the so-called doctrine of *Adoption*. When a heart hears that it is not the child of God by origin, from the first of its being, but may possibly be adopted into his family, its love sinks at once in a cold faint: where is its own father, and who is this that would adopt it? Whatever any company of good men thinks or believes, is to be approached with respect; but nothing must come between the soul and spirit of the father, who is himself the teacher of his children.

As no scripture is of private interpretation, so is there no feeling in human heart which exists in that heart alone, which is not, in some form or degree, in every heart; and thence I conclude that many must have groaned like myself under the supposed authority of this doctrine. The refusal to look up to God as our Father is the one central wrong in the whole human affair; the inability, the one central misery: whatever serves to clear any difficulty from the way of the recognition of the Father, will therefore more or less undermine every difficulty in life.

MAY 29TH

I s God not my very own Father? Is he my Father only in a sort or fashion—by a legal contrivance? The adoption of God would indeed be a blessed thing if another than he had given me being! But if he gave me being, then it means no reception, but repudiation. "O Father, am I not your child?"

It avails nothing to answer that we lost our birthright by the fall, that I have been cast out: can any repudiation, even that of God, undo the facts of my origin? Nor is it merely that he made me: by whose power do I go on living? When he cast me out, did I then begin to draw my being from myself—or from the devil? It cannot be that I am not the creature of God. Creation in the image of God is fatherhood. To be fit to receive his word implies being of his kind. No matter how his image may have been defaced in me: the thing defaced is his image, remains his defaced image. What makes me evil and miserable is, that the thing spoiled in me is the image of the Perfect. In whatever manner I may have become an unworthy child, I cannot thereby have ceased to be a child of God. Is it not proof, this complaint of my heart at the word Adoption? Is it not the spirit of the child, crying out, *Abba, Father*? However bad I may be, I am the child of God, and therein lies my blame. Ah, I would not lose my blame, for in my blame lies my hope. It is the pledge of what I am, and what I am not; the pledge of what I am meant to be, what I shall one day be, the child of God in spirit and in truth.

MAY 30TH

Our English presentation of St. Paul's teaching is in this point very misleading. In the New Testament the word adoption is used only by the apostle Paul. The Greek word might be variously meant; the English can mean but one thing, and that is not what St. Paul means. "The spirit of adoption" Luther translates "The spirit of a child;" *adoption* he translates *kindschaft*, or *childship*. The word used by St Paul does not imply that God adopts children that are not his own, but rather that a second time he fathers his own; that a second time they are born—this time from above; that he will make himself tenfold, yea, infinitely their father: he will have them back into the very bosom whence they issued; he will have them one with himself. It was for the sake of this that, in his Son, he died for them.

Consider, in the apostle's letter to the Galatians, 4:1-7, the last line of which reads "So that thou art no longer a bondservant, but a son; and if a son, then an heir through God." It is as plain as St. Paul could make it that, by the word translated adoption, he means the raising of a father's own child from the condition of subjection to others—a state which, he says, is no better than that of a slave—to the position and rights of a son. None but a child could become a son—the idea is a spiritual coming of age; *only when the child is a man is he really and fully a son.*

MAY 31ST

To be a child is not necessarily to be a son or daughter. The childship is the lower condition of the upward process towards the sonship. God can no more than an earthly parent be content to have only children: he must have sons and daughters—children of his soul, of his spirit, of his love---not merely in the sense that he loves them, or even that they love him, but in the sense that they love like him, love as he loves. For this he does not adopt them; he dies to give them himself, thereby to raise his own to his heart; he gives them a birth from above; they are born again out of himself and into himself. His children are not his real, true sons and daughters until they think like him, feel with him, judge as he judges, are at home with him and without fear before him because he and they love the same things, seek the same ends. For this are we created; it is the one end of our being. He is our father all the time, for he is true; but until we respond with the truth of children, he cannot let all the father out to us; there is no place for the dove of his tenderness to alight. He is our father, but we are not his children. Because we are his children, we must become his sons and daughters. Nothing will satisfy him, or do for us, but that we be one with our father! What else could serve! How else should life ever be a good! Because we are the sons of God, we must become the sons of God.

JUNE 1ST

The Father would make to himself sons and daughters as shall be his sons and daughters not merely by having *come* from his heart, but by having *returned* thither—children in virtue of being such as whence they came, such as choose to be what he is. He will have them share in his being and nature—strong wherein he cares for strength; tender and gracious as he is tender and gracious; angry where and as he is angry Even in the small matter of power, he will have them able to do whatever his Son Jesus could on the earth, whose was the life of the perfect man, whose works were those of perfected humanity. Everything must at length be subject to man, as it was to The Man. When God can do what he will with a man, the man may do what he will with the world; he may walk on the sea like his Lord; the deadliest thing will not be able to hurt him: "He that believeth on me, the works that I do shall he do also; and greater than these shall he do."

He has made us, but we have to *be*. Those who live as Jesus lived—by obedience, namely, to the Father, have a share in their own making; the light becomes life in them. "As many as received him, to them gave he power to become the sons of God." He does not *make* them the sons of God, but he gives them power to *become* the sons of God: in choosing and obeying the truth, man becomes the true son of the Father of lights.

JUNE 2ND

In keeping with St. Paul's epistle to the Galatians, 4:1-7, while we but obey the law God has laid upon us, without knowing the heart of the Father whence comes the law, we are but slaves—not necessarily ignoble slaves, yet slaves; but when we come to think *with* him, when the mind of the son is as the mind of the Father, then is the son *of* the Father, then are we the sons of God.

Children we were; true sons we could never be, save through The Son. He brothers us. He takes us to the knees of the Father, beholding whose face we grow sons indeed. Never could we have known the heart of the Father, never felt it possible to love him as sons, but for him who cast himself into the gulf that yawned between us. In and through him we were foreordained to the sonship: sonship, even had we never sinned, never could we reach without him. We should have been little children loving the Father indeed, but children far from the sonhood that understands and adores. "For as many as are led by the spirit of God, these are sons of God;" "If any man hath not the spirit of Christ, he is none of his." There is no unity but having the same spirit. There is but one spirit, that of truth.

JUNE 3RD

The putting of a son in his true, his foreordained place, has outward relations as well as inward reality; the outward depends on the inward, arises from it, and reveals it. When the child takes his position as a son, he would naturally change his dress and modes of life: when God's children cease to be slaves doing right from law and duty, and become his sons doing right from the essential love of God and their neighbor, they too must change the garments of their slavery for the robes of liberty, lay aside the body of this death, and appear in bodies like that of Christ.

We are the sons of God the moment we lift up our hearts, seeking to be sons—the moment we begin to cry *Father*. But as the world must be redeemed in a few men to begin with, so the soul is redeemed in a few of its thoughts and wants and ways, to begin with: it takes a long time to finish the new creation of this redemption. The apostle Paul speaks at one time of the thing as to come, at another time as done, when it is but commenced: our ways of thought are such. A man's heart may leap for joy the moment when, amidst the sea-waves, a strong hand has laid hold of the hair of his head; he may cry aloud, "I am saved;" and he may be safe, but he is not saved; this is far from a salvation to suffice. So are we sons when we begin to cry *Father*, but we are far from perfected sons. So long as there is in us the least taint of distrust, the least lingering of hate or fear, we have not received the sonship; we have not such life in us as raised the body of Jesus.

JUNE 4TH

Until our outward condition is that of sons royal, sons divine; so long as we groan under sickness and weakness and weariness, old age, and all heavy things; so long we have not yet received the sonship in full—we are but getting ready one day to creep from our chrysalis, and spread the great heaven-storming wings of the psyches of God. We groan, waiting for the redemption of the body, the uplifting of the body to be a fit house and revelation of the indwelling spirit—nay, like that of Christ, a fit temple and revelation of the deeper indwelling God. Hence the revealing of the sons of God, spoken of in Romans 8:19, is the same thing as the redemption of the body; the body is redeemed when it is made fit for the sons of God; then it is a revelation of them—the thing it was meant for. When we are the sons of God in heart and soul, then shall we be the sons of God in body, too: "we shall be like him, for we shall see him as he is."

The redeemed body will show the same self as before, but it will show the being truly—without the defects and imperfections of the former bodily revelation. Even through their corporeal presence shall we then know our own infinitely better, and find in them endlessly more delight, than before. Until the redemption of the body arrives, the true sonship is not wrought out, is only upon the way. Nor can it come but by our working out the salvation he is working in us.

JUNE 5TH

In Romans 8:19, the apostle Paul writes, "For the earnest expectation of the creation waiteth for the revealing *(the outshining)* of the sons of God." When the sons of God show as they are, taking, with the character, the appearance and the place that belong to their sonship; when the sons of God sit with the Son of God on the throne of their Father; then shall they be in potency of fact the lords of the lower creation, the bestowers of liberty and peace upon it; then shall the creation find its freedom in their freedom, its gladness in their sonship. The animals will glory to serve them, will joy to come to them for help. Let the heartless scoff, the unjust despise! The heart that cries *Abba, Father,* cries to the God of the sparrow and the oxen; nor can hope go too far in hoping what God will do for the creation that now groaneth and travaileth in pain because our higher birth is delayed. Shall not the judge of all the earth do right? Shall my heart be more compassionate than his?

Until Christ is born in me, until I am revealed a son of God, pain and trouble will endure—and God grant they may! Until you yourself are the son of God you were born to be, you will never find life a good thing. Thus have both Jesus Christ and his love-slave Paul represented God—as a Father perfect in love, grand in self-forgetfulness, supreme in righteousness, devoted to the lives he has uttered.

JUNE 6TH

It comes to this, then, after the grand theory of the apostle: The world exists for our education; it is the nursery of God's children, served by troubled slaves, troubled because the children are themselves slaves—children, but not good children. Beyond its own will or knowledge, the whole creation works for the development of the children of God into the sons of God. When at last the children have arisen and gone to their Father; when they are clothed in the best robe, with a ring on their hands and shoes on their feet, shining out at length in their natural, their predestined sonship; then shall the mountains and the hills break forth before them into singing, and all the trees of the field shall clap their hands. Then shall the wolf dwell with the lamb, and the leopard lie down with the kid and the calf, and the young lion and the fatling together, and a little child shall lead them. Then shall the fables of a golden age, which faith invented, and unbelief threw into the past, unfold their essential reality, and the tale of paradise prove itself a truth by becoming a fact. Then shall every ideal show itself a necessity, aspiration although satisfied put forth yet longer wings, and the hunger after righteousness know itself blessed. Then first shall we know what was in the Shepherd's mind when he said, "*I came that they may have life and may have it abundantly.*"

LIFE

"I came that they may have life and may have it abundantly."

St. John 10:10

JUNE 7TH

He came to supply all our lack, from the root outward: for what is it we need but more life? What does the infant need but more life? What does the old man need, whose limbs are weak and whose pulse is low, but more of the life which seems ebbing from him? Weary with feebleness, he calls upon death, but in reality it is life he wants. It is but the encroaching death in him that desires death. He longs for rest, but death cannot rest; it takes strength as well as weariness to rest. Low-sunk life imagines itself weary of life, but it is death, not life, it is weary of. Why does the poor, out-worn suicide seek death? Is it not in reality to escape from death—from the death of homelessness and hunger and cold; the death of failure and disappointment; the death of madness, the death of crime and fear of discovery? He seeks the darkness because it seems a refuge from the death which possesses him. What he calls his life is but a dream full of horrible phantasms.

"More life!" is the unconscious prayer of all creation, groaning and travailing for the redemption of its lord. All things are possible with God, but all things are not easy. It is not easy for him to create—that is, after the grand fashion which alone will satisfy his glorious heart and will, the fashion in which he is now creating us.

JUNE 8TH

Divine history shows how hard it is to for God to create that which shall not be himself, yet like himself. The problem is, so far to separate from himself that which must yet on him be ever and utterly dependent, that it shall have the existence of an individual, and be able to turn and regard him—choose him, and say, "I will arise and go to my Father," and so develop in itself the highest *Divine* of which it is capable—the will for the good against the evil—the will to be one with the life whence it has come, and in which it still is—to be the thing the maker thought of when he willed, ere he began to work its being.

I imagine the difficulty of effecting this creation, this separation from himself such that *will* in the creature shall be possible—difficulty of creation so great, that for it God must begin inconceivably far back in the infinitesimal regions of beginnings—not to say before anything in the least resembling man--to set in motion that division from himself which in its grand result should be individuality, consciousness, choice—choice at last pure, being the choice of the right, the true, the divinely harmonious. Hence the final end of the separation is not individuality; that is but a means to it; the final end is oneness—an impossibility without it. For there can be no unity, no delight of love, no harmony, no good in being, where there is but one. Two at least are needed for oneness; and the greater the number of individuals, the greater, the lovelier, the richer, the diviner is the possible unity.

JUNE 9TH

God is life, and the will-source of life. In the outflowing of the life, I know him; and when I am told that he is love, I see that if he were not love he would not, could not, create. The being of God is love, therefore creation. I imagine that from all eternity he has been creating. As he saw it was not good for man to be alone, so has he never been alone himself; from all eternity the father has had the Son, and the never-begun existence of that Son I imagine an easy outgoing of the Father's nature; while to make other beings like us, I imagine the labor of a God, an eternal labor. I imagine that God has never been contented to be alone even with the Son of his love, the prime and perfect idea of humanity, but that he has from the first willed and labored to give existence to other creatures who should be blessed with his blessedness—creatures whom he is now and has always been developing into likeness with that Son—a likeness for long to be distant and small, but forever growing.

Let no soul think that to say God undertook a hard labor in willing that many sons and daughters should be sharers of the divine nature, is to abate his glory! The greater the difficulty, the greater is the glory. He knew what it would cost! Sore suffering such as we cannot imagine, and could only be God's, in the bringing out of the God-life in the individual soul. Man finds it hard to get what he wants, because he does not want the best; God finds it hard to give, because he would give the best, and man will not take it.

JUNE 10TH

What Jesus did, was what the Father is always doing; the suffering he endured was that of the Father from the foundation of the world, reaching its climax in the person of his Son. God provides the sacrifice; the sacrifice is himself. He is always, and has ever been, sacrificing himself to and for his creatures. It lies in the very essence of his creation of them. The worst heresy, next to that of dividing religion and righteousness, is to divide the Father from the Son, in thought or feeling or action or intent; to represent the Son as doing that which the Father does not himself do. If Jesus suffered for men, it was because his Father suffers for men; only he came close to men through his body and their senses, that he might bring their spirits close to his Father and their Father, so giving them life. He is God our Savior: it is because God is our Savior that Jesus is our Savior. The God and Father of Jesus Christ could never possibly be satisfied with less than giving himself to his own! Not the lovingest heart that ever beat can even reflect the length and breadth and depth and height of that love of God which shows itself in his Son—one, and of one mind, with himself.

JUNE 11TH

The Father has given to the Son to have life in himself; that life is our light. We know life only as light; it is the life in us that makes us see. All the growth of the Christian is the more and more life he is receiving. At first his religion may hardly be distinguishable from the mere prudent desire to save his soul; but at last he loses that very soul in the glory of love, and so saves it; self becomes but the cloud on which the white light of God divides into harmonies unspeakable.

"In the mist of life we are in death," said one; it is truer that in the midst of death we are in life. Life is the only reality; what men call death is but a shadow—a word for that which cannot be—a negation, owing the very idea of itself to that which it would deny. But for life there could be no death. If God were not, there would not even be nothing. Death can be the cure for nothing, the cure for everything must be life. The ills which come with existence are from its imperfection, not of itself—what we need is more of it. Life is the law, the food, the necessity of life. Life is everything. Many doubtless mistake the joy of life for life itself; and, longing after the joy, languish with a thirst at once poor and inextinguishable; but even that thirst points to the one spring. These love self, not life, and self is but the shadow of life. When it is taken for life itself, and set as the man's center, it becomes a live death in the man, a devil he worships as his god; the worm of the death eternal he clasps to his bosom as his one joy!

JUNE 12TH

The man who loves his fellow is infinitely more alive than he whose endeavor is to exalt himself above him; the man who strives to be better, than he who longs for the praise of the many; but the man to whom God is all in all, who feels his life-roots hid with Christ in God, who knows himself the inheritor of all wealth and worlds and ages, that man has begun to be alive indeed. Let us in all the troubles of life remember that what we need is more life, more of the life-making presence in us making us more alive. When most suppressed, when most weary of life, as our unbelief would phrase it, let us bethink ourselves that it is in truth the inroad and presence of death we are weary of. When most inclined to sleep, let us rouse ourselves to live. Of all things, let us avoid the false refuge of a weary collapse, a hopeless yielding to things as they are. It is the life in us that is discontented; we need more of what is discontented, not more of the cause of its discontent. He has the victory who, in the midst of pain and weakness, cries out, not for death, not for the repose of forgetfulness, but for strength to fight; for more God in him; who, when sorest wounded, says with Sir Andrew Barton in the old ballad:

> *Fight on my men, says Sir Andrew Barton,*
> *I am hurt, but I am not slain;*
> *I'll lay me down and bleed awhile,*
> *And then I'll rise and fight again.*

184

JUNE 13TH

If, in the extreme of our exhaustion, there should come to us, as to Elijah when he slept in the desert, an angel to rouse us, and show us the waiting bread and water, how would we carry ourselves? Would we, in faint unwillingness to rise and eat, answer, "Lo, I am weary unto death! Let me be gathered to my fathers and be at rest!"? I should be loath to think that, if the enemy came roaring upon us, we would not, like the Red Cross Knight, stagger, heavy sword in nerveless arm, to meet him; but, in the feebleness of foiled effort, it wants yet more faith to rise and partake of the food that shall bring back more effort, more travail, more weariness. The true man trusts in a strength which is not his, and which he does not feel, does not even always desire. To trust in the strength of God in our weakness; to seek from him who is our life, as the natural, simple cure of all that is amiss with us; this is the victory that overcometh the world. To believe in God our strength in the face of all seeming denial, to believe in him out of the heart of weakness and unbelief, these are the broken steps up to the high fields where repose is but a form of strength, strength but a form of joy, joy but a form of love. "I am weak," says the true soul, "but not so weak that I would not be strong; not so sleepy that I would not see the sun rise; not so lame but that I would walk! Thanks be to him who perfects strength in weakness, and gives to his beloved while they sleep!"

JUNE 14TH

If we will but let our God and Father work his will with us, there can be no limit to his enlargement of our consciousness. We have no conception of what life might be, of how vast is the consciousness of which we could be made capable. As little as any man or woman would be inclined to call the existence of a dog an existence to be satisfied with, as little could I, looking on the common human endeavor around me, consent to regard them as worthy the name of life. What in them is true dwells amidst an unchallenged corruption, demanding repentance and labor and prayer for its destruction. The condition of most men and women seems to me a life in death, a possession of withering forms by spirits that slumber, and babble in their dreams. That they do not feel it so, is nothing. The day must come when they will hide their faces with such shame as the good man yet feels at the memory of the time when he lived like them. There is nothing for man worthy to be called life, but the life eternal—God's life, that is, after his degree shared by the man made to be eternal also. For he is in the image of God, intended to partake of the life of the most high, to be alive as he is alive. Of this life the outcome and the light is righteousness, love, grace, and truth. The ignorant soul understands by this life eternal only an endless elongation of consciousness; what God means by it is a being like his own, a being beyond the attack of decay or death, a being which came out of the heart of Life, the heart of God, the fountain of being; an existence having nothing in common, any more than the Eternal himself, with what can pass or cease.

JUNE 15TH

This life, this eternal life, consists for man in absolute oneness with God and all divine modes of being, oneness with every phase of right and harmony. It consists in a love as deep as it is universal, as conscious as it is unspeakable; a love that can no more be reasoned about than life itself. What then is our practical relation to the life original? What have we to do towards the attaining to the resurrection from the dead? If we did not make ourselves, how can we, now we are made, do anything at the unknown roots of our being? What relation of conscious unity can be betwixt the self-existent God, and beings who live at the will of another?

For the link in our being to close the circle of immortal oneness with the Father, we must search the deepest of man's nature: there only can it be found. And there we do find it. For the *will* is the deepest, the strongest, the divinest thing in man; so, I presume, is it in God, for such we find it in Jesus Christ. Here, and here only, in the relation of God's will and his own, can a man come into vital contact with the All-in-all. When a man can and does entirely say, "Not my will, but thine be done"—when he so wills the will of God as to do it, then is he one with God, one, as a true son with a true father, and an heir of all he possesses. By the obedience of a son, he receives into himself the very life of the Father. Will is God's will, obedience is man's will; the two make one. By willed obedience we may share in the bliss of God's essential self-ordained being.

JUNE 16TH

If we do the will of God, eternal life is ours—no mere continuity of existence, for that in itself is worthless as hell, but a being that is one with the essential Life, and so within his reach to fill with the abundant and endless out-goings of his love. Our souls shall be vessels ever growing, filled with more and more life proceeding from the Father and the Son. What abundance of life he came that we might have, we can never know until we have it. But to be for one moment aware of such pure simple love towards but one of my fellows as I trust I shall one day have towards each, must of itself bring a sense of life such as the utmost effort of my imagination can but feebly shadow now. There would be, even in that one love, an expansion of life inexpressible. For we are made for love, not for self. Our neighbor is our refuge; *self* is our demon-foe. Every man is the image of God to every man, and in proportion as we love him, we shall know that sacred fact.

If there are readers to whom my words seem but foolish excitement, it can be nothing to them to be told that I seem to myself to speak only the words of truth and soberness. Such as they have not yet begun to live. Little can they, with minds full of petty cares, or still more petty ambitions, understand the groaning and travailing of the creation. It may be that they are honestly desirous of saving their own wretched souls, but as yet can they know but little of their need of him who is *the first and the last and the living one.*

THE FEAR OF GOD

"And when I saw him, I fell at his feet as one dead. And he laid his right hand upon me, saying, Fear not; I am the first and the last and Living one."

Revelation 1:17-18

JUNE 17TH

I t is not alone the first beginnings of religion that are full of fear. So long as love is imperfect, there is room for torment. That love only which fills the heart—and nothing but love can fill any heart—is able to cast out fear. The thing that is unknown, yet known to be, will always be more or less formidable. When it is known as immeasurably greater than we, and as having claims and making demands upon us, the more vaguely they are apprehended, the more room is there for anxiety; and when the conscience is not clear, this anxiety may well mount to terror. Those fear him most who most imagine him like their own evil selves, only beyond them in power. Power without love, dependence where is no righteousness, wake a worship without devotion. Neither, where the notion of God is better, but the conscience is troubled, will his goodness do much to exclude apprehension. The same consciousness of evil and of offence which gave rise to the bloody sacrifice is still at work in the minds of most who call themselves Christians. Naturally, the first emotion of man towards the being he calls God, but of whom he knows so little, is fear.

Where it is possible that fear should exist, it is well it should exist, cause continual uneasiness, and be cast out by nothing less than love.

JUNE 18TH

In him who does not know God, and must be anything but satisfied with himself, fear towards God is as reasonable as it is natural, and serves powerfully towards the development of his true humanity. Neither the savage nor the self-sufficient sage is rightly human. The humanity has to be born in each, and for this birth everything natural must do its part. Until love, which is the truth towards God, is able to cast out fear, it is well that fear should hold. It is a bond between man and God that can be broken only by the tightening of an infinitely closer bond. God must be terrible to those that are far from him; they must prefer a devil, because of his supreme selfishness, to a God who will die for his creatures, and insists upon giving himself to them, insists upon their being unselfish and blessed like himself. They love their poor existence as it is; God loves it as it must be—and they fear him.

Although he loves them utterly, God does not tell them there is nothing in him to make them afraid. That would be to drive them from him forever. To remove that fear from their hearts, save by letting them know his love with its purifying fire, would be to give them up utterly to the power of evil.

JUNE 19TH

God being a God who loves righteousness, a God who, that his creature might not die of ignorance, died as much as a God could die, and that is divinely more than man can die, to give him himself; such a God may well look fearful from afar to the creature who recognizes in himself no good that must be done; who fears only suffering, and has no aspiration—only wretched ambition! But in proportion as such a creature comes nearer, grows towards him in whose likeness he was begun; in proportion, that is, as the eternal right begins to disclose itself to him, that his individuality can be perfected only in the love of his neighbor, and that his being can find its end only in oneness with the source from which it came; in proportion as he nears the possibility of seeing these things, will his terror at the God of his life abate.

The fire of God, which is his essential being, his love, is a fire unlike its earthy symbol in this, that it is only at a distance it burns—that the farther from him, it burns the worse, and that when we turn and begin to approach him, the burning begins to change to comfort, which will grow to such bliss that the heart at length cries out with supreme gladness, "Whom have I in heaven but thee? And there is no one upon earth that I desire besides thee!"

JUNE 20TH

When a man's evil is burned away, that is when the man yields his self and returns to his lord and God; and that is when that which, before, he was aware of only as burning, he will feel as love, comfort, strength—an eternal, ever-growing life in him. If then any child of the Father finds that he is afraid before him, that the thought of God is a discomfort to him, or even a terror, let him make haste—let him not linger to put on any garment, but rush at once in his nakedness, a true child, for shelter from his own evil and God's terror, into the salvation of the Father's arms.

When John saw the glory of the Son of Man, he fell at his feet as one dead. Why was he overcome with terror? Why was he, who had borne witness to his resurrection and suffered for his sake, afraid? The glory that he saw, the head and hair pouring from it such a radiance of light that they were white as wool, was but the radiant splendor of the Father, which should have taken from him all fear. *"He laid his right hand upon me, saying unto me, Fear not; I am the first and the last, and the living one."* Fear cannot stand before strength; the one and only safety in the universe is the perfect nearness of the Living One! Oh, the joy, to be told, by Power itself, that the cure for trembling is the presence of Power. He told his servant Paul that strength is made perfect in weakness; here he instructs his servant John that the thing to be afraid of is weakness, not strength.

JUNE 21ST

The glory of the mildest show of the Living One is such that even the dearest of his apostles, the best of the children of men, is cowed at the sight. He has not yet learned that glory itself is a part of his inheritance, that there is nothing in a man made in the image of God alien from the most glorious of heavenly shows: he falls as dead before it, when lo, the voice of him that was and is and is forevermore, telling him not to be afraid, for the very reason, that he is the first and the last, the living one! For what shall be the joy, the peace, the completion of him that lives, but closest contact with his Life? Rather than trembling, because he on whose bosom he had leaned when the light of his love was all but shut in now stands with the glory of that love streaming forth, John Boanerges ought to have felt the more joyful and safe as the strength of the living one was more manifested. It was never because Jesus was clothed in the weakness of the flesh that he was fit to be trusted, but because he was strong with a strength able to take the weakness of the flesh for the garment wherein it could best work its work: that strength was now shining out with its own light. Had John been as close in spirit to the Son of Man as he had been in bodily presence, he would have indeed fallen at his feet, but as one too full of joy to stand before the life that was feeding his; he would have fallen to embrace and kiss the feet of him who had now a second time, as with a resurrection from above, arisen before him, in yet heavenlier plenitude of glory.

JUNE 22ND

If God were no longer ruler of the world, and there were another stronger than he, then would be the time to stand in dread of power. But even then the bad man would have no security against the chance of crossing some scheme of the lawless moment, and being ground up and destroyed by the Power of darkness. And then would be the time for the good, not to tremble, but to resolve with the Lord of light to endure all, to let every billow of evil dash and break upon him, nor do the smallest ill, tell the whitest lie for God—knowing that any territory so gained could belong to no kingdom of heaven, could be but a province of the kingdom of darkness. But Good only can create; and if Evil were ever so much the stronger, the duty of men would remain the same—to hold by the Living one, and defy power to its worse—like Prometheus on his rock, defying Jove, and forever dying—thus forever foiling the Evil. For Evil can destroy only itself and its own; it could destroy no enemy—could at worst but cause a succession of deaths, from each of which the defiant soul would rise to loftier defiance, to more victorious endurance—until at length it laughed Evil in the face, and the demon-god shrunk withered before it. In those then who believe that good is the one power, and that evil exists only because for a time it subserves the good, what place can there be for fear? The strong and the good are one; and if our hope coincides with that of God, if it is rooted in his will, what should we do but rejoice in the radiant glory of the First and the Last?

JUNE 23RD

The reason for not fearing before God is that he is all-glorious, all-perfect. Our being needs the all-glorious, all-perfect God. The children can do with nothing less than the Father; they need the infinite one. Beyond all wherein the poor intellect can descry order; beyond all that the rich imagination can devise; beyond all that hungriest heart could long, fullest heart thank for—beyond all these, as the heavens are higher than the earth, rise the thought, the creation, the love of the God who is in Christ, his God and our God, his Father and our Father.

Ages before the birth of Jesus, while, or at least where yet even Moses and his law were unknown, the suffering heart of humanity saw and was persuaded that nowhere else lay its peace than with the first, the last, the living one:

O that thou wouldest hide me in the grave...and remember me!...

Thou shalt call, and I will answer thee: thou wilt have a desire to the work of thine hands.

THE VOICE OF JOB

"O that thou wouldst hide me in the grave, that thou wouldst keep me secret, until thy wrath be past, that thou wouldst appoint me a set time, and remember me! If a man die, shall he live again? All the days of my appointed time will I wait, till my change come. Thou shalt call, and I will answer thee: thou wilt have a desire to the work of thine hands."

Job 14: 13-15

JUNE 24TH

The book of Job seems to me the most daring of poems: from a position of the most vantageless realism, it assaults the very citadel of the ideal! Its hero is a man seated among the ashes, covered with loathsome boils from head to foot, scraping himself with a potsherd. Sore in body, mind, and spirit, he is the instance-type of humanity in the depths of its misery. Job is *the human being*—a center to the sickening assaults of pain, the ghastly invasions of fear: these one time or another, threaten to overwhelm every man, reveal him to himself as enslaved to the external, and stir him up to find some way out into the infinite, where alone he can rejoice in the liberty that belongs to his nature. Job cries aloud to the Might unseen, in infinite perplexity as well as pain. Before the Judge he asserts his innocence, and will not grovel, knowing indeed that to bear himself so would be to insult the holy. He feels he has not deserved such suffering, and will neither tell nor listen to lies for God. Job is nothing of a Stoic, but bemoans himself like a child—a brave child who seems to himself to suffer wrong, and recoils with horror-struck bewilderment from the unreason of the thing. He will not believe God a tyrant; but, while he pleads against his dealing with himself, loves him, and looks to him as the source of life, the gladness of being.

JUNE 25TH

Job dares not think God unjust, but not therefore can he allow that he has done anything to merit the treatment he is receiving at his hands. How can the two things be reconciled? The thought has not yet come to him that that which it would be unfair to lay upon him as punishment, may yet be laid upon him as favor—blessing he would not dare to ask if he saw the means necessary to its giving, but blessing for which, once known and understood, he would be willing to endure all yet again. While he must not think of God as having mistaken him, the discrepancy that looks like mistake forces itself upon him through every channel of thought and feeling. The worst of all with which fear could have dismayed him is come upon him; and worse now than all, death is denied him! He is left to linger in self-loathing, to encounter at every turn of agonized thought the awful suggestion that God has cast him off! He does not deny that there is evil in him, but he does deny that he has been a wicked man. The contradiction between Job's idea of the justice of God and things which had befallen him is constantly haunting him; it has a sting in it far worse than all the other misery with which he is tormented; but it is not fixed in the hopelessness of hell by an accepted explanation more frightful than itself. Job refused the explanation of his friends because he knew it false; to have accepted such as would by many in the present day be given him, would have been to be devoured at once by the monster. He simply holds on to the skirt of God's garment, keeps putting his question again and again. No answer will do for him but the answer that God only can give.

JUNE 26TH

Job cherishes as his one hope the idea that, if he might but lay his case clear before him, God would not fail to see how the thing was, and would explain the matter to him; the man in the ashes would know that God has not closed his eyes, or—horror of all horrors—ceased to be just! Surely the Just would set the mind of his justice-loving creature at rest! His friends, good men, but of the pharisaic type—that is, men who would pay their court to God, instead of coming into his presence as children; men anxious to appease God rather than trust in him; men who would rather receive salvation from God, than God their salvation—these would persuade Job to the confession that he was a hypocrite, insisting that such things could not have come upon him but because of wickedness, for some secret vileness. They grow angry when he refuses to be persuaded. They insist on his hypocrisy, he on his righteousness. And indeed, God has said thus to the accuser of men: "Hast thou considered my servant Job, that there is none like him in the earth, a perfect and an upright man?" God gives Job into Satan's hand with confidence in the result; and at the end of the trial approves of what Job has said concerning himself. But the very appearance of God is enough to make Job turn against himself: his part was to have trusted God altogether, in spite of every appearance, in spite of very reality! He sees that though God has not been punishing him for his sins, yet is he far from what he ought to be, and must become. "Behold," he says, "I am vile; what shall I answer thee? I will lay mine hand upon my mouth."

JUNE 27TH

Let us look closer at Job's way of thinking and speaking about God, and his manner of addressing him, so different from the pharisaic in all ages. Waxing indignant at the idea that his nature required such treatment, he cries out "Am I a sea or a whale, that thou settest a watch over me?" *Thou knowest that I am not wicked.* To his friends he cries: "Will ye speak wickedly for God? And talk deceitfully for him?"*Do you not know that I am the man I say?* Such words are pleasing in the ear of the father of spirits. He is not a God to accept the flattery which declares him above obligation to his creatures; a God to demand of them a righteousness different from his own. Job is confident of receiving justice. There is a strange but most natural conflict of feeling in him. His faith is in truth profound, yet is he always complaining. It is but the form his faith takes in his trouble. He is sure that, to get things set right, all he needs is admission to the presence of God. He uses language which, used by any living man, would horrify the "religious", in proportion to the lack of truth in them, just as it horrified his three friends, whose religion was "doctrine" and rebuke. God speaks not a word of rebuke to Job for the freedom of his speech. It is those who know and respect only the outsides of religion, such as never speak or think of God but as the Almighty or Providence, who will say of the man who would go close up to God, and speak to him out of the deepest in the nature he has made, "he is irreverent." They pay court to God, not love him; they treat him as one far away, not as the one whose bosom is the only home.

JUNE 28TH

L ike a child escaping from the dogs of the street, Job flings the door to the wall, and rushes to seek the presence of the living one. He would cast his load at the feet of his maker! But alas—nowhere can he see his face! He has hid himself from him! "Oh that I knew where I might find him! That I might come even to his seat! Will he plead against me with his great power? No! but he would put strength in me. There the righteous might dispute with him; so should I be delivered forever from my judge. Behold, I go forward, but he is not there; and backward, but I cannot perceive him; but he knoweth the way that I take: when he hath tried me, I shall come forth as gold."

He cannot find him! Yet is he in his presence all the time, and his words enter into the ear of God his Savior. The grandeur of the poem is that Job pleads his cause with God against all the remonstrance of religious authority, recognizing no one but God. And grandest of all is that he implies that God *owes* something to his creature. This is the beginning of the greatest discovery of all— that God owes *himself* to the creature he has made in his image, for so he has made him incapable of living without him. This, his creatures' highest claim upon him, is his divinest gift to them. For the fulfilling of their claim he has sent his son, that he may himself, the father of him and of us, follow into our hearts.

JUNE 29TH

A re we not the clay, and he the potter? How can the clay claim from the potter? We are the clay, it is true, but *his* clay, spiritual clay, with needs and desires—and rights; clay worth the Son of God's dying for, that it might learn to consent to be shaped unto honor. We can have no merits—a *merit* is a thing impossible; but God has given us rights. Out of him we have nothing; but, created by him, come forth from him, we have even rights towards him—ah, never *against* him! His whole desire and labor is to make us capable of claiming, and induce us to claim of him the things whose rights he bestowed in creating us. Being made, we have claims on him who made us: our needs are our claims. A man who will not provide for the hunger of his child is condemned by the whole world. It is God to whom every hunger, every aspiration, every longing of our nature is to be referred; he made all our needs, made us the creatures of a thousand necessities. When doubt and dread invade, and the voice of love in the soul is dumb, what can please the father of men better than to hear his child cry to him from whom he came, "Here I am, O God! Thou hast made me; give me that which thou hast made me needing." What would he have, but that his children should claim their father? God is the origin of both need and supply, the father or our necessities, the abundant giver of the good things. Right gloriously he meets the claims of his child! The story of Jesus is the heart of his answer, not primarily to the prayers, but to the divine necessities of the children he has sent out into his universe.

JUNE 30TH

In light of the truth, that God's nature is that of Jesus Christ, of absolute love and devotion—let us look at the words *"Oh that thou wouldst hide me in the grave!"* Job appeals to his creator, whom his sufferings compel him to regard as displeased with him, though he knows not why. He prays to forget him for a time, that the desire of the maker to look again upon the creature he had made may awake within him, and make the heart of the parent remember and long after the face of the child; then will he rise in joy, to plead with confidence the cause of his righteousness. For God is closer to the man than is anything God has made: what can be closer than the making and the made? The whole existence of a creature is a unit, an entirety of claim upon his creator: just *therefore*, let him do with me as he will—even to seating me in the ashes, and seeing me scrape myself with a potsherd! Not the less but ever the more will I bring forward my claim. Is it not the sweetest music ear of maker can her? Except the word of perfect son, "Lo, I come to do thy will, O God!" We, imperfect sons, shall learn to say the same words, too: that we may grow capable and say them, and so enter into our birthright, become partakers of the divine nature in its divinest element, that Son came to us—died for the slaying of our selfishness, the destruction of our mean hollow pride. We are his father's debtors for our needs, our rights, our claims, and he will have us pay the uttermost farthing. So true is the father, he will even compel us, through misery if needful, to put in our claims, for he knows we have eternal need of these things: without the essential rights of his being, who can live?

JULY 1ST

I protest, therefore, against all teaching which gives the impression that the exceeding goodness of God towards man is not the natural and necessary outcome of his being. As if the idea of God admitted of his being less than he is, less than perfect, less than Jesus Christ! Less than Love absolute, less than entire unselfishness! As if the God revealed to us in the new Testament were not his own perfect necessity of loving-kindness, but one who has made himself better than, by his own nature, by his own love, by the laws which he willed the laws of his existence, he needed to be!

If it be answered that we have fallen, and God is thereby freed from any obligation, that is but a lie. No amount of wrong-doing in a child can ever free a parent from the divine necessity of doing all he can to deliver his child; the bond between them cannot be broken. It is the vulgar, worldly idea that freedom consists in being bound to nothing. Not such is God's idea of liberty! The more children he creates, with the more claims upon him, the freer is he as creator and giver of life, which is the essence of his Godhead: to make scope for his essence is to be free. Our Lord teaches us that the truth, known by obedience to him, will make us free: our freedom lies in living the truth of our relations to God and man. God could not be satisfied with himself without doing all that a God and Father could do for the creatures he had made—that is, without doing just what he had done, what he is going to and will do, to deliver his sons and daughters, and bring them home with rejoicing.

JULY 2ND

To answer the cry of the human heart, "Would that I could see him! Would that I might come before him, and look upon him face to face!" God sent his son, the express image of his person. And that we might not be limited in our understanding of God by the constant presence to our weak spiritual sense of any embodiment whatever, he took him away. Having seen him, in his absence we understand him better. That we might know him he came; that we might go to him he went. If we dare, like Job, to plead with him in any of the heart-rending troubles that arise from the impossibility of loving such misrepresentation of him as is held out to us by some; if we think and speak out before him that which seems to us to be right, will he not be heartily pleased with his children's love of righteousness? Verily he will not plead against us with his great power, but will put strength in us, and where we are wrong will instruct us. For the heart that wants to do and think aright, that seeks to worship him as no tyrant, but as the perfectly righteous God, is the delight of the Father. To the heart that will not call that righteousness which it feels to be unjust, but clings to the skirt of his garment, and lifts pleading eyes to his countenance, to that heart he will lay open the riches of his being.

JULY 3RD

"O Lord, they tell me I have so offended against thy law that, as I am, thou canst not look upon me, but threatenest me with eternal banishment from thy presence. But I have never known myself clean: how can I cleanse myself? Thou must take me as I am and cleanse me. Thou requirest of us to forgive: surely thou forgivest freely! Bound thou may be to destroy evil, but art thou bound to keep the sinner alive that thou may punish him, even if it make him no better? Sin cannot be deep as life, for thou art the life; and sorrow and pain go deeper than sin, for they reach to the divine in us. To see men suffer might make us shun evil, but it never could make us hate it. We might see thereby that thou hatest sin, but we never could see that thou lovest the sinner. Chastise us in loving kindness, and we shall not faint. Art not thou thyself, in thy Son, the sacrifice for our sins, the atonement of our breach? Could we ever have come to know good as thou knowest it, save by passing through the sea of sin and the fire of cleansing? They tell me I must say *for Christ's sake*, or thou wilt not pardon: it takes the very heart out of my poor love to hear that thou wilt not pardon me except because Christ has loved me; but I give thee thanks that nowhere in the record of thy gospel, does one of thy servants say any such word. Thou bearest our griefs and carriest our sorrows; and surely thou wilt one day enable us to pay every debt we owe to each other! We run within the circle of what men call thy wrath, and find ourselves clasped in the zone of thy love!"

JULY 4ᵀᴴ

When I speak of *rights*, I do not mean *merits*—of any sort. We can deserve from God nothing at all, in the sense of any right proceeding from ourselves. All our rights are such with which the bounty of love inconceivable has glorified our being—rights so deep, so high, that their satisfaction cannot be given until we long for them with our deepest desire. The giver of them came to men, lived with men, and died by the hands of men, that they might possess these rights abundantly. Our rights have God himself at the heart of them. But as to deserving, that is absurd; he had to die to make us listen and receive.

But, lest it should be possible that any unchildlike soul might, in arrogance and ignorance, think to stand upon his rights *against* God, and demand of him this or that after the will of the flesh, I will say this: He has a claim on God, a divine claim, for any pain, disappointment, or misery that would help to show him to himself as the fool he is; he has a claim to be punished, to be spared not one pang that may urge him towards repentance; yea, he has a claim to be sent out into the outer darkness, whether what we call hell, or something speechlessly worse, if nothing less will do. He has a claim to be compelled to repent; to have one after another of the sharp-toothed sheepdogs of the great shepherd sent after him, until he comes to see that nothing will ease his pain, nothing make a life worth having, but the presence of the living God within him.

JULY 5TH

I t is not at first easy to see wherein God gives Job any answer; I cannot find that he offers him the least explanation of why he has so afflicted him. He says Job has spoken what is right concerning him, and his friends have not; and he calls up before him, one after another, the works of his hands. The answer, like some of our Lord's answers if not all of them, seems addressed to Job himself, not to his intellect; to the revealing, God-like imagination in the man, and to no logical faculty whatever. It consists in a setting forth of the power of God, as seen in his handiwork; and all that is said concerning them has to do with their show of themselves to the eyes of men. In what belongs to the deeper meanings of nature and her mediation between us and God, the appearances of nature are the truths of nature, far deeper than any scientific discoveries concerning them. The show of things is that for which God cares most, for their show is the face of far deeper things; we see in them, as in a glass darkly, the face of the unseen. What they say to the childlike soul is the truest thing to be gathered of them. To know a primrose is a higher thing than to know all the botany of it—just as to know Christ is an infinitely higher thing than to know all theology. So Nature exists primarily for her look, her appeals to the heart and the imagination, her simple service to human need, and not for the secrets to be discovered in her and turned to man's further use. What is our knowledge of the elements of the atmosphere, its oxygen, hydrogen, nitrogen, and all the rest, to the blowing of the wind in our faces?

JULY 6TH

The argument implied in the poem seems to be this: that Job, seeing God so far before him in power, and his works so far beyond his understanding that they filled him with wonder and admiration, ought to have reasoned that he who could work so grandly must certainly use wisdom in things that touched him nearer, though they came no nearer his understanding. In this world, power is no *proof* of righteousness; but was it likely that he who could create should be unrighteous? Did not all he made delight the beholding man? Did such things foreshadow injustice towards the creature he had made in his image? If Job could not search his understanding in these things, why should he conclude his own case wrapt in the gloom of injustice? Might he not trust him to do him justice? God's ways with him might well be beyond his comprehension! The true child, the righteous man, will trust absolutely, against all appearances, the God who has created in him the love of righteousness.

God does not tell Job why he had afflicted him: he rouses his child-heart to trust. All the rest of Job's life on earth, I imagine, his slowly vanishing perplexities would yield him ever fresh meditations concerning God and his ways, new opportunities of trusting him. Everything which we cannot understand is a closed book of larger knowledge, whose clasps the blessed perplexity urges us to open. That God knows is enough for me; I *shall* know, if I *can* know.

JULY 7TH

How much more than Job are we bound, who know him in his Son as Love, to trust God in all the troubling questions that force themselves upon us! In the confusion of Job's thoughts, in the presence of two such facts, that God was just, yet punishing a righteous man as if he were wicked, while he was not yet able to receive the thought that approving love itself might be inflicting or allowing the torture—that such suffering as his was granted only to a righteous man that he might be made perfect—I can well imagine that at times, as the one moment he doubted God's righteousness, and the next cried aloud, "Though he slay me, yet will I trust in him," there must have mingled some element of doubt as to the existence of God. To deny the existence of God may involve less unbelief than the smallest yielding to doubt of his goodness. I say *yielding*; for a man may be haunted by doubts, and only grow thereby in faith. Doubts are the messengers of the Living One to rouse the honest. Doubt must precede every deeper assurance; for uncertainties are what we first see when we look into a region hitherto unknown. In all Job's begging and longing to see God, then, may well be supposed to mingle the mighty desire to be assured of God's being. One great point in the poem is that when Job hears the voice of God, though it utters no word of explanation, it is enough to him to hear it: he knows that God is, and that he hears the cry of his creature. That he is there, knowing all about him, is enough; he needs no more to reconcile seeming contradictions, and the worst ills of outer life become endurable.

JULY 8TH

Even if Job could not at first follow his argument, God settled everything for him when, by answering him out of the whirlwind, he showed him that he had not forsaken him. It is true that nothing but a far closer divine presence can ever make life a thing fit for a son of man—for while he has it not in him, his conscious self is but a mask, a spiritual emptiness; but for the present, Job, yielding to God, was satisfied. Perhaps he came at length to see that, if anything God could do to him would trouble him so as to make him doubt God, then it was time that he should be so troubled, that his lack of faith should be revealed to him. To know that our faith is weak is the first step towards its strengthening; to be capable of distrusting is death; to know that we are, and cry out, is to begin to live—to begin to be made such that we cannot distrust, such that God may do anything with us and we shall never doubt him. Until doubt is impossible, we are lacking in the true, the childlike knowledge of God; for either God is such that one may distrust him, or he is such that to distrust him is the greatest injustice of which a man can be guilty. If we are able to distrust him, either we know God imperfectly, or we do not know him. Perhaps Job learned something like this; anyhow, the result of what Job had to endure was a greater nearness to God. But all that he was required to receive at the moment was the argument of God's loving wisdom in his power, to his loving wisdom in everything else. In a very deep sense, power and goodness are one. In the deepest fact they are one.

JULY 9TH

S eeing God, Job forgets all he wanted to say. The close of the poem is grandly abrupt. To justify himself in the presence of Him who is Righteousness seems to him what it is— foolishness and worthless labor. If he is righteous, God knows it better than he does himself. All the evils and imperfections of his nature rise up before him in the presence of the one pure, the one who has no selfishness in him. "Behold," he cries, "I am vile; what shall I answer thee? I will lay mine hand upon my mouth." Then again, after God has called to witness for him behemoth and leviathan, he replies, "I know that thou canst do everything, and that no thought can be withholden from thee. Who is he that hideth counsel without knowledge?" This question was the word with which first God made his presence known to him; and in the mouth of Job now repeating the question, it is the humble confession, "*I am that foolish man.*" "Therefore," he goes on, "have I uttered that I understood not; things too wonderful for me, which I knew not." He had not knowledge enough to have a right to speak. "Hear, I beseech thee, and I will speak:" In the time to come, he will yet cry—to be taught, not to justify himself. "I will demand of thee, and declare thou unto me." The more diligently yet will he seek to know the counsel of God. That he cannot understand will no longer distress him; it will only urge him to fresh endeavor after the knowledge of him who in all his doings is perfect.

JULY 10TH

Job had his desire: he saw the face of God—and abhorred himself in dust and ashes. He sought justification; he found self-abhorrence. Was this punishment? The farthest from it possible. It was the best thing that the God could do for him. Blessedest gift is self-contempt, when the giver of it is the visible glory of the Living One. To be able to behold that glory is to live; to run from self is to begin to be pure of heart. By very means of the sufferings against which he had cried out, the living one came near to him, and he was silent. God had laid all these troubles upon him that He might through them draw nigh to him, and enable Job to know him.

Any man may, like Job, plead his cause with God: he gives us liberty to speak, and will hear with absolute fairness. But, blessed be God, the one result for all who so draw nigh to him will be to see him plainly, the perfect Savior, the profoundest refuge even from the wrongs of their own being; so seeing him, they will abhor themselves, and rejoice in him. When we turn from ourselves to him, becoming true, that is, being to God and to ourselves what we are, he will turn again our captivity; they that have sown in tears shall reap in joy; they shall doubtless come again with rejoicing, bringing their sheaves with them. Then will the waters that rise from God's fountains run in God's channels.

JULY 11TH

The prosperity that follows upon Job's submission is the embodiment of a great truth. Although a man must do right even if it were to send him to hell forever, yet we need not fear: all good things must grow out of and hang upon the one central good, the one law of life—the Will, the One Good. To submit absolutely to him is the only reason: circumstance as well as all being must then bud and blossom as the rose. And they will! What matter whether in this world or the next, if one day I know my life as a perfect bliss?

Friends, our cross may be heavy, and the *via dolorosa* rough; but we have claims on God, yea, the right to cry to him for help. He has spent, and is spending himself to give us our birthright, which is righteousness. Though we shall not be condemned for our sins, we cannot be saved but by leaving them; though we shall not be condemned for the sins that are passed, we shall be condemned if we love the darkness rather than the light, and refuse to come to him that we may have life. God is offering us the one thing we cannot live without—his own self: we must make room for him; we must cleanse our hearts that he may come in; we must do as the Master tells us, who knew all about the Father and the way to him—*we must deny ourselves, and take up our cross daily, and follow him.*

SELF-DENIAL

"And he said unto all, If any man would come after me, let him deny himself, and take up his cross daily, and follow me. For whosoever would save his life shall lose it; but whosoever shall lose his life for my sake, the same shall save it."

St. Luke 9:23-24

JULY 12TH

Christ is the way out, and the way in; the way from slavery, conscious or unconscious, into liberty; the way to the home we desire but do not know. We must become as little children, and Christ must be born in us: we must learn of him, and the one lesson he has to give is himself: he does first all he wants us to do; he is first all he wants us to be. We must not merely do as he did; we must see things as he saw them, regard them as he regarded them; we must take the will of God as the very life of our being; we must neither try to get our own way, nor trouble ourselves as to what may be thought or said of us. *The world* must be to us as nothing--not the world God makes and means, but the world man makes by choosing the perversion of his own nature—a world apart from and opposed to God's world. By *the world* I mean all ways of judging, regarding, and thinking, whether political, economical, ecclesiastical, social, or individual, which are not divine, which are not God's ways of thinking, regarding, or judging; which do not take God into account, do not set his will supreme, as the one only law of life; which do not care for the truth of things, but the customs of society or the practice of the trade; which heed not what is right, but the usage of the time. From everything that is against the teaching and thinking of Jesus, from the world in the heart of the best man in it, and especially from the world in his own heart, the disciple must turn to follow him. The first thing in all progress is to leave something behind; to follow him is to leave one's self behind. *"If any man would come after me, let him deny himself."*

JULY 13TH

S ome think Jesus means that the disciple must go against his likings because they are his likings; that something is gained by abstinence from what is pleasant, or by the doing of what is disagreeable—that to thwart the lower nature is in itself a good. Now, I will not dare say what a man may not get good from, if the thing be done in simplicity and honesty. When a man, for the sake of doing what is right, does in mistake that which is not right, God will take care that he be shown the better way. The mere effort of will, arbitrary and uninformed of duty, may add to the man's power over his lower nature; but in that nature it is God who must rule, and not the man. From a man's rule of himself, in smallest opposition, however devout, to the law of his being, arises the huge danger of nourishing, by the pride of self-conquest, a far worse than even the animal self—the demonic self. True victory over self is the victory of God in the man, not of the man alone. In whatever man does without God, he must fail miserably. In crossing his natural, therefore, in themselves, *right* inclinations, a man may develop a self-satisfaction which in its very nature is a root of all sin. Doing the thing God does not require of him, he puts himself in the place of God, becoming one who commands, not one who obeys. To enjoy heartily and thankfully, and do cheerfully without, when God wills we should, is the way to live in regard to things of the lower nature; these must not be confounded with the things of *the world*. The law of God is enough for me, and for laws invented by man, I will none of them. They are false, and come all of rebellion. God, not man, is our judge.

JULY 14TH

It is not to thwart or tease the poor self that Jesus tells the would-be disciple to deny himself; he tells us we must leave it altogether—yield it, refuse it, lose it: thus only shall we save it, thus only have a share in our own being. The self is given to us that we may sacrifice it; it is ours that we like Christ may have something to offer—not that we should torment it, but that we should abandon it utterly. The self is to be no longer the ruler of our action. We are no more to think, "What would I like to do?" but "What would the Living one have me do?" The Self is God's making—only it must be the "slave of Christ," that the Son may make it also the free son of the same Father; it must receive all from him; it must follow him, not its own desires. Christ must be its law. The time will come when it shall be so possessed by the indwelling God that there will be no longer any enforced denial of it needful; it has been finally denied and refused, learned to receive with thankfulness, to demand nothing. God's eternal denial of himself, revealed in him who for our sakes in the flesh took up his cross daily, will have been developed in the man; his eternal rejoicing will be in God—and in his fellows, before whom he will cast his glad self to be a carpet for their walk, a footstool for their rest, a stair for their climbing.

JULY 15TH

To deny oneself is to act no more from the standing-ground of self; to allow no passing influence between the self and the will; not to let the right hand know what the left hand doeth. No grasping or seeking shall give motion to the will; no desire to be conscious of worthiness shall order the life; no ambition whatever shall be a motive of action; no longing after the praise of men influence a single throb of the heart. To deny the self is to not shrink from condemnation or contempt of the community or country which is against the mind of the Living one; for no love or entreaty of father or mother, wife or child, friend or lover, to turn aside from following him, but forsake them all as any ruling power in our lives; we must do nothing to please them that would not first be pleasing to him. Right deeds, and not the judgment thereupon; true words, and not what reception they may have, shall be our care. Not merely shall we not love money, or trust in it, but, whether we have it or not, we must never think of it as a windfall from event or circumstance, but as the gift of God. It is God feeds us, warms us, quenches our thirst. The will of God must be to us all in all; the life of the Father must be the joy of the child; we must know our very understanding his—that we live and feed on him every hour in the closest way. To know these things in the depth of our knowing is to deny ourselves and take God instead. To try after them is to begin the denial, to follow him who never sought his own.

JULY 16TH

We must deny all anxieties and fears. When young we must not mind what the world calls failure; as we grow old, we must not be vexed that we cannot remember, must not regret that we cannot do, must not be miserable because we grow weak or ill: we must not mind anything. We have to do with God who can, not with ourselves where we cannot. He is our care; we are his; our care is to will his will; his care, to give us all things. This is to deny ourselves. "Self, you may be my consciousness, but you are not my being. If you were, what a poor miserable, weak wretch I should be! But my life is hid with Christ in God, whence it came, and whither it is returning—with you certainly, but as an obedient servant, not a master. For God is more to me than my consciousness of myself. He is my life; you are only so much of it as my poor half-made being can grasp. Because I have treated you as if you were indeed my own self, you have dwindled yourself and lessened me, till I am ashamed of myself. If I were to mind what you say, I should soon be sick of you. No! Let me have the company of the Perfect One, not of you! Of my elder brother, the Living one! Goodbye, self, I deny you, and will do my best every day to leave you behind me."

JULY 17TH

When Jesus tells us we must follow him, he speaks first and always as *the Son* of the Father—and that in the active sense, as the obedient God, the Son who came expressly and only to do the will of the Father. At the moment he says *Follow me*, he is following the Father. It is nothing even thus to think of him, except thus we *believe* in him—that is, we do as he does. We must believe in him *practically*; we do not follow him by holding this or that theory about why he died, or wherein lay his atonement: such things can be revealed only to those who follow him in his active being and the principle of his life—who do as he did, live as he lived. There is no other following. He is all for the Father; we must be all for the Father too, else are we not following him. To follow him is to be learning of him, to think his thoughts, use his judgments, feel things as he felt them, that we may be of the same mind with his Father. Busy from morning to night doing great things for him on any other road, we should but earn the reception, "I never knew you." When he says, "Take my yoke upon you," he does not mean a yoke which he would lay upon our shoulders; it is the yoke he himself is carrying that he tells us to take. He says, "The yoke *I carry* is easy, the burden *on my shoulders* is light." With the garden of Gethsemane before him, with the hour and the power of darkness waiting for him, he declares his yoke easy, his burden light. He first denies himself, and takes up his cross, then tells us to do the same. The Father magnifies the Son, not the Son himself; the Son magnifies the Father.

JULY 18TH

We must be jealous for God against ourselves, and look well to the cunning and deceitful Self, until it is thoroughly and utterly denied, and God is to it also All-in-all—till we have left it quite empty of our will, and God has come into it. Until then, its very denials, its very turnings from things dear to it for the sake of Christ, will tend to foster its self-regard, and generate in it a yet deeper self-worship. The Self will please itself with the thought of its unselfishness, its devotion to God, its forsakings for his sake. It may not *call* itself, but it will soon *feel* itself a saint, looking down upon the foolish world and its ways. In a thousand ways will Self delude itself. Christ sought not his own, not anything but the will of his Father: we have to grow diamond-clear, true as the white light of the morning. Hopeless task! –were it not that he offers to come himself, and dwell in us.

We must note that the thing has to be done *daily*: we must keep on denying. It is a deeper and harder thing than any sole effort of most herculean will may finally effect. For the will is not pure, is not free, until the Self is absolutely denied. It takes long for the water of life that flows from the well within us, to permeate every outlying portion of our spiritual frame, subduing everything, until at last we are delivered into the liberty of the glory of the children of God. Every day till then we have to take up our cross; every hour to see that we are carrying it.

JULY 19TH

Here is the promise to those who will leave all and follow him: "*Whosoever shall lose his life, for my sake, the same shall save it,*"—in St. Matthew, "*Find it.*" To lose ourselves in the salvation of God's heart! To be no longer any care to ourselves, but know God taking divinest care of us, his own! To revel in the unsought love of those who love us as we love them! To know that we are in the child's secret of existence, that we are pleasing in the eyes and to the heart of the Father! What a self is this to receive again from him for that we forsook! We left it paltry, low, mean; he took up the poor cinder of a consciousness, carried it back to the workshop of his spirit, made it a true thing, and restored it to our having forever!

All high things can be spoken only in figures of speech; and these cannot *fit* intellectually; they can be interpreted truly only by such as have the spiritual fact in themselves. When we speak of a man and his soul, we imply two selves; but we cannot divide ourselves so, and the figure suits but imperfectly. It was never the design of the Lord to explain things to our understanding—we require a means, a word, whereby to think of high things: that is what a true figure, while far from perfect, will always be to us. And the true soul sees, or will come to see, that the Lord's words, his figures, always represent more than they are able to present; for, as the heavens are higher than the earth, so are the heavenly things higher than the earthly signs of them, let the signs be good as ever sign may be.

JULY 20TH

There is no joy belonging to human nature, as God made it, that shall not be enhanced a hundredfold to the man who gives up himself—though, in so doing, he may seem to be yielding the very essence of life. To yield self is to give up grasping at things as if they came from nowhere, because no one appears presenting them, and to receive them direct from their source. The careless soul receives the Father's gifts as if they dropped into his hand. He thus grants himself a slave, dependent on chance and his own blundering endeavor. For the good that comes to him, he gives no thanks; at the disappointments that befall him he grumbles—there must be someone to blame! He does not think what Power would not be worse than squandered to sustain him after his own fashion in his paltry, low-aimed existence! The hour is coming when all that art, science, nature, and animal nature can afford us, in ennobling subjugation to the higher even as man is subject to the Father, shall be the possession of the sons and daughters of God, to their endless delight. God is able to give these things to those to whom he is all in all; to others he cannot give them, for they are unable to receive them who are outside the truth of them. We are not to love God for the sake of what he can give us, for it is impossible to love him save because he is our God, and altogether good and beautiful; but neither may we forget that, in the end, God will answer his creature in the joy of his heart. The good Father made his children to be joyful; only, ere they can enter into his joy, they must be like himself, ready to sacrifice joy to truth.

JULY 21ST

Every reward held out by Christ is a pure thing; nor can it enter the soul save as a death to selfishness. It is not selfish to be joyful. What power could prevent him who sees the face of God from being joyful? The one bliss of the universe is the presence of God, which is simply God being to the man the indwelling power of his life. Where can be the selfishness in being so made happy? It may be deep selfishness to refuse to be happy. Selfishness consists in taking the bliss from another; to find one's bliss in the bliss of another is not selfishness. The one bliss, next to the love of God, is the love of our neighbor. If any say, "You love because it makes you blessed," I deny it: We are blessed because we love. Love is unselfishness. In the main we love because we cannot help it. There is no merit in it-- how should there be in any love?—but neither is it selfish. There are many who confound righteousness with merit. "If it makes you happy to love," they say, "where is your merit? It is only selfishness!" There is no merit, I reply, yet the love that is born in us is our salvation from selfishness. It is of the very essence of righteousness. Because a thing is joyful, it does not follow that I do it for the joy of it; yet when the joy is in others, the joy is pure. That *certain* joys should be joys is the very denial of selfishness. A man would be demonically selfish, whom love itself did not make joyful.

JULY 22ND

S ome of the things a man may have to forsake in following Christ, he has not to forsake because of what they are in themselves. Neither nature, art, science, nor fit society, is of those things a man will lose in forsaking himself: they are God's, and have no part in the world of evil, the false judgments, low wishes and unrealities that make up the conscious life of the self which has to be denied. But in forsaking himself to do what God requires of him, a man may find he has to leave some of God's things, not to repudiate them, but because they draw his mind from the absolute necessities of the true life in himself or in others. Then he who knows God will find that knowledge opens the door of his understanding to all things else. He will become able to behold them from within, instead of having to search wearily into them from without. Then will the things he has had to leave be restored to him a hundredfold. So will it be in the forsaking of friends. It is not to cease to love them, "for he that loveth not his brother whom he hath seen, how can he love God whom he hath nor seen?" It is to not allow their love to cast even a shadow between us and our Master; to be content to lose their approval, even their affection, where the Master says one thing and they another. It is to learn to love them in a far higher, deeper, tenderer, truer way than before—a way which keeps all that was genuine in the former way, and loses all that was false. We shall love their selves, and disregard our own.

JULY 23RD

There is another kind of forsaking that may fall to the lot of some, and which they may find very difficult: the forsaking of such notions of God and his Christ as they were taught in their youth, of which they have begun to doubt the truth, but which to cast away seems like parting with every assurance of safety. By holding with a school he supposes to be right, a man but bolsters himself with the worst of all unbelief—opinion calling itself faith, unbelief calling itself religion. But for him who is in earnest about the will of God, it is of endless consequence that he should think rightly of God. He cannot truly know his will while his notion of him is in any point that of a false god. If such a man seem to himself to be giving up even his former assurance of salvation, in yielding such ideas of God as are unworthy of God, he must none the less, if he would enter into life, take up that cross also. He will come to see that he must follow no doctrine, be it true as word of man could state it, but the living Truth, the Master himself. Many good souls will one day be horrified at the things they now believe of God. If they have not thought about them, but given themselves to obedience, they may not have done them much harm as yet. But there are those who find them a terrible obstruction, and yet imagine, or at least fear them true; such must take courage to forsake the false in any shape, to deny their old selves in the most seemingly sacred of prejudices, and follow Jesus as he is presented by himself, his apostles, and the spirit of truth. We must look to *how we have learned Christ.*

THE TRUTH IN JESUS

"But ye did not so learn Christ; if so be that ye heard him, and were taught in him, even as truth is in Jesus: that ye put away, as concerning your former manner of life, the old man, which waxeth corrupt after the lusts of deceit[2]."

Eph. 4:20-22

---

[2]   That is, "which is still going to ruin through the love of the lie."

JULY 24TH

How have we learned Christ? It ought to be a startling thought, that we may have learned him wrong. That must be far worse than not to have learned him at all: his place is occupied by a false Christ, hard to exorcise! Have we learned Christ as he taught himself, or as men have taught him who did not understand him? Have we learned Christ in false statements and corrupted lessons about him, or have we learned *himself*? And is only our brain full of things concerning him, whether true or false, or does he himself dwell in our hearts, a learnt, and ever being learnt lesson, the power of our life? Consider the following utterance, from one in the front rank of those skeptical of Christianity: "*The visiting on Adam's descendants through hundreds of generations of dreadful penalties for a small transgression which they did not commit; the damning of all men who do not avail themselves of an alleged mode of obtaining forgiveness, which most men have never heard of; and the effecting of reconciliation by sacrificing a son who was perfectly innocent, are actions which, ascribed to a human ruler, would call forth expressions of abhorrence; and the ascription of them to the Ultimate Cause of things must become impossible.*" I do not quote the passage with the design of opposing it, for I entirely agree with it; the system it assails is a false one, and I have never heard a word from skeptics such as this writer which even touched anything I hold; yet the beliefs that he attacks are, alas, those held by many so-called Christians.

JULY 25TH

Rather than believe a single point involving the spirit of such a system of belief as represented in the quotation above, even with the assurance thereby of such salvation as it offers, I would set myself with hopeless heart to what I am now trying, with an infinite hope in the help of God: to get rid of my miserable mean self, comforted only by the chance that death would either leave me without thought more, or reveal something of God which it would not be an insult to hold concerning him. Even such a chance might enable one to live. And if had I to do with the writer, I would ask: if he will allow that there was a man named Jesus, who died of the truth he taught, can he believe he died for such alleged truth as these abominable dogmas? But it is to those who call themselves Christians that I would speak.

Of those whose presentation of Christian doctrine is the same as the writer's, there are two classes: such as are content it should be so, and such to whom those things are grievous, but who do not see how to get rid of them. To the latter it may be some little comfort to have one who has studied the New Testament for many years and loves it beyond the power of speech to express, declare to them his conviction that there is not an atom of such teaching in the whole lovely, divine utterance; that such things are all and altogether the invention of men—honest invention, I grant, but yet not true.

JULY 26TH

I s Christianity a system of articles of belief, let them be however correct? Never. I would rather have a man holding what seem to me the most obnoxious untruths, opinions the most irreverent and gross, if at the same time he lived in the faith of the Son of God, that is, trusted in God as the Son of God trusted in him, than I would have a man with every one of whose formulas of belief I agreed, but who knew nothing of a daily life and walk with God. The one, holding doctrines of devils, is yet a child of God; the other, holding the doctrines of Christ and his Apostles, is of the world, yea, of the devil. For to hold a thing with the intellect is not to *believe* it. A man's real belief is that which he lives by; and that which the man I mean lives by, is the love of God, and obedience to his law, so far as he has recognized it. Those hideous doctrines are outside of him; he *thinks* they are inside, but no matter; they are not true, and they cannot really be inside any good man. This man would shrink with loathing from actions such as he thinks God justified in doing; like God, he loves and helps and saves. Will the living God let such a man's opinions damn him? No more than he will let the correct opinions of another, who lives for himself, save him. When some say that, to be saved, a man must hold this or that, then they are leaving the living God and his will, and putting trust in some notion *about* him or his will. We are told to believe in the living Lord, who, by his presence with and in us, and by our obedience to him, lifts us out of darkness into light, leads us from the kingdom of Satan into the glorious liberty of the sons of God.

JULY 27TH

No preaching of any plan of salvation is the preaching of the glorious gospel of the living God. Even if a plan, a theory, were absolutely true, the holding of it with sincerity, the trusting in this or that about Christ, or in anything he did or could do, the trusting in anything but himself, his own living self, is a delusion. Many will grant this heartily, and yet the moment you come to talk with them, you find they insist that to believe in Christ is to believe in the atonement, meaning by that only and altogether their special theory about the atonement; and when you say we must believe in the atoning Christ, and cannot possibly believe *in* any theory concerning the atonement, they go away and denounce you. Because I refuse an explanation which is not in the New Testament, though they believe it is, because they can think of no other, one which seems to me as false in logic as detestable in morals, therefore I am not a Christian! I do not say that with this sad folly may not mingle a potent faith in the Lord himself; but I do say that the importance they place on theory is even more sadly obstructive to true faith than such theories themselves. While the mind is occupied in enquiring, "Do I believe or feel this thing right?" the true question is forgotten: "Have I left all to follow him?" To the man who gives himself to the living Lord, every belief will necessarily come right; the Lord himself will see that his disciple believe aright concerning him.

JULY 28TH

What I insist upon is that a man's faith shall be in the living, loving, ruling, helping Christ, devoted to us as much as ever he was. It is not faith that he did this, that his work wrought that—it is faith in the man who did and is doing everything for us that will save a man: without this he cannot work to heal spiritually, any more than he would heal physically, when he was present to the eyes of men. Do you ask, "What is faith in him?" I answer, the leaving of your way, your objects, your self, and the taking of his and of him; the leaving of your trust in men, in money, in opinion, in character, in atonement itself, *and doing as he tells you.* I can find no words strong enough to serve for the weight of this necessity—this obedience. It is the one terrible heresy of the church, that it has always been presenting something other than obedience as faith in Christ. The work of Christ is not the Working Christ, any more than the clothing of Christ is the body of Christ. If the woman who touched the hem of his garment had trusted in the garment and not in him who wore it, would she have been healed? And the reason that so many who believe *about* Christ rather than in him, get the comfort they do, is that, touching thus the mere hem of his garment, they cannot help believing a little in the live man inside the garment. It is not surprising that such believers should so often be miserable; they lay themselves down to sleep with nothing but the skirt of his robe in their hand—a robe too, I say, that never was his, only by them is supposed his—when they might sleep in peace with the living Lord in their hearts.

JULY 29TH

S ome Christians, instead of so knowing Christ that they have him in them saving them, lie wasting themselves in self-examination as to whether they are believers, whether they are really trusting in the atonement, whether they are truly sorry for their sins—the way to madness, to despair of the heart. Some even ponder the imponderable—whether they are of the elect, whether theirs is a saving faith—when all the time the man who died for them is waiting to begin to save them from every evil; and first from this self which is consuming them with trouble about its salvation; he will set them free and begin at once to fill them with the fullness of God, if only they will mind what he says to them, which is the beginning, middle, and end of faith. Get up, and do something the master tells you, and so make yourself his disciple at once. Instead of asking yourself whether you believe or not, ask yourself whether you have this day done one thing because he said, Do it, or once abstained because he said, Do not. It is simply absurd to say you believe, or even want to believe in him, if you do not anything he tells you. What though you should succeed in persuading yourself that you are his disciple, if, after all, he says to you, "Why did you not do the things I told you? Depart from me; I do not know you!" You can begin at once to be a disciple of the Living One by obeying him in the first thing you can think of in which you are not obeying him. We must learn to obey him in everything, and so must begin somewhere: let it be at once, and in the very next thing that lies at the door of our conscience!

JULY 30TH

If you think of nothing but Christ, and do not set yourself to do his words, you but build your house on sand. What have such teachers not to answer for, who have turned their pupils' regard from the direct words of the Lord, which are spirit and life, to contemplate plans of salvation tortured out of the words of his apostles, even were those plans as true as they are false! There is but one plan of salvation, and that is to believe in the Lord Jesus Christ; that is, to take him for what he is—our master, and his words as if he meant them, which assuredly he did. To do his words is to enter into vital relation with him, to obey him is the only way to be one with him. There can be no truth, no reality, in any initiation of at-one-ment with him, that is not obedience.

I know what the father of lies whispers to those to whom such teaching is distasteful: "It is the doctrine of works!" But one word of the Lord humbly heard and received will suffice to send all the demons of false theology into the abyss. He says the man that does not do the things he tells him builds his house to fall in utter ruin. He instructs his messengers to go and baptize all nations, "teaching them to observe all things whatsoever I have commanded you." Tell me it is faith he requires: do I not know it? But faith in what? Faith in what he is, in what he says--a faith which can have no existence except in obedience, a faith which *is* obedience.

JULY 31ST

Do you put your faith in *Christ*, I ask those who doubt what I have been saying above, or in the doctrines and commandments of men? If you say, "In him," is it then possible that you do not see that, above all things and all thoughts, you are bound to obey him? Do you not mourn that you cannot trust in him as you would, that you find it too hard? Too hard it is for you, and too hard it will remain, while the things he tells you to do you do not try! How should you be capable of trusting in the true one while you are nowise true to him? The very thing to make you able to trust in him, and so receive all things from him, you turn your back upon: obedience you decline, or at least neglect. You say you do not refuse to obey him? I care not whether you refuse or not, while you do not obey. Remember the parable: "I go, sir, and went not." What have you done this day because it was the will of Christ? Have you dismissed an anxious thought for the morrow? Have you ministered to any needy soul or body, and kept your right hand from knowing what your left hand did? Have you begun to leave all and follow him? Are you being wary of covetousness? Have your forgiven your enemy? Are you seeking the kingdom of God and his righteousness before all other things? Have you given to someone that asked of you? If you do nothing that he says, it is no wonder that you cannot trust in him, and are therefore driven to seek refuge in the atonement, as if something he had *done*, and not he himself *in his doing* were the atonement.

AUGUST 1ST

What does it matter how a man understands the atonement, so long as he is not of one mind with the Truth, so long as he and God are not at one, do not atone together? Knowing that a man does not heed his word, why should I heed his explanation of it? He does not his will, and so cannot understand him; he does not know him, and that is why he cannot trust in him. Does a man think his common sense enough to let him know what the Lord means? His common sense ought to be enough to know itself unequal to the task. It is the heart of the child that alone can understand the Father. Would a man have me think him guilty of the sin against the Holy Ghost—that he *understands* Jesus Christ and yet will not obey him? That were too dreadful. I believe he does not understand him.

No man can do yet what he tells him—but are you trying? Obedience is not perfection, but trying. Do you suppose he ever gave a commandment knowing it was of no use for it could not be done? He tells us a thing knowing that we must do it, or be lost; that not his Father himself could save us but by getting us at length to do everything he commands, for not otherwise can we learn the holy secret of divine being. He knows that you can try, and that in your trying and failing he will be able to help you, until at length you shall do the will of God even as he does it himself. The most correct notions without obedience are worthless. The doing of the will of God is the way to oneness with God, which alone is salvation.

AUGUST 2ND

W ell do I know it is faith that saves us—but not faith in any work of God—faith in God himself. If I did not believe God as good as the tenderest, purest, most unselfish human heart could imagine him, yea, an infinitude better, higher than we as the heavens are higher than the earth—if I did not feel every fiber of heart and brain and body safe with him because he is the Father who made me that I am—I would not be saved, for this faith is salvation; it is God and the man one. God and man together, the vital energy flowing unchecked from the creator into his creature—that is the salvation of the creature. But the poorest faith in the living God, the God revealed in Christ Jesus, if it be true, that is obedient, is the beginning of the way to know him, and to know him is eternal life. If you mean by faith anything of a different kind, that faith will not save you. Any other kind of faith will not save you. A faith, for instance, that God does not forgive me because he loves me, but because he loves Jesus Christ, cannot save me, because it is a falsehood against God: such a gospel would be the preaching of a God that was not love, therefore in whom was no salvation. Such a faith would damn, not save a man; for it would bind him to a God who was anything but perfect. Such assertions are nothing but the poor remnants of paganism, and it is only with that part of our nature not yet Christian that we are able to believe them.

AUGUST 3RD

We must forsake all our fears and distrusts for Christ. We must receive his teaching heartily, and not let the interpretation of it attributed to his apostles make us turn aside from it. I say *attributed* to them, for what they teach is never against what Christ taught, though very often the exposition of it is. We may be sure of this, that no man will be condemned for any sin that is past; that, if he be condemned, it will be because he would not come to the light when the light came to him; because he would not cease to do evil and learn to do well; because he hid his unbelief in the garment of a false faith, and would not obey; because he imputed to himself a righteousness that was not his; because he preferred imagining himself a worthy person, to confessing himself everywhere in the wrong, and repenting. If we do what the Lord tells us, his light will go up in our hearts. Till then we could not understand even if he explained to us. So long as a man will not set himself to obey the word spoken, written, read, of the Lord Christ, I would not take the trouble to convince him concerning the most obnoxious doctrines that they were false as hell. It is those who would fain believe, but who by such doctrines are hindered, whom I would help; those whom the false teaching has driven away from God. Any man who has been strenuously obeying Jesus receives the truth that God is light, and in him is no darkness—a truth which is not acknowledged by calling the darkness attributed to him light, and the candle of the Lord in the soul of man darkness.

240

AUGUST 4TH

The whole secret of progress is the doing of the thing we know. There is no other way of progress in the spiritual life; only as we do, can we know. Is there anything you will not leave for Christ? You cannot know him—and yet he is the Truth, the one thing alone that can be known! Do you not care to be imperfect? Would you rather keep this or that, with imperfection, than part with it to be perfect? You cannot know Christ, for the very principle of his life was the simple absolute relation of realities; his one idea was to be a perfect child to his Father. He who will not part with all for Christ, is not worthy of him, and cannot know him; how could he receive to his house a man who prefers something to his Father; a man who will strike a bargain with God, and say, "I will give up so much, if thou wilt spare me!" The man will have to be left to himself. He must find what it is to be without God!

To let their light shine, not to force on them their interpretations of God's designs, is the duty of Christians towards their fellows. If those who set themselves to explain their theories of Christianity had set themselves instead to do the will of the Master, how different would now be the condition of that portion of the world with which they came into contact! In how many a heart would the name of the Lord be loved where now it remains unknown!

AUGUST 5TH

Do not deter men with worthless explanations of Christianity, but attract them by your behavior, your doing of the Lord's will, and they will draw nigh to behold how Christians love one another, how just they are; how their goods are the best, their prices most reasonable, their word most certain! That in their families is neither jealousy nor emulation! That mammon is not there worshipped, that in their homes selfishness is neither the hidden nor the openly ruling principle; that their children are as diligently taught to share as some are to save, that in no house of theirs is religion one thing, and the daily life another.

Some will say, *"How then shall the world go on?"* The Lord's world will go on, and that without such men; the devil's world will go on, and that with them. Their objection is but proof of their unbelief. Either they do not believe the Lord—that if we seek first the kingdom of God, all things needful will be added to us; or what he undertakes does not satisfy them; they prefer the offers of Mammon. They would not live under such restrictions as the Lord might choose to lay upon them if he saw that something might be made of them precious in his sight! They would inherit the world, and not by meekness. They say, "Christ has satisfied the law," but they will not satisfy him! They say, "Lord I believe; help mine unbelief," but when he says, "Leave everything behind you, and be as I am towards God," they turn away, muttering about *figurative language.*

AUGUST 6TH

Those who live *the* life, who are Christians indeed, draw the world after them. In their churches they receive truest nourishment, strength to live—thinking far less of serving God on Sunday, and far more of serving their neighbors during the week. The sociable vile, the masterful rich, the deceitful trader, the ambitious poor, who are attracted by offers of a salvation other than deliverance from sin, are nowhere to be found, and all are the cleaner and stronger for their absence; while the publicans and the sinners are drawn instead, and turned into true men and women.

If any tell me my doctrine is presumptuous and contrary to what is taught in the New Testament, I will not defend my beliefs, the principles on which I try to live. I appeal to them instead, whether or not I have spoken the truth concerning our paramount obligation to do the word of Christ. If they say I have not, I have nothing more to say; there is no other ground on which we can meet. But if they allow that it is a prime, even if not *the* prime duty, then what I insist upon is, that they should do it, so and not otherwise recommending the knowledge of him. If your opinions are wrong, the obedience alone on which I insist will set them right; no one can know Christ to be right until he does as Christ does, as he tells us to do. For him who does not see that Christ must be obeyed, he must be left to the teaching of the Father, who brings all that hear and learn of him to Christ; He will leave no man to his own way, however much the man may prefer it.

AUGUST 7TH

The Lord did not die to provide a man with the wretched heaven he may invent for himself, or accept invented for him by others; he died to give him life, and bring him to the heaven of the Father's peace; the children must share in the essential bliss of the Father and the Son. This is and has been the Father's work from the beginning—to bring us into the home of his heart, where he shares the glories of life with the Living One. This is our destiny; and however a man may refuse, he will find it hard to fight with God—useless to kick against the goads of his love. For the Father is goading him, or will goad him, if needful, into life by unrest and trouble; hell-fire will have its turn if less will not do: can any need it more than such as will neither enter the kingdom of heaven themselves, nor suffer them to enter it that would? The old race of the Pharisees is by no means extinct; they were St. Paul's great trouble, and are yet to be found in every religious community under the sun.

AUGUST 8TH

The one thing truly to reconcile all differences is to walk in the light. So St. Paul teaches us in Philippians 3:16. After setting forth the loftiest idea of human endeavor in declaring the summit of his own aspiration he says, not "This must be your endeavor also, or you cannot be saved;" but, "If in anything ye be otherwise minded, God shall reveal even this unto you. Nevertheless whereto we have already attained, let us walk by that same." Observe what widest conceivable scope is given by the apostle to honest opinion, even in things of grandest import! The one essential point with him is that whereto we have attained, what we have seen to be true, *we walk by that.* In such walking, and in such walking only, love will grow, truth will grow; the soul, then first in its genuine element and true relation to God, will see into reality that was before but a blank to it; and he who has promised to teach, will teach abundantly. Faster and faster will the glory of the Lord dawn upon the hearts and minds of his people so walking; fast and far will the knowledge of him spread, for truth of action, both proceeding and following truth of word, will prepare the way before him. Only when a man begins to do the thing he knows, does he begin to be able to think aright; then God comes to him in a new and higher way. When man joins with God, then is all impotence and discord cast out. Until then, God is in contest with the gates of hell that open in the man, and can but hold his own; when the man joins him, then is Satan foiled.

AUGUST 9TH

The law of all laws, the necessity of nature, is that God and man are one. Until they begin to be one in the reality as in the divine idea, in the flower as in the root, in the finishing as in the issuing creation, nothing can go right with the man, and God can have no rest from his labor in him. As the greatest orbs in heaven are drawn by the least, God himself must be held in divine disquiet until every one of his family be brought home to his heart, to be one with him in a unity too absolute, profound, far-reaching, fine, and intense, to be understood by any but the God from whom it comes, yet to be guessed at by the soul from the unspeakableness of its delight when at length it is with the *only* that can be its own, the one that it can possess, the one that can possess it. For God is the heritage of the soul in the owness of origin; man is the offspring of his making will, of his life; God himself is his birthplace; God is the self that makes the soul able to say, *I too, I myself*. This absolute unspeakable bliss of the creature is that for which the Son died, for which the Father suffered with him. Then only is life itself; then only is it right, is it one; then only is it as designed and necessitated by the eternal life-outgiving Life.

Whereto then we have attained, let us *walk* by that same!

THE CREATION IN CHRIST

"All things were made by him, and without him was not anything made that was made. In him was life, and the life was the light of men."

John 1:3-4

AUGUST 10TH

It seems to me that any lover of the gospel can hardly have failed to feel dissatisfaction with the close of the third verse of John 1: "All things were made by him, and without him was not anything made *that was made*." That it is no worse than redundant can be no satisfaction to the man who would find perfection, if he may, in the words of him who was nearer the Lord than any other. My hope was therefore great when I saw, in reading the Greek, that the shifting of a period would rid me of the redundancy. And I found the change did unfold such a truth as showed the rhetoric itself in accordance with the highest thought of the apostle. Let us then look at the passage as I think it ought to be translated, and then seek the meaning for the sake of which it was written. It is a meaning indeed by no means dependent on this passage, belonging as it does to the very truth as it is in Jesus; but it is therein magnificently expressed by the apostle, and differently from anywhere else:

"All things were made through him, and without him was made not one thing. That which was made in him was life, and the life was the light of men."

Note the antithesis of the *through* and the *in*. In this grand assertion seems to me to lie, more than shadowed, the germ of creation and redemption—of all the divine in its relation to all the human.

248

AUGUST 11TH

I believe that Jesus Christ is the eternal son of the eternal father; that from the first, Jesus is the son, because God is the father. I believe, therefore, that the Father is the greater, that if the Father had not been, the Son could not have been. In saying what I do, I only say what Paul implies when he speaks of the Lord giving up the kingdom to his father, that God may be all in all. I worship the Son as the human God, the divine, the only Man, deriving his being and power from the Father, equal with him as a son is the equal at once and the subject of his father—but *making himself the equal of his father in what is most precious in Godhead, namely, Love*—which is indeed, the essence of the statement of the evangelist we have been considering—a higher thing than the making of the worlds and the things in them, which he did by the power of the Father, not by a self-existent power in himself, whence the apostle, to whom the Lord must have said things he did not say to the rest, or who was better able to receive what he said to all, says, "All things were made" not *by*, but "*through* him." The Father made essential use of the Son, so that all that exists was created *through* him. What was the part in creation of the Father and the part of the Son, who can understand?—but perhaps we may one day come to see into it a little; for I dare hope that, through our willed sonship, we shall come far nearer ourselves to creating. The word *creation* applied to the loftiest success of human genius seems to me a mockery of humanity, itself in the process of creation.

AUGUST 12TH

L et us read the text again: "All things were made *through* him, and without him was made not one thing. That which was made *in* him was life." The power by which he created the worlds was given him by his father; he had in himself a greater power than that by which he made the worlds. There was something made, not *through* but *in* him; something brought into being by himself. Here he creates in his grand way, in himself, as did the Father. "That which was made *in* him was *life*." What is the *life* the apostle intends? Many forms of life have come to being through the Son, but those were results, not forms of the life that was brought to existence *in* him. He could not have been employed by the Father in creating, save in virtue of the life that was *in* him. As to what the life of God is to himself, we can only know that we cannot know it. As to what the life of God is in relation to us, we know that it is the causing life of everything that we call life—of everything that is; and in knowing this, we know something of that life, by the very forms of its force. But the one interminable mystery is first, how can he be self-existent, and next, how he can make other beings exist: self-existence and creation no man will ever understand. The cause of our being is antecedent to our being; we can therefore have no knowledge of our own creation; neither can we understand that which we can do nothing like. If we could make ourselves, we should understand our creation, but to do that we must be God. Nevertheless, if I be a child of God, I must be *like* him, even in the matter of creative energy.

AUGUST 13TH

What was the life, the thing made in the Son—made by him inside himself, not outside him—made not *through* but *in* him—the life that was his own, as God's is his own? It was that act in him that corresponded in him, as the son, to the self-existence of his father. Now what is the deepest in God? His power? No, for power could not make him what we mean when we say *God*. Evil could, of course, never create one atom; but let us understand very plainly, that a being whose essence was only power would be such a negation of the divine that no righteous worship could be offered him: his service must be fear, and fear only. Such a being, even were he righteous in judgment, yet could not be God. In one word, God is Love. Love is the deepest depth, the essence of his nature, at the root of all his being. It is not merely that he could not be God, if he had made no creatures to whom to be God; but love is the heart and hand of his creation; it is his right to create, and his power to create as well. The love that foresees creation is itself the power to create. Neither could he be righteous—that is, fair to his creatures—but that his love created them. His perfection is his love. All his divine rights rest upon his love. Ah, he is not the great monarch! The simplest peasant loving his cow is more divine than any monarch whose monarchy is his glory. If God would not punish sin, or if he did it for anything but love, he would not be the father of Jesus Christ, the God who works as Jesus wrought.

AUGUST 14TH

What in Christ is correspondent to the creative power of God? It must be something that comes also of love; and in the Son the love must be to the already existent. Because of that eternal love which has not beginning, the Father must have the Son. God could not love, could not be love, without making things to love: Jesus has God to love; the love of the Son is responsive to the love of the Father. The response to self-existent love is self-abnegating love. The refusal of himself is that in Jesus which corresponds to the creation of God. His love takes action, creates, in self-abjuration, in the death of self as motive; in the drowning of self in the life of God, where it lives only as love. What is life in a child? Is it not perfect response to his parents, through oneness with them? A child at strife with his parents, one in whom their will is not his, is no child; as a child he is dead. His spiritual order is on the way to chaos. Disintegration has begun. Death is at work in him. See the same child yielding to the will that is righteously above his own; see the life begin to flow from the heart through the members; see the light rise like a fountain in his eyes, and flash from his face! Life has again its lordship!

The life of Christ is this—negatively, that he does nothing, cares for nothing for his own sake; positively, that he cares with his whole soul for the will, the pleasure of his father. Because his father is his father, therefore he will be his child.

AUGUST 15TH

The truth in Jesus is his relation to his father; the righteousness of Jesus is his fulfilment of that relation. Meeting this relation, loving his father with his whole being, he is not merely alive as born of God; but, giving himself with perfect will to God, choosing to die to himself and live to God, he therein creates in himself a new and higher life; and, standing upon himself, has gained the power to awake life, the divine shadow of his own, in the hearts of us his brothers and sisters, who have come from the same birth-home as himself, namely, the heart of his God and our God, his father and our father, but who, without our elder brother to do it first, would never have chosen that self-abjuration which is life, never have come alive like him. To will, not from self, but with the Eternal, is to live.

This active willing to be the Son of the Father, perfect in obedience, is that in Jesus which responds and corresponds to the self-existence of God. Jesus rose to the height of his being, set himself down on the throne of his nature, in the act of subjecting himself to the will of the Father as his only good, the only *reason* of his existence. When he died on the cross, he did in the torture of the body of his revelation what he had done at home in glory and gladness. From the infinite beginning he completed and held fast the eternal circle of his existence in saying, "Thy will, not mine, be done!"

AUGUST 16TH

Jesus made himself what he is by dying into the will of the eternal Father, through which will he was the eternal Son—thus plunging in to the fountain of his own life, the everlasting Fatherhood, and taking the Godhead of the Son. This is the life that was made *in* Jesus. This life, self-willed in Jesus, is the one thing that makes such life, the eternal life, the true life, possible—nay imperative, essential, to every man, woman, and child, whom the Father has sent into the outer, that he may go back into the inner world, his heart. As the self-existent life of the Father has given us being, so the willed devotion of Jesus is his power to give us eternal life like his own—to enable us to do the same. There is no life for any man, other than the same kind that Jesus has; his disciple must live by the same absolute devotion of his will to the Father's. Because we come out of the divine nature, which chooses to be divine, we must *choose* to be divine, to be one with God, or we perish. While God is the father of his children, Jesus is the father of their sonship. We are not and cannot become true sons without our will willing his will. It was the will of Jesus to be the thing God willed and meant him, that made him the true son of God. So with us: we must *be* the sons we are. We are not made to be what we cannot help being; sons and daughters are not after such fashion! We must be sons and daughters in our will. And we can be such only by choosing God for the father he is, and doing his will. Therein lies human bliss. The working out of this our salvation must be pain, but the eternal form of the will of God in and for us, is intensity of bliss.

AUGUST 17TH

The life of which I have spoken became light to men in the appearing of him in whom it came into being. The life became a light that men might see it, and themselves live by choosing that life also, by choosing so to live, such to be. There is always something deeper than anything said, something through which the central reality shines more or less plainly. Light itself is but the poor outside form of a deeper, better thing, namely, life. The life is Christ. The light too is Christ, but only the body of Christ. The life is Christ himself. The light is what we *see* and shall see in him; the life is what we may *be* in him. The obedient human God appeared as the obedient divine man, doing the works of his father—the things, that is, which his father did—doing them humbly before unfriendly brethren. The Son of the Father must take his own form in the substance of flesh, that he may be seen of men, and so become the light of men—not that men may have light, but that men may have life; that through the life that is in them, they may begin to hunger after the life of which they are capable, and which is essential to their being; that the life in them may long for him who is their life, and thirst for its own perfection, even as root and stem may thirst for the flower for whose sake, and through whose presence in them, they exist. That the child of God may become the son of God by beholding *the* Son, the life revealed in light; that the radiant heart of the Son of God may be the sunlight to his fellows; that the idea may be drawn out by the presence and daring of the Ideal—that Ideal, the perfect Son of the Father, was sent to his brethren.

AUGUST 18TH

Let us not forget that the devotion of the Son could never have been but for the devotion of the Father, who never seeks his own glory one atom more than does the Son; who is devoted to the Son, and to all his sons and daughters, with a devotion perfect and eternal, with fathomless unselfishness. The whole being and doing of Jesus on earth is a being like God, a doing of the will of God; a shining out of that life that men might see it, an unveiling of the Father in the Son, that men may know him. It is the prayer of the Son to the rest of the sons to come back to the Father. He seems to me to say, "I know your father, for he is my father; I know him because I have been with him from eternity. You do not know him; I have come to tell you that as I am, such is he, only greater and better. He only is the true, original good; I am true because I seek nothing but his will. He only is all in all; I am not all in all, but he is my father, and I am the son in whom his heart of love is satisfied. Come home with me and sit with me on the throne of my obedience. Together we will do his will, and be glad with him, for his will is the only good. You may do with me as you please; I will not defend myself. I bear witness that my father is such as I. In the face of death I assert it, and dare death to disprove it. Death can only kill my body; he cannot make me his captive. Father, thy will be done! Gladly will I suffer that men may know that I live, and that thou art my life."

AUGUST 19TH

The bond of the universe, the harmony of things, the negation of difference, the fact at the root of every vision, revealing that love is the only good in the world, and selfishness the one thing hateful, in the city of the loving God, is the devotion of the Son to the Father. It is the life of the universe. It is not the fact that God created all things that makes the universe a whole; but that he through whom he created them loves him perfectly, is satisfied to be because his father is with him. For there can be no unity, no oneness where there is only one. For the very beginnings of unity there must be two. Without Christ, therefore, there could be no universe. The reconciliation wrought by Jesus was the necessary working out of the eternal antecedent fact, that God and Christ are one, the Son loving the Father and the Father loving the Son as only the Father and Son can love. The prayer of the Lord for unity between men and the Father and himself springs from the eternal need of love. But for the Father and the Son, no two would care a jot the one for the other. It might be right for creatures to love because of mere existence, but what two creatures would ever have originated the loving? But if the Father loves the Son, if the very music that make the harmony of life lies in the burning love in the hearts of Father and Son, then glory be to the Father and the Son, drawing us up into the glory of their joy, to share in the thoughts of love that pass between them, in their thoughts of delight and rest in each other, in their thoughts of joy in all the little ones. The life of Jesus is the light of men, revealing to them the Father.

AUGUST 20TH

L ight is not enough; light is for the sake of life. We too must have life in ourselves. We too must, like the Life himself, live. We can live in no way but that in which Jesus lived, in which life was made in him. That way is to give up our life. This is the one supreme action of life possible to us for the making of life in ourselves. Christ did it of himself, and so became light to us, that we might be able to do it in ourselves, after him, and through his originating act. The help that he has given and gives, the spirit, in our hearts, is all in order that we may, as we must, do it ourselves. Till then we are not alive; life is not made in us. The whole strife and labor and agony of the Son with every man, is to get him to die as he dies. All preaching that aims not at this is a building with wood and hay and stubble. If I say not with whole heart, "My father, do with me as thou wilt, only help me against myself and for thee," if I cannot say, "Let me be thy dog, thy horse, thy anything thou willest; let me be thine in any shape the love that is my Father may please to have me;" if we cannot, fully as this, give ourselves to the Father, then we have not yet laid hold upon that for which Christ has laid hold upon us. The faith that a man must put in God reaches above earth and sky, stretches beyond the farthest outlying star of the creatable universe. The question is not at present, however, of removing mountains, a thing that will one day be simple to us, but of waking and rising from the dead *now*.

AUGUST 21ST

When a man truly and perfectly says with Jesus, "Thy will be done," he closes the ever-lasting life circle; the life of the Father and the Son flows through him; he is a part of the divine organism. Then is the prayer of the Lord in him fulfilled: "I in them and thou in me, that they may be made perfect in one." The Christ in us is the spirit of the perfect child toward the perfect father, our own true nature made to blossom in us by the Lord, whose life is the light of men that it may become the life of men; for our true nature is childhood to the Father. Let us then arise and live—arise even in the darkest moments of spiritual stupidity, when hope itself sees nothing to hope for. Let us go at once to the Life. Let us comfort ourselves in the thought of the Father and the Son. So long as the Son loves the Father with all the love the Father can welcome, all is well with the little ones. God is all right—why should we mind standing in the dark for a minute outside his window? Of course we miss the *insideness*, but there is a bliss of its own in waiting. What if the rain be falling, and the wind blowing; what if we stand alone, or, more painful still, have some dear one beside us, sharing our *outsideness*; what even if the window be not shining, because of the curtains drawn across it; let us think to ourselves, or say to our friend, "God is; Jesus is not dead; nothing can be going wrong, however it may look to hearts unfinished in childness." Let us say to the Lord, "Jesus, art thou loving the Father in there? Then we out here will do his will, patiently waiting till he open the door."

AUGUST 22ND

Perhaps the Son is saying to the Father, "Thy little ones need some wind and rain: their buds are hard; the flowers do not come out. I cannot get them made blessed without a little more winter weather." Then perhaps the Father will say, "Comfort them, my son Jesus, with the memory of thy patience when thou wast missing me." In a word, let us be at peace, because peace is at the heart of things—peace and utter satisfaction between the Father and the Son—in which peace they call us to share; in which peace they promise that at length, when they have their good way with us, we shall share. Before us, then, lies a bliss unspeakable, a bliss beyond the thought or invention of man, to every child who will fall in with the perfect imagination of the Father. His imagination is one with his creative will. The thing that God imagines, that thing exists. When the created falls in with the will of him who "loved him into being," then all is well; thenceforward the mighty creation goes on in him upon higher and yet higher levels, in more and yet more divine airs. Thy will, O God, be done! Nought else is other than loss, decay, and corruption. There is no life but that born of the life that the Word made in himself by doing thy will, which life is the light of men. Through that light is born the life of men—the same life in them that came first into being in Jesus. As he laid down his life, so must men lay down their lives, that as he liveth they may live also. That which was made in him was life, and the life is the light of men; and yet his own, to whom he was sent, *did not believe him.*

THE KNOWING OF THE SON

"And the Father himself which hath sent me, hath borne witness of me. Ye have neither heard his voice at any time, nor seen his shape. And ye have not his word abiding in you; for whom he hath sent, him ye believe not."

John 5:37-38

AUGUST 23RD

We shall know one day just how near we come in the New Testament to the very words of the Lord. That we have them with a difference, I cannot doubt. For one thing I do not believe he spoke in Greek. That the thoughts of God would come to of the heart of Jesus in anything but the mother-tongue of the simple men to whom he spoke, I cannot think. Are we bound to believe that John Boanerges, who indeed best, and in some things alone, understood him, was able, after such a lapse of years, to give us in his gospel, the *very* words in which he uttered the simplest profundities ever heard in the human world? I do not say he was not able; I say, Are we bound to believe he was able? The gospel of John is the outcome of years and years of remembering, recalling, and pondering the words of the Master. We cannot tell of how much the memory, with God in the man, may be capable; but I do not believe that John would have always given us the very words of the Lord. God has not cared that we should anywhere have assurance of his very words; and that not merely, perhaps, because of the tendency in his children to word-worship, false logic, and corruption of the truth, but because he would not have them oppressed by words, seeing that words, being human, therefore but partially capable, could not absolutely express what the Lord meant, and that even he must depend for being understood upon the spirit of his disciple. Seeing it could not give life, the letter should not be throned with power to kill; it should be but the handmaid to open the door of the truth to the mind that was *of* the truth.

AUGUST 24ᵀᴴ

D o I then believe in an individual inspiration to anyone who chooses to lay claim to it? Yes—to everyone who claims it from God; not to everyone who claims from men the recognition of his possessing it. He who has a thing does not need to have it recognized. If I did not believe in a special inspiration to every man who asks for the holy spirit, I should have to throw aside the whole tale as an imposture; for the Lord has, according to that tale, promised such inspiration to those who ask it. If an objector has not this spirit, is not inspired with the truth, he knows nothing of the words that are spirit and life. His assent equally is but the blowing of an idle horn. And how is one to tell whether it be in truth the spirit of God that is speaking in a man? You are not called upon to tell. The question for you is whether you have the spirit of Christ yourself. The question is for you to put to yourself, to answer for yourself: Am I alive with the life of Christ? Is his spirit dwelling in me? Everyone who desires to follow the Master has the spirit of the Master, and will receive more that he may follow in his very footsteps. He is not called upon to prove to this or that or any man that he has the light of Jesus; he has to let his light shine. It does not follow that his work is to teach others. When the truth urges him, let him speak it out and not be afraid— content to be condemned for it; comforted that if he mistake, the Lord himself will condemn him, and save him "as by fire." If he speaks true, the Lord will say "I sent him." For all truth is of him; no man can see a true thing to be true but by the Lord, the spirit.

AUGUST 25TH

How is one to know that a thing is true? By doing what you know to be true, and calling nothing true until you see it to be true; by shutting your mouth until the truth opens it. "But if I do not take the words attributed to him by the evangelists for the certain, absolute, very words of the Master, how am I to know that they represent his truth?" By seeing in them what corresponds to the plainest truth he speaks, and commends itself to the power that is working in you to make of you a true man; by their appeal to your power of judging what is true; by their rousing of your conscience. If they do not seem to you true, either they are not the words of the Master, or you are not true enough to understand them. Be certain of this, that if any words that are his do not show their truth to you, you have not received his message in them; they are not yet to you the word of God. They may be the nearest to the truth that words can come; they may have served to bring many into contact with the heart of God; but for you they remain as yet sealed. If yours be a true heart, it will revere them because of the probability that they are words with the meaning of the Master behind them. If you wait, your ignorance will not hurt you; if you presume to reason from them, you are a blind man disputing what you never saw. Humble mistake will not hurt us: the truth is there, and the Lord will see that we come to know it. The error of a true heart will not be allowed to ruin it. Certainly that heart would not have mistaken the truth except for the untruth yet remaining in it; but he who casts out devils will cast out that devil as well.

AUGUST 26TH

n the words of John 5:37-38, I see enough to enable me to believe that its words embody the mind of Christ. If I could not say this, I should say, "The apostle has here put on record a saying of Christ's; I have not yet been able to recognize the mind of Christ in it; therefore I conclude that I cannot have understood it, for to understand what is true is to know it true." I have yet seen no words credibly reported as the words of Jesus, concerning which I dared to say, "His mind is not therein, therefore the words are not his." The mind of man can receive any word only in proportion as it is the word of Christ, and in proportion as he is one with Christ. To him who does verily receive his word, it is a power, not of argument, but of life. The words of the Lord are not for the logic that deals with words as if they were things; but for the spiritual logic that reasons from divine thought, dealing with spiritual facts. And no thought can be conveyed save through the symbolism of the creation. The heavens and the earth are around us that it may be possible to speak of the unseen by the seen; for the outermost husk of creation has correspondence with the deepest things of the Creator. There are things with which an enemy hath meddled; but there are more things with which no enemy could meddle, and by which we may speak of God. They may not have revealed him to us, but at least when he is revealed, they show themselves so much of his nature, that we at once use them as spiritual tokens to help convey to other minds what we may have seen of the unseen. Belonging to this sort of mediation are the words of the Lord quoted by St. John above.

AUGUST 27TH

If Jesus said the words quoted in John 5:37-38, he meant more, not less, than lies on their surface. They cannot be mere assertion of what everybody knew. They were not intended to inform the Jews of a fact they would not have dreamed of denying. Who among them would say he had ever heard God's voice, or seen his shape? John himself says "No man hath seen God at any time." (1:18) What is the tone of the passage? It is reproach. The word *see* in the one statement (John 1:18) means *see with the eyes*; in the other (John 5: 37-38), *with the soul*. The one statement is made of all men; the other is made to certain of the Jews of Jerusalem concerning themselves. It is true that no man hath seen God, and true that some men ought to have seen him. No man hath seen him with his bodily eyes; these Jews ought to have seen him with their spiritual eyes. No man has ever seen God in any outward, visible, form of his own; he is revealed in no shape save that of his son. But multitudes of men have with their mind's, or rather their heart's eye, seen more or less of God; and perhaps every man might have and ought to have seen something of him. We cannot follow God into his infinitesimal intensities of spiritual operation; God may be working in the heart of a savage in a way that no wisdom of his wisest, humblest child can see. Many who have never beheld the face of God, may yet have caught a glimpse of the hem of his garment; many who have never seen his shape, may yet have seen the vastness of his shadow; some have dreamed his hand laid upon them, who never knew themselves gathered to his bosom.

AUGUST 28TH

The reproach in the words of the Lord is the reproach of men who ought to have had an experience they had not had. Let us look a little closer at his words. "Ye have not heard his voice at any time," might mean, *Ye have never listened, or obeyed, his voice*; but the following phrase, "nor seen his shape," keeps us rather to the primary sense of the word *hear.* Plainly he implies, *You ought to know his voice; you ought to know what he is like.* "You have not his word abiding in you": *The word that is in you from the beginning, the word of God in your conscience, is not dwelling in you; the scripture in which you think you have eternal life does not abide with you. You do not dwell with it, brood upon it, and obey it. You are not of those to whom the word of God comes. Their ears are ready to hear; they hunger after the word of the Father.* On what does the Lord found his accusation of them? "For whom he hath sent, him ye believe not." "How so?" the Pharisees might answer. "Have we not asked from thee a sign from heaven, and hast thou not point-blank refused it?"

The argument of the Lord was indeed of small weight with those to whom it most applied, for the more it applied, the more incapable were they of seeing that it did apply; but it would be of great force upon some that stood listening, their minds open to the truth, and their hearts drawn to the man before them.

AUGUST 29TH

The Lord's argument was this: "If ye had ever heard the Father's voice, known his call; if you had ever imagined him, or a God anything like him; if you had cared for his will so that his word was at home in your hearts, you would have known me when you saw me—known that I must come from him, that I must be his messenger, and would have listened to me. The least acquaintance with God, such as any true heart must have, would have made you recognize that I came from the God of whom you knew that something. You would have been capable of knowing me by the light of his word abiding in you; by the shape you had beheld however vaguely; by the likeness of my face and my voice to those of my father. You would have seen my father in me; you would have known me by the little you knew of him. The family feeling would have been awake in you, the holy instinct of the same spirit, making you know your elder brother. That you do not know me now, as I stand here speaking to you, is that you do not know your own father, even my father; that throughout your lives you have refused to do his will, and so have not heard his voice; that you have shut your eyes from seeing him, and have thought of him only as a partisan of your ambitions. If you had loved my father, you would have known his son." And I think he might have said, "If even you had loved your neighbor, you would have known me, neighbor to the deepest and best in you."

AUGUST 30TH

If the Lord were to appear this day in your land as once in Palestine, he would not come in the halo of the painters, or with that wintry shine of effeminate beauty, of sweet weakness, in which it is their helpless custom to represent him. Neither would he likely come as carpenter, or mason, or gardener. He would come in such form and condition as might bear to the present America, or England, or France, a relation like that which the form and condition he then came in, bore to the motley Judea, Samaria, and Galilee. If he came thus, in form altogether unlooked for, who would they be that recognized and received him? The idea involves no absurdity. He is not far from us at any moment—if the old story be indeed more than the best and strongest of the fables that possess the world. He might at any moment appear: who, I ask, would be the first to receive him? Now, as then, it would of course be the childlike in heart, the truest, the least selfish. They would not be the highest in the estimation of any church, for the childlike are not yet the many. It might not even be those that knew most about the former visit of the Master. It would certainly be those who were most like the Master—those that did the will of the Father, that built their house on the rock by hearing and doing his sayings. But are there any enough like him to know him at once by the sound of his voice, by the look of his face? There are multitudes who would at once be taken by a false Christ fashioned after their fancy, and would reject the Lord as a poor impostor. One thing is certain: they who first recognized him would be those that most loved righteousness and hated iniquity.

AUGUST 31ST

I would not forget that there are many in whom foolish forms cover a live heart, warm toward everything human and divine; but let each be true after the fashion possible to him, and he shall have the Master's praise. If the Lord were to appear, he has been so misrepresented by such as have claimed to present him, and especially in the one eternal fact of facts—the relation between him and his father—that it is impossible for many that they should see any likeness. For my part, I would believe in no God rather than in such a God as is generally offered for believing in. How far those may be to blame who, righteously disgusted, cast the idea from them, nor make inquiry whether something in it may not be true, though most must be false, neither grant it any claim to investigation on the chance that some that call themselves his prophets may have taken spiritual bribes "to mingle beauty with infirmities, and pure perfection with impure defeature"--how far those may be to blame, it is not my work to inquire. Some would grasp with gladness the hope that such chance might be proved a fact; others would not care to discern upon the palimpsest, covered but not obliterated, a credible tale of a perfect man revealing a perfect God: they are not true enough to desire that to be fact which would immediately demand the modelling of their lives upon a perfect idea, and the founding of their every hope upon the same.

But we all, beholding the glory of the Lord, are changed into the same image.

THE MIRRORS OF THE LORD

"But we all, with open face beholding as in a glass the glory of the Lord, are changed into the same image from glory to glory, even as by the spirit of the Lord."

2 Corinthians 3:18

SEPTEMBER 1ST

Of all writers I know, Paul seems to me the most plainly practical in his writing. What has been called his mysticism is at one time the exercise of a power of seeing, as by spiritual refraction, truths that had not, perhaps have not yet, risen above the human horizon; at another, the result of a wide-eyed habit of noting the analogies and correspondences between the concentric regions of creation; it is the working of a poetic imagination divinely alive, whose part is to foresee and welcome approaching truth; to discover the same principle in things that look unlike; to embody things discovered, in forms and symbols heretofore unused, and so present to other minds the deeper truths to which those forms and symbols owe their being. I find in Paul's writing the same artistic fault, with the same resulting difficulty, that I find in Shakespeare's—a fault springing from the admirable fact that the man is much more than the artist—the fault of trying to say too much at once, of pouring out the plethora of a soul swelling with life and its thought, through the too narrow neck of human utterance. Thus we are at times bewildered between two or more meanings, equally good in themselves; but the uncertainty lies always in the intellectual region, never in the practical. What Paul cares about is plain enough to the true heart, however far from plain to the man whose desire to understand goes ahead of his obedience, who starts with the notion that Paul's design was to teach a system, to explain instead of help to see God, a God that can be revealed only to childlike insight, never to keenest intellect.

SEPTEMBER 2ND

The energy of the apostle, like that of his master, went forth to rouse men to seek the kingdom of God over them, his righteousness in them; to dismiss the lust of possession and passing pleasure; to look upon the glory of the God and Father, and turn to him from all that he hates; to recognize the brotherhood of men, and the hideousness of what is unfair, unloving, and self-exalting. His design was not to teach any plan of salvation other than obedience to the Lord of Life. Let us see then what Paul teaches us in this passage about the life which is the light of men. It is his form of bringing to bear upon men the truth announced by John.

When Moses came out from speaking with God, his face was radiant; its shining was a wonder to the people, and a power upon them. But the radiance began at once to diminish and die away, for it was not indigenous in Moses. Therefore Moses put a veil upon his face that they might not see it fade. Paul says that the veil which obscured the face of Moses lies now upon the hearts of the Jews, so that they cannot understand him, but that when they turn to the Lord, go into the tabernacle with Moses, the veil shall be taken away, and they shall see God. Then will they understand that the glory is indeed faded upon the face of Moses, but by reason of the glory that excelleth, the glory of Jesus that overshines it. The sight of the Lord will take that veil from their hearts. Where he is, there is no more bondage, no more wilderness or Mt. Sinai. The Son makes free with sonship.

SEPTEMBER 3RD

Consider the words of 2 Corinthians 3:18. *"We need no Moses,"* Paul is, in essence, saying, *"no earthly mediator, to come between us and the light, and bring out for us a little of the glory. We go into the presence of the Son revealing the Father--into the presence of the Light of men. Our mediator is the Lord himself, the spirit of light, a mediator not sent by us to God to bring back his will, but come from God to bring us himself. We enter, like Moses, into the presence of the visible, radiant God—only how much more visible, more radiant! As Moses stood with uncovered face receiving the glory of God full upon it, so full in the light of the glory of God we stand— you and I, Corinthians. It is no reflected light we see, but the glory of God shining in and from the face of Christ, the glory of the Father, one with the Son. Israel saw but the fading reflection of the glory of God on the face of Moses; we see the glory itself in the face of Jesus."* But translations that have "beholding as in a glass," or "reflecting as a mirror," miss the meaning. The idea, with the figure, is that of a poet, not a man of science. The poet deals with the outer show of things, which is infinitely deeper in its relation to truth, as well as more practically useful, than the analysis of the man of science. Paul never thought of the mirror as reflecting, as throwing back the rays of light from its surface; he thought of it as receiving, taking into itself, the things presented to it—as filling its bosom with the glory it looks upon. Imagine the face of your friend in a mirror: the mirror seems to hold it in itself, to surround the visage with its liquid embrace.

SEPTEMBER 4TH

The best word to represent the Greek, and the most literal as well by which to translate it, is the verb *mirror*, so that 2 Cor. 3:18 would read "But we all, with unveiled face, mirroring the glory of the Lord..." The prophet-apostle seems to me to say "We all, with clear vision of the Lord, mirroring in our hearts his glory, even as a mirror would take into itself his face, are thereby changed into his likeness, his glory working our glory, by the present power, in our inmost being, of the Lord, the spirit." Our mirroring of Christ, then, is one with the presence of his spirit in us. The idea, you see, is not the reflection, the radiating of the light of Christ on others, though that were an image true enough; but the taking into, and having in us, him working to the changing of us. It is but according to the law of symbol, that the thing symbolized by the mirror should have properties far beyond those of leaded glass or polished metal, seeing it is a live soul understanding that which it takes into its deeps. It mirrors by its will to hold in its mirror. Unlike its symbol, it can hold not merely the outward resemblance, but the inward likeness of the person revealed by it; it is open to the influences of that which it embraces, and is capable of active cooperation with them. Paul's idea is that when we take into our understanding, our heart, the glory of God, namely Jesus Christ as he shows himself to our eyes, our hearts, our consciences, he works upon us, and will keep working, till we are changed to the very likeness we have thus mirrored in us; for with his likeness he comes himself, and dwells in us.

SEPTEMBER 5TH

The Lord will work until the image of the humanity of God is wrought out and perfected in us, the image we were made at first, but which could never be developed in us except by the indwelling of the perfect likeness. By the power of Christ thus received and at home in us, we are changed—the glory in him becoming glory in us, his glory changing us to glory. But we must beware of receiving this or any symbol *after the flesh*, beware of interpreting it in any fashion that partakes of the character of the mere physical or psychical. The symbol deals with things far beyond the deepest region whence symbols can be drawn. The indwelling of Jesus in the soul of man, who shall declare! But let us note this, that the dwelling of Jesus in us is the power of the spirit of God upon us; for the "the Lord is that spirit," and the Lord dwelling in us, we are changed "even as from the Lord the spirit." When we think Christ, Christ comes; when we receive his image into our spiritual mirror, he enters with it. Our open receiving thought is his door to come in. When our hearts turn to him, that is opening the door to him, that is holding up our mirror to him; then he comes in, not by our thought only, but he comes himself, and of his own will—comes in as we could not take him, but as he can come and we receive him—enabled to receive by his very coming the one welcome guest of the whole universe. Thus the Lord, the spirit, becomes the soul of our souls, becomes spiritually what he always was creatively; and as our spirit informs, gives shape to our bodies, in like manner his soul informs, gives shape to our souls.

SEPTEMBER 6TH

The Lord, the spirit, is but the deeper soul that willed and wills our souls, which rises up, the infinite Life, into the Self we call *I* and *me*, but which lives immediately from him, and is his very own property and nature—unspeakably more his than ours: this deeper creative soul, working on and with his creation upon higher levels, makes the *I* and *me* more and more his, and himself more and more ours; until at length the glory of our existence flashes upon us, we face full to the sun that enlightens what it sent forth, and know ourselves alive with an infinite life, even the life of the Father; know that our existence is not the moonlight of a mere consciousness of being, but the sun-glory of a life justified by having become one with its origin, thinking and feeling with the primal Sun of life, from whom it was dropped away that it might know and bethink itself, and return to circle forever in exultant harmony around him. Then indeed we *are;* then indeed we have life; the life of Jesus has, through light, become life in us; the glory of God in the face of Jesus, mirrored in our hearts, has made us alive; we are one with God forever and ever.

SEPTEMBER 7TH

What less than such a splendor of hope would be worthy of the revelation of Jesus? Filled with the soul of their Father, men shall inherit the glory of their Father; filled with themselves, they cast him out and rot. The company of the Lord, soul to soul, is that which saves with life, his life of God-devotion, the souls of his brethren. No other saving can save them. They must receive the Son, and through the Son the Father. What it cost the Son to get so near to us that we could say *Come in,* is the story of his life. He stands at the door and knocks, and when we open to him he comes in, and dwells with us, and we are transformed to the same image of truth and purity and heavenly childhood. Where power dwells, there is no force; where the spirit-Lord is, there is liberty. The Lord Jesus, by free, potent communion with their inmost being, will change his obedient brethren till in every thought and impulse they are good like him, loving the Father perfectly like him, ready to die for the truth like him, caring like him for nothing in the universe but the will of God, which is love, harmony, liberty, beauty, and joy. I do not know if we may call this having life in ourselves; but it is the waking up, the perfecting in us of the divine life inherited from our Father in heaven, who made us in his own image, whose nature remains in us, and makes it the deepest reproach to a man that he has neither heard his voice at any time, nor seen his shape. He who would thus live must, as a mirror draws into its bosom an outward glory, receive into his "heart of hearts" the inward glory of Jesus Christ, *the Truth.*

THE TRUTH

"I am the truth."

John 14:6

SEPTEMBER 8TH

When the man of the five senses talks of *truth,* he regards it but as a predicate of something historical or scientific proved a fact; or, if he allows that, for all he knows, there may be higher truth, yet, as he cannot obtain proof of it from without, he acts as if under no conceivable obligation to seek any other satisfaction concerning it. Whatever appeal be made to the highest region of his nature, such a one behaves as if it were the part of a wise man to pay it no heed, because it does not come within the scope of the lower powers of that nature. According to the word of *the* man, however, truth means more than fact, more than relation of facts of persons, more than loftiest abstraction of metaphysical entity—it means being and life, will and action; for he says, "*I am the truth.*" I desire to help those whom I may to understand more of what is meant by *the truth,* not for the sake of definition, or logical discrimination, but that, when they hear the word from the mouth of the Lord, the right idea may rise in their minds; that the word may neither be to them a void sound, nor call up either a vague or false notion of what he meant by it. If he says, "I am the truth," it must, to say the least, be well to know what he means by the word with whose idea he identifies himself. And at once we may premise that he can mean nothing merely intellectual, such as may be set forth and left there; he means something vital, so vital that it includes everything else which, in any lower plane, may go or have gone by the same name. Let us endeavor to arrive at his meaning by a gently ascending stair.

SEPTEMBER 9TH

A thing being so, the word that says it is so is the truth. But the fact may be of no value in itself, and our knowledge of it of no value either. Of most facts it may be said that the truth concerning them is of no consequence. For instance, it cannot be in itself important whether on a certain morning I took one side of the street or the other. It may be of importance to someone to know which I took, but in itself it is of none. It would therefore be felt unfit if I said, "It is *a truth* that I walked on the sunny side." The correct word would be *a fact*, not *a truth*. If the question arose whether a statement concerning the thing were correct, we should still be in the region of fact; but when we come to ask whether the statement was true or false, then we are concerned with the matter as the assertion of a human being, and ascend to another plane of things. It may be of no consequence which side I was upon, or it may be of consequence to someone to know which, but it is of vital importance to the witness and to any who love him, whether or not he believes the statement he makes—whether the man himself is true or false. Concerning the thing it can be but a question of fact; it remains a question of fact even whether the man has or has not spoken the truth; but concerning the man it is a question of truth: he is either a pure soul, so far as this thing witnesses, or a false soul, capable and guilty of a lie. In this relation it is of no consequence whether the man spoke the fact or not; if he meant to speak the fact, he remains a true man.

SEPTEMBER 10TH

L et us go from the region of facts that seem casual, to those facts that are invariable, which therefore involve what we call *law*. It will be seen at once that the truth or falsehood of a statement in this region is of more consequence. It is a small matter whether the water in my jug was frozen this morning; but it is a fact of great importance that at thirty-two degrees Fahrenheit water always freezes. Is it then a truth that water freezes at thirty-two degrees? The principle that lies at the root of it in the mind of God must be a truth, but to the human mind the fact is as yet only a fact. Call it a law if you will—a law of nature if you choose—that it always is so, but not a truth. It cannot be to us a truth until we discern the reason for its existence. Tell us why it *must* be so, and you state a truth. When we come to see that a law is such because it is the embodiment of a certain eternal thought, a fact of the being of God, the facts of which alone are truths, then indeed it will be to us, not a law merely, but an embodied truth. A law of God's nature is a way he would have us think of him; it is a necessary truth of all being. When we say, I understand that law; I see why it ought to be; it is just like God; then it rises to a revelation of character, nature, and will in God. It is a picture of something in God, a word that tells a fact about God, and is therefore far nearer being called a truth than anything below it. As a simple illustration: What notion should we have of the unchanging and unchangeable, without the solidity of matter? If we had nothing solid about us, where would be our thinking about God and truth and law?

282

SEPTEMBER 11TH

E very fact in nature is a revelation of God, is there such as it is because God is such as he is; and I suspect that all its facts impress us so that we learn God unconsciously. True, we cannot think of any one fact thus, except as we find the soul of it—its fact of God; but from the moment when first we come into contact with the world, it is to us a revelation of God, his things seen, by which we come to know the things unseen. What idea could we have of God without the sky? The truth of the sky is what it makes us feel of the God that sent it out to our eyes. In its discovered laws, light seems to me to be such because God is such. Its so-called laws are the waving of his garments, waving so because he is thinking and loving and walking inside them. We are here in a region far above that commonly claimed for science, open only to the heart of the child and the childlike man and woman. Facts and laws are but a means to an end; in the perfected end we find the intent, and there God. For that reason, human science cannot discover God; for science is but the backward undoing of the tapestry-web of God's science; it will never find the face of God, while those who would reach his heart will find also the spring-head of his science. The work of science is a following back of his footsteps, too often without appreciation of the result for which the feet took those steps. If a man could find out why God worked so, then he would be discovering God; but even then he would not be discovering the best and deepest of God; for his means cannot be so great as his ends.

SEPTEMBER 12TH

A sk a man of mere science, what is the truth of a flower: he will pull it to pieces, show you its parts, explain how they operate, how they minister each to the life of the flower; he will tell you what changes are wrought in it by scientific cultivation; and many more facts about it. Ask the poet what is the truth of the flower, and he will answer: "Why, the flower itself, the perfect flower, and what it cannot help saying to him who has ears to hear it." The truth of the flower is not the facts about it, but the shining, glowing, gladdening, patient thing throned on its stalk—the compeller of smile and tear from child and prophet. The man of science laughs at this, because he does not know what it means; but the poet and the child care as little for his laughter as the birds of God, as Dante calls the angels, for his treatise on aeronautics. The children of God must always be mocked by the children of the world, whether in the church or out of it—children with sharp ears and eyes, but dull hearts. Those that hold love the only good in the world, understand and smile at the world's children, and can do very well without anything the world has to tell them. In the higher state to which their love is leading them, they will speedily outstrip the men of science, for they have that which is at the root of science, that for the revealing of which God's science exists. What shall it profit a man to know all things, and lose the bliss, the consciousness of well-being, which alone can give value to knowledge?

SEPTEMBER 13TH

If we understand, if we love the flower, we have that for which the science is there, that which alone can equip us for true search into the means and ways by which the divine idea of the flower was wrought out to be presented to us. The idea of God *is* the flower; his idea is not the botany of the flower. Its botany is but a thing of ways and means—of canvas and color and brush in relation to the picture in the painter's brain. The mere intellect can never find out that which owes its being to the heart supreme. The idea of God is the flower: he thought it, invented its means, sent it, a gift of himself, to the eyes and hearts of his children. When we see how they are loved by the ignorant and degraded, we may well believe the flowers have a place in the history of the world which we are yet a long way from understanding, and which science could not, to all eternity, understand. Watch that child! He has found one of his silent and motionless brothers, with God's clothing upon it, God's thought in its face. In what a smile breaks out the divine understanding between them! Watch his mother when he takes it home to her—no nearer understanding it than he! It is no old association that brings those tears to her eyes; it is God's thought, unrecognized as such, holding communion with her. She weeps with a delight inexplicable. It is only a daisy! Only a lily of the field! But here is a truth of nature, a perfect thought from the heart of God, a divine fact, a dim revelation! Who but a father could think the flowers for his little ones? We are close to the region now in which the Lord's word is at home—"I am the truth."

SEPTEMBER 14TH

What is the truth of water? Is it that it is formed of hydrogen and oxygen? Is oxygen and hydrogen the divine idea of water? Or has God put the two together only that man might separate and find them out? He allows his child to pull his toys to pieces; but he were a child not to be envied for whom his inglorious father would make toys to such an end! Find for us what in the constitution of the two gases makes them fit and capable to be thus honored in forming the lovely thing, and you will give us a revelation about more than water, namely about the God who made oxygen and hydrogen. The water itself, that dances, and sings, and slakes the wonderful thirst—symbol and picture of that draught for which the woman of Samaria made her prayer to Jesus—this lovely thing itself, whose very wetness is a delight to every inch of the human body in its embrace—this water is its own self its own truth, and is therein a truth of God. Let him who would know the love of the maker, become sorely athirst, and drink of the brook by the way—then lift up his heart to the inventor and mediator of thirst and water, that man might foresee a little of what his soul may find in God. Let a man go to the hillside and let the brook sing to him till he loves it, and he will find himself far nearer the fountain of truth than the triumphal chemist will ever lead the shouting crew of his half-comprehending followers. He will draw from the brook the water of joyous tears, "and worship him that made heaven, and earth, and the sea, and the fountains of waters."

SEPTEMBER 15TH

The truth of a thing is the blossom of it, the thing it is made for, the topmost stone set on with rejoicing; truth in a man's imagination is the power to recognize this truth of a thing; and wherever, in anything that God has made, in the glory of it, be it sky or flower or human face, we see the glory of God, there a true imagination is beholding a truth of God. We have seen that the moment whatever goes by the name of truth comes into connection with man; the moment that, instead of merely mirroring itself in his intellect as a thing outside of him, it comes into contact with him as a being of action; the moment the knowledge of it affects his sense of duty, it becomes a thing of far nobler import; the question of truth enters upon a higher phase, looks out of a loftier window. A fact which in itself is of no value, becomes at once a matter of life and death—moral life and death, when a man has the choice, the imperative choice of being true or false concerning it. When the truth of a thing is perceived by a man, he approaches the fountain of truth whence the thing came, and perceiving God by understanding what is, becomes more of a man, more of the being he was meant to be. In virtue of this truth perceived, he has relations with the universe undeveloped in him till then. But far higher will the doing of the least, the most insignificant duty rise him. He begins thereby to be a true man. A man may delight in the vision and glory of a truth, and not himself be true. The man whose vision is weak, but who, as far as he sees, and desirous to see farther, does the thing he sees, is a true man.

SEPTEMBER 16TH

The man who recognizes the truth of any human relation, and neglects the duty involved, is not a true man. The man who takes good care of himself, and none of his brother and sister, is false. A man may be a poet, aware of the highest truth of a thing, he may be a man who would not tell a lie, or steal, or slander—and yet he may not be a true man, inasmuch as the essentials of manhood are not his aim: having nowise come to the flower of his own being, nowise attained the truth of that for which he exists—neither is he striving after the same. Man is man only in the doing of the truth, perfect man only in the doing of the highest truth, which is the fulfilling of his relations to his origin. But he has relations with his fellow man, to many a man far plainer than his relations with God. Now the nearer is plainer that he may step on it, and rise to the higher, to the less plain. The very nature of a man depends upon these relations. They are *truths,* and the man is a true man as he fulfils them. Fulfilling them perfectly, he is himself a living truth. The fulfilments of these truths are duties. Man is so constituted as to understand them at first more than he can love them, with the resulting advantage of having thereby the opportunity of choosing them purely because they are true; so doing he chooses to love them, and is enabled to love them in the doing, which alone can truly reveal them to him, and make the loving of them possible. Then they cease to show themselves in the form of duties, and appear as they more truly are, absolute truths, essential realities, eternal delights.

SEPTEMBER 17TH

The man is a true man who chooses duty; he is a perfect man who at length never thinks of duty, who forgets the name of it. The duty of Jesus was the doing in lower forms than the perfect that which he loved perfectly, and did perfectly in the highest forms also. Thus he fulfilled all righteousness. One who went to the truth by mere impulse, would be a holy animal, not a true man. Relations, truths, duties, are shown to the man away beyond him, that he many choose them, and be a child of God, choosing righteousness like him. The moral philosopher who regards duties only as facts of his system; even the man who rewards them as truths, essential realities of his humanity, but goes no farther, is essentially a liar, a man of untruth. He is a man in possibility, but not a real man yet. The recognition of these things is the imperative obligation to fulfil them. Not fulfilling these relations, the man is undoing the right of his own existence, destroying his *raison d'etre,* making of himself a monster, a live reason why he should not live, for nothing on those terms could ever have begun to be. His presence is a claim upon his creator for destruction. The facts of human relation, then, are truths indeed, and of most awful import. "Whosoever hateth his brother is a murderer; and ye know that no murderer hath eternal life abiding in him!" The man who lives a hunter after pleasure, not a laborer in the fields of duty, is in himself a lie. Hence all the holy—that is, healing—miseries that come upon him; they are for the compelling of the truth he will not yield—a painful suasion to be himself, to be a truth.

SEPTEMBER 18TH

Suppose a man did everything required of him, fulfilled all the duties of his relations with this fellows—was toward them at least, a true man; he would yet feel that something was lacking to his necessary well-being. Like a live flower, he would feel that he had not yet blossomed, and could not tell what the blossom ought to be. In this direction the words of the Lord point, when he says to the youth, "If thou wouldst be perfect." The man would feel that the truth of his being and nature was not yet revealed to his consciousness. He would remain unsatisfied, because there was in him the deepest, closest, strongest relation which had not yet come into live fact, which had not yet become a truth in him, toward which he was not true, whereby his being remained untrue, he was not himself, was not yet ripened into the divine idea, which alone can content itself. A child with a child's heart who does not even know that he has a father, yet misses him. This relation has not yet so far begun to be fulfilled in him, as that the coming blossom should send before it patience and hope enough to enable him to live by faith without sight. When the flower begins to come, the human plant begins to rejoice in the glory of God not yet revealed, the inheritance of the saints in light; with uplifted stem and forward-leaning bud expects the hour when the lily of God's field shall know itself alive, with God himself for its heart and its atmosphere; the hour when God and the man shall be one, and all that God cares for shall be the man's.

SEPTEMBER 19TH

The highest truth to the intellect is the relation in which man stands to the source of his being—his love to the love that kindled his power to love, his intellect to the intellect that lighted his. If a man deal with these things only as ideas to be analyzed, he treats them as facts and not as truths, and is no better—probably much the worse—for his converse with them, for he is false to all that is most worthy of his faithfulness. But when the soul becomes aware that he needs someone above him, whom to obey, in whom to rest, from whom to seek deliverance from what in himself is despicable; when he is aware of an opposition in him, that, while he hates it, is yet present with him, and seeming to be himself, what sometimes he calls *the old Adam*, sometimes *the flesh,* sometimes *his lower nature*, sometimes *his evil self;* then indeed is the man in the region of truth, and beginning to come true in himself. Nor will it be long ere he discover that there is no part in him with which he would be at strife, so God were there, so that it were true, what it ought to be; for, by whatever name called—the old Adam, or antecedent dog, or tiger, it would then fulfil its part holily, intruding upon nothing, subject utterly to the rule of the higher; dog or tiger, it would be good dog, good tiger.

SEPTEMBER 20TH

When the man bows down before a power to whom he is no mystery as he is to himself; a power that knows whence he came and whither he is going; why and where he began to go wrong; who can set him right, longs indeed to set him right, making of him a creature to look up to himself without shadow of doubt, anxiety or fear, confident as a child whom his father is leading by the hand to the heights of happy-making truth, knowing that where he is wrong, the father will set him right--then the man is bursting into his flower; then the truth of his being, the eternal fact at the root of his new name, his real nature, begins to show itself; than his nature is almost in harmony with itself. For, obeying the will that is the cause of his being, and that will being righteousness and love and truth, he beings to stand on the apex of his being, to know himself divine. He begins to feel himself free. The truth—not as known to his intellect, but as revealed in his own sense of being true, known by his essential consciousness of his divine condition, without which his nature is neither his own nor God's—trueness has made him free. Not any abstract truth, not truth its very metaphysical self, can make any man free; but the truth done, the truth loved, the truth lived by the man; the truth *of* and not merely *in* the man himself; the honesty that makes the man himself a child of the honest God.

SEPTEMBER 21ST

When a man is, with his whole nature, loving and willing the truth, he is then a live truth. But this he has not originated in himself. He has seen it and striven for it, but not originated it. The one originating, living, visible truth, embracing all truths in all relations, is Jesus Christ. He is true; he is the live Truth. His truth, chosen and willed by him, the flower of his sonship which is his nature, is his absolute obedience to his father. The obedient Jesus is Jesus the Truth. He is true and the root of all truth and development of truth in men. Their very being, however far from the true human, is the undeveloped Christ in them, and his likeness to Christ is the truth of a man, even as the perfect meaning of a flower is the truth of a flower. Every man, according to the divine idea of him, must come to the truth of that idea; and under every form of Christ is the Christ. As Christ is the blossom of humanity, so the blossom of every man is the Christ perfected in him. The vital force of humanity working in him is Christ; he is his root—the generator and perfecter of his individuality. The stronger the pure will of the man to be true; the freer and more active his choice; ever the more is the man and all that is his, Christ's. Without him he could not have been; being, he could not have become capable of truth; capable of truth, he could never have loved it; loving and desiring it, he could not have attained to it. Nothing but the heart presence betwixt the creating Truth and the responding soul could make a man go on hoping, until at last he forget himself, and keep open house for God to come and go.

SEPTEMBER 22ND

The Lord gives us the will wherewith to will, and the power to use it, and the help needed to supplement the power; but we ourselves must will the truth, and for that he is waiting, for the victory of God his father in the heart of his child. In this alone can he be satisfied. The work is his, but we must take our willing share. When the blossom breaks forth in us, the more it is ours the more it is his, for the highest creation of the Father, and that preeminently through the Son, is the being that can, like the Father and the Son, of his own self will what is right. When my being is consciously in the hands of him who called it to live and think and suffer and be glad—given back to him by a perfect obedience—I thenceforward breathe the breath, share the life of God himself. Then I am free, in that I am true—which means one with the Father. When a man is true, if he were in hell he could not be miserable. He is right with himself because right with him whence he came. To be right with God is to be right with the universe; one with the power, the love, the will of the mighty Father, the cherisher of joy, the lord of laughter, whose are all glories, all hopes, who loves everything and hates nothing but selfishness, which he will not have in his kingdom. Christ then is the Lord of life; his life is the light of men; the light mirrored in them changes them into the image of him, the Truth; and thus *the truth, who is the Son, makes them free.*

FREEDOM

"The Truth shall make you free...Whoseoever committeth sin, is the servant of sin. And the servant abideth not in the house forever; but the Son abideth ever. If the son therefore shall make you free, ye shall be free indeed."

John 8: 32, 34-36.

SEPTEMBER 23RD

As the passage from John stands, I have not been able to make sense of it. No man could be in the house of the Father in virtue of being the servant of sin; yet this man is in the house as a servant, and the house in which he serves is not the house of sin, but the house of the Father. The utterance is confused at best, and the reasoning faulty. He must be in the house of the Father on some other ground than sin. Most difficulties of similar nature, where the words of the Lord may have been misrepresented, likely originated with some scribe who, desiring to explain what he did not understand, wrote his worthless gloss on the margin: the next copier took the words for an omission that ought to be replaced in the body of the text. What do we not owe to the critics who have searched the scriptures, and found what really was written! In the present case, Dr. Wescott's notation gives a reading with a difference indeed small to the eye, but great enough to give us fine gold. What I take for the true reading in English, then, is: "Everyone committing sin is a slave. But the slave does not remain in the house forever; the son remaineth forever. If then the son shall make you free, you shall in reality be free." The words of the Lord here are not that he who sins is the slave of sin, true utterly as that is; but that he is a slave, and the argument shows that he means a slave to God. The two are perfectly consistent. No amount of slavery to sin can keep a man from being as much the slave of God as God chooses in his mercy to make him. It is his sin makes him a slave instead of a child. His slavery to sin is his ruin; his slavery to God is his only hope.

SEPTEMBER 24TH

God indeed does not love slavery; he hates it; he will have children, not slaves; but he may keep a slave in his house a long time in the hope of waking up the poor slavish nature to aspire to the sonship which belongs to him, which is his birthright. But the slave is not to be in the house forever. The father is not bound to keep his son a slave because the foolish child prefers it. Whoever will not do what God desires of him, is a slave whom God can compel to do it, however he may bear with him. He who, knowing this, or fearing punishment, obeys God, is still a slave, but a slave who comes within hearing of the voice of his master. There are, however, far higher than he, who yet are but slaves. Those to whom God is not all in all, are slaves. They may not commit great sins; they may be trying to do right; but so long as they *serve* God, from duty, and do not know him as their father, the joy of their being, they are slaves—good slaves, but slaves. They are by no means so slavish as those that serve from fear, but they are slaves; and because they are but slaves, they can fulfil no righteousness, can do no duty perfectly, but must ever be trying after it warily and in pain, knowing well that if they stop trying, they are lost. They are slaves indeed, for they would be glad to be adopted by one who is their own father! Where then are the sons? I know none, I answer, who are yet utterly and entirely sons or daughters. But I do know some who are enough sons and daughters to be at war with the slave in them, who are not content to be slaves to their father.

SEPTEMBER 25TH

Nothing I have seen or known of sonship comes near the glory of the thing; but there are thousands of sons and daughters who are siding with the father of their spirits against themselves, against all that divides them from him from whom they have come, but out of whom they have never come, seeing that in him they live and move and have their being. Such are not slaves; they are true though not perfect children; they are fighting along with God against the evil separation; they are breaking at the middle wall of partition. Only the rings of their fetters are left, and they are struggling to take them off. They are children—with more or less of the dying slave in them; they know it is there, and what it is, and hate the slavery in them, and try to slay it. The real slave is he who does not desire to end his slavery; who looks upon the claim of the child as presumption; who cleaves to the traditional authorized service of forms and ceremonies, and does not know the will of him who made the seven stars and Orion, much less cares to obey it; who never lifts up his heart to cry, "Father, what wouldst thou have me to do?" When they are sons and daughters, they will no longer complain of the hardships, and miseries, and troubles of life; no longer grumble at their aches and pains, at the pinching of their poverty; no longer be indignant at their rejection by what is called Society. Those who believe in their own perfect father can ill blame him for anything they do not like. Ah, friend, it may be you and I are slaves, but there are such sons and daughters as I speak of.

SEPTEMBER 26TH

The slaves of sin rarely grumble at that slavery; it is their slavery to God they grumble at; of that alone they complain—of the painful messengers he sends to deliver them from their slavery both to sin and to himself. They must be sons or slaves. They cannot rid themselves of their owner. Whether they deny God, or mock him by acknowledging and not heeding him, or treat him as an arbitrary, formal monarch; whether, taking no trouble to find out what pleases him, they do dull things for his service he cares nothing about, or try to propitiate him by assuming with strenuous effort some yoke the Son never wore, and never called on them to wear, they are slaves, and not the less slaves that they are slaves to God; they are so thoroughly slaves, that they do not care to get out of their slavery by becoming sons and daughters, by finding the good of life where alone it can or could lie. Could a creator make a creature whose well-being should not depend on himself? And if he could, would the creature be the greater for that? Which, the creature he made more, or the creature he made less dependent on himself, would be the greater? The slave in heart would immediately, with Milton's Satan, reply, that the farthest from him who made him must be the freest, thus acknowledging his very existence a slavery, and but two kinds of being—a creator, and as many slaves as he pleases to make, whose refusal to obey is their unknown protest against their own essence.

SEPTEMBER 27TH

To the slave at heart, God had no right to create beings less than himself; and as he could not create equal, he ought not to have created! But they do not complain of having been created; they complain of being required to do justice. They will not obey, but, his own handiwork, ravish from his work every advantage they can! They desire to be free with another kind of freedom than that with which God is free; unknowing, they seek a more complete slavery. There is, in truth, no midway between absolute harmony with the Father and the condition of slaves— submissive, or rebellious. If the latter, their very rebellion is by the strength of the Father in them. They do not see that, if his work, namely, they themselves, are the chief joy to themselves, much more might the life that works them be a glory and joy to them. For nothing can come so close as that which creates; the nearest, strongest, dearest relation possible is between creator and created. Where this is denied, the schism is the widest; where it is acknowledged and fulfilled, the closeness is unspeakable. The liberty of the God that would have his creature free is in contest with the slavery of the creature who would cut his own stem from his root that he might call it his own and love it; who rejoices in his own consciousness, instead of the life of that consciousness; who poises himself on the tottering wall of his own being, instead of the rock on which that being is built.

SEPTEMBER 28TH

The slavish man regards his own dominion over himself as a freedom infinitely greater than the range of the universe of God's being. If he says, "At least I have it my own way!" I answer, you do not know what is your way and what is not. You know nothing of whence your impulses, your desires come. They may spring now from some chance, as of nerves diseased; now from some infant hate in your heart; now from the greed or lawlessness of some ancestor you would be ashamed of if you know him; or it may be now from some far-piercing chord of a heavenly orchestra: the moment it comes up into your consciousness, you call it your own way, and glory in it! Two devils amusing themselves, one at each ear, might soon make that lordly *me* you are so in love with rejoice in the freedom of willing the opposite each alternate moment. The whole question rests on the relation of creative and created, of which few seem to have the consciousness yet developed. Freedom from God can only mean an incapacity for seeing the facts of existence, an incapability of understanding the glory of the creature who makes common cause with his creator in his creation of him, who wills that the lovely will calling him into life and giving him choice, should finish making him, should draw him into the circle of the creative heart, to joy that he lives by no poor power of his own, but is one with the causing life of his life. Such a creature knows the life of the infinite Father as the very flame of his life, and joys that nothing is done in the universe which the Father will not share with him as much as perfect generosity can make possible.

SEPTEMBER 29TH

One may call out, in the agony and thirst of a child waking from a dream of endless seeking and no finding, "I am bound like Lazarus in his grave-clothes! What am I to do?" Here is the answer, drawn from this parable of our Lord; for the saying is much like a parable, teaching more than it utters, appealing to the conscience and heart, not to the understanding: "You are a slave; the slave has no hold on the house; only the sons and daughters have an abiding rest in the home of their father. God cannot have slaves about him always. You must give up your slavery, and be set free from it. That is what I am here for. If I make you free, you shall be free indeed; for I can make you free only by making you what you were meant to be, sons like myself. But it is you who must become sons; you must will it, and I am here to help you." It is as if he said, "You shall have the freedom of my father's universe; for, free from yourselves, you will be free of his heart. Yourselves are your slavery. That is the darkness which you have loved rather than the light. You have given honor to yourselves, and not to the Father; you have sought honor from men, and not from the Father! Therefore, even in the house of your father, you have been but sojourning slaves. We in his family are all one; we have no party-spirit; we have no self-seeking: fall in with us, and you shall be free as we are free."

SEPTEMBER 30TH

If, told to give up his slavery, the poor starved child cry, "How Lord?" the answer will depend on what he means by that *how*. If he means, "What plan wilt thou adopt? What is thy scheme for cutting my bonds and setting me free?" the answer may be a deepening of the darkness, a tightening of the bonds. But if he means, "Lord, would wouldst thou have me do?" the answer will not tarry. "Give yourself to me to do what I tell you, to understand what I say, to be my good, obedient little brother, and I will wake in you the heart that my father put in you, the same kind of heart that I have, and it will grow to love the Father, altogether and absolutely, as mine does, till you are ready to be torn to pieces for him. Then you will know that you are at the heart of the universe, at the heart of every secret—at the heart of the Father. Not till then will you be free, then free indeed!"

Christ died to save us, not from suffering, but from ourselves; not from injustice, far less from justice, but from being unjust. He died that we might live—but live as he lives, by dying as he died who died to himself that he might live unto God. If we do not die to ourselves, we cannot live to God, and he that does not live to God, is dead.

OCTOBER 1ST

"Ye shall know the truth," the Lord says, "and the truth shall make you free. I am the truth, and you shall be free as I am free. To be free, you must be sons like me. To be free, you must *be* that which you have to be, that which you are created to be. To be free, you must give the answer of sons to the Father who calls you, fear nothing but evil, care for nothing but the will of the Father, hold to him in absolute confidence and infinite expectation. He alone is to be trusted." He has shown us the Father, not only by doing what the Father does, not only by loving his Father's children even as the Father loves them, but by his perfect satisfaction with him, his joy in him, his utter obedience to him. He has shown us the Father by the absolute devotion of a perfect son. He is the Son of God because the Father and he are one, have one thought, one mind, one heart. Upon this truth hangs the universe; and upon the recognition of this truth—that is, upon their becoming this true—hangs the freedom of the children, the redemption of their whole world. "I and the Father are one," is the center-truth of the Universe; and the circumfering truth is, "That they also may be one in us." The only free man, then, is he who is a child of the Father. He is a servant of all, but can be made the slave of none: he is a son of the lord of the universe. He is in himself, in virtue of his truth, free. His is in himself a king. For the Son rests his claim to royalty on this, that *he was born and came into the world to bear witness to the truth.*

KINGSHIP

"Art thou a king then? Jesus answered, Thou sayest that I am a king! To this end was I born, and for this cause came I into the world, that I should bear witness unto the truth: everyone that is of the truth hearest my voice."

John 18:37

OCTOBER 2ND

Pilate asks Jesus if he is a king. The question is called forth by what the Lord has just said concerning his kingdom, closing with the statement that it is not of this world. He now answers Pilate that he is a king indeed, but shows him that his kingdom is of a very different kind from what is called kingdom in this world. The rank and rule of this world are uninteresting to him. He might have had them. Calling his disciples to follow him, and his twelve legions of angels to help them, he might soon have driven the Romans into the abyss, piling them on the heap of nations they had tumbled there before. What easier for him than thus to have cleared the way, and over the tributary world reigned the just monarch that was the dream of the Jews, never seen in Israel or elsewhere, but haunting the hopes and longings of the poor and their helpers! He might from Jerusalem have ruled the world, not merely dispensing what men call justice, but compelling atonement. He did not care for government. No such kingdom would serve the ends of his father in heaven, or comfort his own soul. What was perfect empire to the Son of God, while he might teach one human being to love his neighbor, and be good like his father! To be lover-helper to one heart, for its joy, and the glory of his father, was the beginning of true kingship! The Lord would rather wash the feet of his weary brothers than be the one only perfect monarch that ever ruled in the world. It was empire he rejected when he ordered Satan behind him like a dog to his heel. Government, I repeat, was to him flat, stale, unprofitable.

OCTOBER 3RD

What then is the kingdom over which the Lord cares to reign, for he says he came into the world to be a king? I answer, a kingdom of kings, and no other. Where every man is a king, there only does the Lord care to reign, in the name of his father. A king must rule over his own kind. Jesus is a king in virtue of no conquest, inheritance, or election, but in right of essential being; and he cares for no subjects but such as are his subjects in the same right. His subjects must be, in their very nature and essence, kings. The Lord's is a kingdom in which no man seeks to be above another. He says, "I am a king, for I was born for the purpose, I came into the world with the object of bearing witness to the truth. Everyone that is of my kind, that is of the truth, hears my voice. He is a king like me, and makes one of my subjects." Pilate thereupon—as would most Christians nowadays, instead of setting about being true—requests a definition of truth, a presentation to his intellect; but instantly, whether confident of the uselessness of the inquiry, or intending to resume it when he has set the Lord at liberty, goes out to the people to tell them he finds no fault in him. Whatever interpretation we put on his action here, he must be far less worthy of blame than those "Christians" who, instead of setting themselves to be pure "even as he is pure," to be their brother and sister's keeper, and to serve God by being honorable in their place of work, proceed to "serve" him, some by going to church, some by condemning the opinions of their neighbors, some by teaching others what they do not themselves heed.

OCTOBER 4TH

Neither Pilate nor the superficial Christian asks the one true question, "How am I to be a true man? How am I to become a man worth being a man?" The Lord is a king because his life, the life of his thoughts, of his imagination, of his will, of every smallest action, is true—true first to God in that he is altogether his, true to himself in that he forgets himself altogether, and true to his fellows in that he will endure anything they do to him, nor cease declaring himself the son and messenger and likeness of God. They will kill him, but it matters not: the truth is as he says!

Jesus is a king because his business is to bear witness to the truth. What truth? All truth; all verity of relation throughout the universe—first of all, that his father is good, perfectly good; and that the crown and joy of life is to desire and do the will of the eternal source of will, and of all life. He deals thus the death-blow to the power of hell. For the one principle of hell is, "I am my own, my own king and my own subject. My own glory is my chief care; my ambition, to gather the regards of men to the one center, myself. The more self-sufficing I feel or imagine myself, the greater I am. I will be free with the freedom that consists in doing whatever I am inclined to do, from whatever quarter may come the inclination." To all these principles of hell, or of this world—they are the same thing—the Lord, the king, gives the direct lie.

OCTOBER 5TH

The Lord is saying, "I have been from all eternity the son of him from whom you issue, and whom you call your father, but whom you will not have your father: I know all he thinks and is; and I say this, that my perfect freedom, my pure individuality, rests on the fact that I have not another will than his. My will is all for his will, for his will is right. He is righteousness itself. His very being is love and self-devotion, and he will have his children such as himself—creatures of love, of fairness, of self-devotion to him and their fellows. I was born to bear witness to the truth—in my own person to be the truth visible—the very likeness and manifestation of the God who is true. Every fact of me witnesses him. He is the truth, and I am the truth. Kill me, but while I live I say, such as I am, he is. My Father is like me. You do not like to hear it because you are not like him. I am low in your eyes which measure things by their show; therefore you say I blaspheme. I should blaspheme if I said he was such as anything you are capable of imagining him, for you love show, and power, and the praise of men. I do not, and God is like me. I came into the world to show him. I am a king because he sent me to bear witness to his truth, and I bear it. Kill me, and I will rise again. Death is my servant; you are the slaves of Death because you will not be true, and let the truth make you free. Bound, and in your hands, I am free as God, for God is my father. I know I shall suffer, suffer unto death, but if you knew my father, you would not wonder that I am ready; you would be ready, too. He is my strength. My father is greater than I.

OCTOBER 6TH

I am daring to present a shadow of the Lord's witnessing, a shadow surely cast by his deeds and his very words! If I mistake, he will forgive me. I fear only lest I should fail of witnessing, and myself be, after all, no king, but a talker; no disciple of Jesus, ready to go with him to the death, but an arguer about the truth; a hater of the lies men speak for God, and myself a truth-speaking liar, not a doer of the word.

We see, then, that the Lord bore his witness to the Truth, to the one God, by standing just what he was, before the eyes and the lies of men. The true king is the man who stands up a true man and speaks the truth, and will die but not lie. The robes of such a king may be rags or purple; it matters neither way. The rags are the more likely, but neither better nor worse than the robes. Then was the Lord dressed most royally when his robes were a jest, a mockery. Of the men who before Christ bear witness to the truth, some were sawn asunder, some subdued kingdoms; it mattered nothing which: they witnessed. The truth is *God;* the witness to the truth is Jesus. The kingdom of the truth is the hearts of men. The bliss of men is the true God. The thought of God is the truth of everything. All well-being lies in true relation to God. The man who responds to this with his whole being is of the truth. The man who knows these things, and but knows them, the man who sees them to be true, and does not order life and action, judgment and love by them, is of the worst of lying; with hand, and foot, and face he casts scorn upon that which his tongue confesses.

OCTOBER 7TH

L ittle thought the sons of Zebedee and their ambitious mother what the earthly throne of Christ's glory was which they and she begged they might share. For the king crowned by his witnessing, witnessed then to the height of his uttermost argument, when he hung upon the cross—like a sin, as Paul in his boldness expresses it. When his witness is treated as a lie, then most he witnesses, for he gives it still. High and lifted up on the throne of his witness, on the cross of his torture, he holds to it: "I and the Father are one." Every mockery borne in witnessing is a witnessing afresh. Infinitely more than had he sat on the throne of the whole earth, did Jesus witness to the truth when Pilate brought him out for the last time, and perhaps made him sit on the judgment-seat in his mockery of kingly garments and royal insignia, saying, "Behold your king!" Just because of those robes and that crown, that scepter and that throne of ridicule, he was the only real king that ever sat on any throne.

OCTOBER 8TH

I s every Christian expected to bear witness? A man content to bear no witness to the truth is not in the kingdom of heaven. One who believes must bear witness. One who sees the truth, must live witnessing to it. Is our life, then, a witnessing to the truth? Do we carry ourselves in bank, on farm, in house or shop, in study or chamber or workshop, as the Lord would, or as the Lord would not? Are we careful to be true? Do we endeavor to live to the height of our ideas? Or are we mean, self-serving, world-flattering, fawning slaves? When contempt is cast on the truth, do we smile? Wronged in our presence, do we make no sign that we hold by it? I do not say we are called upon to dispute, and defend with logic and argument, but we are called upon to show that we are on the other side. But when I say *truth*, I do not mean *opinion*: to treat opinion as if that were truth, is grievously to wrong the truth. The soul that loves the truth and tries to be true will know when to speak and when to be silent; but the true man will never look as if he did not care. We are not bound to say all we think, but we are bound not even to look what we do not think. The girl who said before a company of mocking companions, "I believe in Jesus," bore true witness to her Master, the Truth. David bore witness to God, the Truth, when he said, "*Unto thee, O Lord, belongeth mercy, for thou renderest to every man according to his work.*"

JUSTICE

"Also unto thee, O Lord, belongeth mercy; for thou renderest to every man according to his work."

Psalm 62 v.12

OCTOBER 9TH

S ome translators have *loving kindness* rather than *mercy* in the quote above from Psalm 62; but I presume there is no real difference as to the character of the word. The religious mind educated upon the theories prevailing in the so-called religious world would here recognize a departure from the presentation to which they have been accustomed: for to fit their way of thinking, the verse would have to be changed thus: "To thee, O Lord, belongeth *justice,* for thou renderest to every man according to his work." Let the reason for my choosing this passage, so remarkable in itself, for a motto to the sermon which follows, remain for the present doubtful; but endeavor to see plainly what we mean when we use the word *justice,* especially the justice of God—for his justice gives existence to the idea of justice in our minds and hearts. Because he is just, we are capable of knowing justice and have the idea of justice so deeply imbedded in us.

What do we mean most often by *justice?* Is it not the carrying out of the law, the infliction of penalty assigned to offence? By a just judge we mean a man who administers the law without prejudice, and where guilt is manifest, punishes as much as, and no more than, the law has lain down. It may not be that justice has therefore been done. The law itself may be unjust, or the working of the law may be foiled by the parasites of law for their own gain,. *But even if the law is good, and thoroughly administered, it does not necessarily follow that justice is done.*

OCTOBER 10TH

S uppose my watch has been taken from my pocket; I lay hold of the thief, who is proved guilty and sentenced to a just imprisonment: have I had justice done me? The thief may have had justice done him—but where is my watch? I remain a man wronged. The thief, the man that did the wrong, is the only one who can set the wrong right. God may be able to move the man to right the wrong, but God himself cannot right it without the man. If my watch is found and returned to me, is the account settled between me and the thief? I may forgive him, but is the wrong removed? By no means. But suppose the thief to repent; suppose that it is out of his power to return the watch, but he comes to me and says he is sorry and begs me to accept what little he is able to give as a beginning of atonement. Should I not feel that he had done more to make up for the injury inflicted than the mere restoration of the watch, even by himself, could accomplish? Would there not lie, in his confession, submission, and initial restoration, an appeal to the divinest in me, a sufficing atonement as between man and man? Should I feel it necessary, for the sake of justice, to inflict some certain suffering as demanded by righteousness? The punishing of the wrong-doer makes no atonement for the wrong done. How could it make up to me for the stealing of my watch that the man was punished? The wrong would be there all the same. I am not saying the man ought not to be punished—far from it; only that the punishment nowise makes up to the man wronged. Punishment may do good to the man who does the wrong, but that is a thing as different as it is important.

OCTOBER 11TH

Even without the material rectification of a wrong when that is impossible, repentance removes the offence which no suffering could. I should even feel that the gift the thief had made me, giving into my heart a repentant brother, was infinitely beyond the restitution of what he had taken from me. If it be objected, "You may forgive, but the man has sinned against God," I answer, then it is not a part of the divine to be merciful, and a man may be more mercifiul than his maker! "Mercy may be against justice." Never—if you mean by justice what I mean. If anything be against justice, it cannot be called mercy, for it is cruelty. "To thee, O Lord, belongeth mercy, for thou renderest every man according to his work." There is *no* opposition, *no* strife whatever, between mercy and justice. Those who say justice means the punishment of sin, and mercy the not punishing of sin, and attribute both to God, would make a schism in the very idea of God. Which brings me to the question, what is meant by divine justice?

Human justice may be a poor distortion, a mere shadow of justice; but the justice of God must be perfect. If you ask the average congregation what is meant by it, would not 19 out of 20 answer that it means his punishing of sin? Yet a Roman emperor might punish every wrong and be the most unjust of men. God is one; and the depth of foolishness is reached by that theology which represents God as having to do that as a magistrate which as a father he would not do! The love of the father makes him desire to be unjust as judge!

OCTOBER 12TH

God is no magistrate, but if he were, it would be a position to which his fatherhood alone gave him the right. The justice of God is this, that he gives every man, woman, child, and beast, everything that has being, fair play; he renders to every man according to his work; and therein lies his perfect mercy; for nothing else could be merciful to the man, and nothing but mercy could be fair to him. Who would say a man was a just man because he insisted on prosecuting every offender? A scoundrel might do that. Punishment of the guilty may be involved in justice, but it does not constitute the justice of God one atom more than it would constitute the justice of a man.

And yet many claim that God does this or that which is not fair. But to say on the authority of the Bible that God does a thing no honorable man would do, is to lie against God. To uphold a lie for God's sake is to be against God, not for him. God is the truth, and truth alone is on his side. While his child could not see the rightness of a thing, he would infinitely rather, even if the thing were right, have him say, God could not do that thing, than have him believe that he did it. If the man were sure God did it, the thing he ought to say would be, "Then there must be something about it I do not know which if I did know, I should see the thing quite differently."

OCTOBER 13TH

Where an evil thing is invented to explain and account for a good thing, and a lover of God is called upon to believe the invention or be cast out, he need not mind being cast out, for it is into the company of Jesus. Where there is no ground to believe that God does a thing except that men who would explain God have believed and taught it, he is not a true man who accepts men against his own conscience of God. I acknowledge no authority calling upon me to believe a thing of God which I could not believe right in my fellow man. If you say, that may be right of God to do which it would not be right of man to do, I answer, yes, because the relation of the maker to his creatures is very different from the relation of those creatures to each other, and he has therefore duties toward his creatures requiring of him what no man would have the right to do to his fellow man; but he can have no duty that is not both just and merciful. More is required of the maker, by his own act of creation, than can be required of men. More and higher justice and righteousness is required of him by himself; greater nobleness, more penetrating sympathy, and *nothing* but what, if an honest man understood it, he would say was right. If it be a thing man cannot understand, then man can say nothing as to whether it is right or wrong. He cannot even know that God does *it*, when the *it* is unintelligble to him. What he calls *it* may be but the smallest facet of a composite action. His part is silence.

OCTOBER 14TH

If it be said by any that God does a thing which seems to me unjust, then either I do not know what the thing is, or God does not do it. If, for instance, it be said that God visits the sins of the fathers on the children, a man who takes *visits upon* to mean *punishes,* and *the children* to mean *the innocent children,* ought to say, "Either I do not understand the statement, or the thing is not true, whoever says it." God may do what seems to a man not right, but it must so seem to him because God works on higher, divine, perfect principles too right for a selfish, unfair, or unloving man to understand. But least of all must we accept some low notion of justice in a man, and argue that God is just in doing after that notion.

The common idea, then, is that the justice of God consists in punishing sin: it is in the hope of giving a larger idea of the justice of God in punishing sin that I ask, *"Why is God bound to punish sin?"* If a man say, "How could a just God not punish sin?" I answer that mercy is a good and right thing, and but for sin there could be no mercy. We are told to forgive, to be as our father in heaven. Two rights cannot possibly be opposed to each other. If God punish sin, it must be merciful to punish sin; and if God forgive sin, it must be just to forgive sin. He cannot be sometimes merciful, and not always merciful. He cannot be just, and not always just. Mercy belongs to him, and needs no contrivance of theological trickery to justify it.

OCTOBER 15TH

God does punish sin, but there is no opposition between punishment and forgiveness. The one may be essential to the possibility of the other. *Why* does God punish sin? Because sin itself deserves punishment? Then how can he tell us to forgive it? Here, then, is the fault with the whole idea: punishment is *nowise* an *offset* to sin. Foolish people sometimes, in a tone of self-congratulatory pity, will say, "If if I have sinned, I have suffered." Yes, verily, but what of that? What merit is there in it? Even had you laid the suffering upon yourself, what did that do to make up for the wrong? That you may have bettered by your suffering is well for you, but what atonement is there in the suffering? The notion is a false one altogether. Punishment, deserved suffering, is not an equal offset for sin; there is no use laying it on the other scale, it will not move it a hair's breadth. Suffering weighs nothing at all against sin. It is not of the same kind, not under the same laws, any more than mind and matter. We may say a man deserves punishment; but when we forgive and do not punish him, we do not always feel that we have done wrong; neither when we do punish him do we feel that any amends have been made for his wrongdoing. If it were an offset to wrong, then God would be bound to punish; but he cannot be, for he forgives. Punishment is not directly for justice, else mercy would involve injustice. Then it is not for the sake of the punishment, as a thing that in itself ought to be done, but as a *means to an end*, that God punishes.

OCTOBER 16TH

God is not bound to *punish* sin; he is bound to *destroy* it. If he were not the Maker, he might not be bound to destroy sin; but seeing he has created creatures who have sinned, and therefore sin has, by the creating act of God, come into the world, God is, in his own righteousness, bound to destroy sin. And God is always destroying sin. He is always saving the sinner from his sins, and that is destroying sin. But vengeance on the sinner, the law of a tooth for a tooth, is not in the heart of God. If the sinner and the sin in him are the concrete object of the divine wrath, then there can be no mercy; indeed, there will be an end put to sin by the destruction of the sin and the sinner together. But thus would no atonement be wrought—nothing be done to make up for the wrong God has allowed to come into being by creating man. There must be an atonement, a making-up, which cannot be made except by the man who has sinned. What better is the world, what better is the sinner, that the sinner should suffer—continue suffering to all eternity? Would there be less sin in the universe? What setting-right would come of the sinner's suffering? To suffer to all eternity could not make up for one unjust word. That word is an eternally evil thing; nothing but God in my heart can cleanse me from the evil that uttered it. Sorrow and confession and self-abasing love will make up for the evil word; suffering will not. I may be saved from evil by learning to loathe it, to shrink from it with an eternal avoidance. The only vengeance worth having on sin is to make the sinner himself its executioner.

OCTOBER 17TH

S in and punishment are in no antagonism to each other in man, any more than pardon and punishment are in God; they can perfectly co-exist. The one naturally follows the other. Sin and suffering are not opposites; the opposite of evil is good, not suffering; the opposite of sin is not suffering, but righteouness. The path across the gulf that divides right from wrong is not the fire, but repentance. If my friend has wronged me, will it console me to see him punished? Will his agony be a balm to my deep wound? But would not the shadow of repentant grief, the light of reviving love on his countenance, heal it at once, however deep? Take any of those wicked people in Dante's hell, and ask wherein is justice served by their punishment. Mind, I am not saying it is not right to punish them; I am saying that justice is not, never can be, satisfied by suffering. Human resentment, human revenge, human hate may be so satisfied. Such justice as Dante's keeps wickedness alive in its most terrible forms. Is God not defeated every time that one of those lost souls defies him? God is triumphantly defeated throughout the hell of his vengeance. The notion that a creature born with impulses to evil not of his own generating, and which he could not help having, a creature to whom the true face of God was never presented, should be thus condemned, is a loathsome lie against God. It never in truth found place in any heart, though in many a pettifogging brain. There is but one thing lower than deliberately to believe such a lie, and that is to worship the God of whom it is believed.

OCTOBER 18TH

The one deepest, highest, truest, most wholesome suffering must be generated in the wicked by a vision of the hideousness of their lives, of the horror of the wrongs they have done. Physical suffering may be a factor in rousing this mental pain; but "I would I had never been born!" must be the cry of Judas, not because of the hell-fire around him, but because he loathes the man that betrayed his friend, the world's friend. When a man loathes himself, he has begun to be saved. Punishment tends to this result. Not for its own sake, not as a make-up for sin, not for divine revenge—horrible word—not for any satisfaction to justice, can punishment exist. It is for the sake of amendment and atonement. God is bound by his love to punish sin in order to deliver his creature; he is bound by his justice to destroy sin in his creation. Love is justice—the fulfilling of the law, for God as well as for his children. This is the reason for punishment; this is why justice requires that the wicked shall not go unpunished—that they, through the eye-opening power of pain, may come to see and do justice, may be brought to desire and make all possible amends, and so become just. Such punishment concerns justice in the deepest degree. For Justice, that is God, is bound in himself to see justice done by his children—not in the mere outward act, but in their very being. He is bound in himself to make up for wrong done by his children, and he can do nothing to make up for wrong done but by bringing about the repentance of the wrong-doer.

OCTOBER 19TH

When the man says, "I did wrong; I hate myself and my deed; I cannot endure to think that I did it!" then is atonement begun. Without that, all that the Lord did would be lost. He would have made no atonement. Repentance, restitution, confession, prayer, forgiveness, righteous dealing thereafter, is the sole possible, the only true make-up for sin. For nothing less than this did Christ die. When a man acknowledges the right he denied before; when he says to the wrong, "I abjure, I loathe you; I see now what you are; I could not see it before because I would not; God forgive me; make me clean, or let me die!" then justice, that is God, has conquered—and not till then. The work of Jesus Christ on earth was the creative atonement, because it works atonement in every heart. He brings and is bringing God and man, and man and man, into perfect unity: "I in them and thou in me, that they may be made perfect in one."

Some may think this a dangerous doctrine—and indeed, it is more dangerous than they think to many things—to every evil, to every lie, to every false trust in what Christ did, instead of in Christ himself. Paul glories in the cross of Christ, but he does not trust in the cross; he trusts in the living Christ and his living father.

OCTOBER 20TH

J ustice then requires that sin should be put an end to; and not that only, but that it should be atoned for; and where punishment can do anything to this end, where it can help the sinner to know what he has been guilty of, where it can soften his heart to see his pride and wrong and cruelty, justice requires that punishment shall not be spared. The more we believe in God, the surer we shall be that he will spare nothing that suffering can do to deliver his child from death. If suffering cannot serve this end, we need look for no more hell, but for the destruction of sin by the destruction of the sinner. That, however, would be for God to suffer defeat, blameless indeed, but defeat.

If God be defeated, he must destroy—that is, he must withdraw life. How can he go on sending forth his life into irreclaimable souls, to keep sin alive in them throughout the ages of eternity? But then, no atonement would be made for the wrongs they have done; God remains defeated, for he has created that which sinned, and which would not repent and make up for its sin. But those who believe that God will thus be defeated by many souls, must surely be of those who do not believe he cares enough to do his very best for them. He *is* their Father; he had power to make them out of himself, separate from himself, and capable of being one with him: surely he will somehow save and keep them! Not the power of sin itself can close *all* the channels between creating and created.

OCTOBER 21ST

The notion of suffering as an offset for sin, the foolish idea that a man by suffering borne may get out from under the hostile claim to which his wrong-doing has subjected him, comes first of all from the satisfaction we feel when wrong comes to grief. Why do we feel this satisfaction? Because we hate wrong, but, not being righteous ourselves, more or less hate the sinner as well as his wrong, hence are not only righteously pleased to behold the law's disapproval proclaimed in his punishment, but unrighteously pleased with his suffering, because of the impact upon us of his wrong. In this way, the inborn justice of our nature passes over to evil. It is no pleasure to God, as it so often is to us, to see the wicked suffer. To regard any suffering with satisfaction, save it be sympathetically with its curative quality, comes of evil, is inhuman because undivine, is a thing God is incapable of. His nature is always to forgive, and just because he forgives, he punishes. Because God is so altogether alien to wrong, because it is to him a heart-pain and trouble that one of his little ones should do the evil thing, there is no extreme of suffering to which, for the sake of destroying the evil thing in them, he would not subject them. A man might flatter, or bribe, or coax a tyrant; but there is no refuge from the love of God; that love will, for very love, insist upon the uttermost farthing.

OCTOBER 22ND

M any there are who do not care for a love that will insist upon the uttermost farthing. They cannot care for it until they begin to know it. But the eternal love will not be moved to yield a man to the selfishness that is killing him. What lover would yield his lady to her passion for morphia? Some may sneer at such love, but the Son of God who took the weight of that love, and bore it through the world, is content with it, and so is everyone who knows it. The love of the Father is a radiant perfection. Love and not self-love is lord of the universe. Justice demands your punishment, because justice demands, and will have, the destruction of sin. It demands that your father should do his best for you. God, being the God of justice, that is, of fair play, and having made us what we are, apt to fall and capable of being raised again, is in himself bound to punish in order to deliver us—else is his relation to us poor beside that of an earthly father. "To thee, O Lord, belongeth mercy, for thou renderest to every man according to his work." A man's work is his character; and God in his mercy is not indifferent, but treats him according to his work.

OCTOBER 23RD

The notion that the salvation of Jesus is a salvation from the consequences of our sins is a false, mean, low notion. The salvation of Christ is salvation from the smallest tendency or leaning to sin. It is a deliverance into the pure air of God's ways of thinking and feeling. It is a salvation that makes the heart pure, with the will and choice of the heart to be pure. To such a heart, sin is disgusting. It sees a thing as it is—that is, as God sees it, for God sees everything as it is. The soul thus saved would rather sink into the flames of hell than steal into heaven and skulk there under the shadow of an imputed righteouness. No soul is saved that would not prefer hell to sin. Jesus did not die to save us from punishment; he was called Jesus because he should save his people from their sins.

I have no desire to change the opinion of man or woman; but I would do my utmost to disable such as think correct opinion essential to salvation from laying any other burden on the shoulders of true men and women than the yoke of their Master; and such burden, if already oppressing any, I would gladly lift. They press their theories upon others, insisting on their thinking about Christ as they think, instead of urging them to go to Christ to be taught by him whatever he chooses to teach them. From such and their false teaching I would gladly help to deliver the true-hearted. Let the dead bury their dead, but I would do what I may to keep them from burying the living.

OCTOBER 24TH

I f there be no satisfaction to justice in the mere punishment of the wrong-doer, what shall we say of the notion of satisfying justice by causing one to suffer who is not the wrong-doer? And what, moreover, shall we say to the notion that, just because he is not the person who deserves to be punished, but is absolutely innocent, his suffering gives perfect satisfaction to the perfect justice? That the injustice be done with the consent of the person maltreated makes no difference: it makes it even worse, seeing, as they say, that justice requires the punishment of the *sinner*, and here is one far more than innocent. They have shifted their ground; it is no more punishment, but mere suffering the law requires! The thing gets worse and worse. Rather than believe in a justice—that is, a God—to whose righteousness, abstract or concrete, it could be any satisfaction for the wrong-doing of a man that a man who did no wrong should suffer, I would be driven from among men, and dwell with the wild beasts that have not reason enough to be unreasonable. What! God, the father of Jesus Christ, like that! The anger of him who will nowise clear the guilty, appeased by the suffering of the innocent! How did it ever come to be imagined? It sprang from the trustless dread that cannot believe in the forgiveness of the Father; cannot believe that even God will do anything for nothing; cannot trust him without a legal arrangement to bind him. It sprang from the pride that will understand what it cannot, before it will obey what it sees. He that insists on understanding *first* will believe a lie—a lie from which obedience alone will at length deliver him.

OCTOBER 25TH

To those who say that they believe in this false doctrine of substitution, I respond: To believe in it is your punishment for being able to believe it; you may call it your reward, if you will. You ought not to be able to believe it. It is the merest, poorest, most shameless fiction, invented without the perception that it was an invention—fit to satisfy the intellect, doubtless, of the inventor, else he could not have invented it. It has seemed to satisfy also many a humble soul, content to take what was given, and not think; content that another should think for him, and tell him what was the mind of his Father in heaven. Let the person who can be so satisfied, be so satisfied; I have not to trouble myself with him. That he can be content with it, argues him unready to receive better. So long as he can believe false things concerning God, he is such as is capable of believing them—with how much or how little of blame, God knows. Opinion, right or wrong, will do nothing to save him. I would that he thought no more about this or any other opinion, but set himself to do the work of the Master. With his opinions, true or false, I have nothing to do. It is because such as he force evil things upon their fellows—utter or imply them from the seat of authority or influence—to their agony, their paralyses, their unbelief, their indignation, their stumbling, that I have any right to speak. I would save my fellows from having what notion of God is possible to them blotted out by a lie.

OCTOBER 26TH

I f it is false, how can the doctrine of substitution have been permitted to remain so long an article of faith to so many? On the same principle on which God took up and made use of the sacrifices men had, in their lack of faith, invented as a way of pleasing him. Some children will tell lies to please the parents that hate lying. They will even confess to having done a wrong they have not done, thinking their parents would like them to say they had done it, because they teach them to confess. God accepted men's sacrifices until he could get them to see—and with how many of them has he not yet succeeded, in the church and out of it!—that he does not care for such things. The potency of that teaching comes from its having in it a notion of God and his Christ, poor indeed and faint, but, by the very poverty and untruth in its presentation, fitted to the weakness and unbelief of men, seeing it was by men invented to meet and ease the demand made upon their own weakness and unbelief. The truth is there; it is Christ, the glory of God. But the ideas that poor souls breed concerning this glory the moment the darkness begins to disperse, is quite another thing. Truth is indeed too good for men to believe; unable to believe in the forgivingness of their father in heaven, they invented a way to be forgiven that should not demand of him so much; which might make it right for him to forgive; which should save them from having to believe downright in the tenderness of his father-heart, for that they found impossible.

OCTOBER 27TH

The weakness and unbelief of men has led them to think of God as bound to punish for the sake of punishing, as an offset to their sin; they could not believe in clear forgiveness; that did not seem divine; it needed itself to be justified; so they invented for its justification a horrible injustice, involving all that was bad in sacrifice, even human sacrifice. They invented a satisfaction for sin which was an insult to God. He sought no satisfaction, but an obedient return to the Father. What satisfaction was needed he made himself in what he did to cause them to turn from evil and go back to him. The thing was too simple for complicated unbelief and the arguing spirit. Gladly would I help their followers to loathe such thoughts of God; but for that, they themselves must grow better men and women. When the heart recoils, discovering how horrible it would be to have such an unreality for God, it will begin to search about and see whether it must indeed accept such statements concerning God; it will search after a real God by whom to hold fast, a real God to deliver them from the terrible idol. It is for those thus moved that I write, not at all for the sake of disputing with those who love the lie they may not be to blame for holding; who, like the Pharisees, would cast out of their synagogue the man who doubts their travesty of the grandest truth in the universe, the atonement of Jesus Christ. Of such a man they will unhesitatingly report that he does not believe in the atonement. But a lie for God is against God, and carries the sentence of death in itself.

OCTOBER 28TH

Instead of giving their energy to do the will of God, men of power have given it to the construction of a system to explain why Christ must die, and the necessities and designs of God in permitting his death; and they have clung to the morally and spiritually vulgar idea of justice and satisfaction held by pagan Rome, buttressed by the Jewish notion of sacrifice. Their system is briefly this: God is bound to punish sin to the uttermost. But Christ takes man's punishment upon himself, and God lets man go unpunished, upon a condition: he must say, "I have sinned, and deserve to be tortured to all eternity. But Christ has paid my debts by being punished instead of me. Therefore he is my Savior. I am now bound by gratitude to him to turn away from evil."

Yet it would be the worst of all wrongs to the guilty to treat them as innocent. To the poorest idea of justice in punishment, it is essential that the sinner should receive the punishment. God is absolutely just, and there is no deliverance from his justice, which is one with his mercy. To believe in a vicarious sacrifice is to think to take refuge with the Son from the righteousness of the Father; with his work instead of with the Son himself; to shelter behind a false quirk of law instead of nestling in the eternal heart of the Father, who is merciful in that he renders to every man according to his work, and compels their obedience. God will never let a man off with any fault. He must have him clean. He will impute to him nothing that he has not, will lose sight of no smallest good that he has. He is God beyond all that heart hungriest for love and righteousness could to eternity desire.

OCTOBER 29TH

Some of the best of men have held the theories I stigmatize, men I have loved and honored, some heartily and humbly— but because of what they *were,* not because of what they *thought;* and they were what they were in virtue of their obedient faith, not of their opinion. They were not better men because of holding these theories. In virtue of knowing God by obeying his son, they rose above the theories they had never looked in the face, and so had never recognized as evil. Many have arrived, in the natural progress of their sacred growth, at the point where they must abandon them. The man of whom I knew the most good gave them up gladly. Good to worshipfulness may be the man that holds them, and I hate them the more therefore; they are lies that, working under cover of the truth mingled with them, burrow as near the heart of the good man as they can go. Whoever, from whatever reason of blindness, may be the holder of a lie, the thing is a lie, and no falsehood must mingle with the justice we mete out to it. There is nothing for any lie but the pit of hell. Yet until the man sees the thing to be a lie, how shall he but hold it! Are there not mingled with it shadows of the noblest truth in the universe? So long as a man is able to love a lie, he is incapable of seeing it is a lie. He who is true, out and out, will know at once an untruth; and to that vision we must all come.

OCTOBER 30TH

I write for those for whom such teaching as the doctrine of substitution has folded in a cloud through which they cannot see the stars of heaven, so that some of them even doubt if there be any stars of heaven. For the holy ones who believed and taught these things in days gone by, all is well. Many of the holiest of them cast the lies from them long ere the present teachers of them were born. Many who would never have invented such lies for themselves, yet receiving them with the seals affixed of so many good men, took them in their humility as recognized truths, instead of inventions of men; and, oppressed by the authority of men far inferior to themselves, did not dare dispute them, but proceeded to order their lives by what truths they found in their company, and so had their reward, the reward of obedience, in being by that obedience brought to know God, which knowledge broke for them the net of a presumptuous self-styled orthodoxy. Every man who tries to obey the Master is my brother, whether he counts me such or not, and I revere him; but dare I give quarter to what I see to be a lie, because my brother believes it? The lie is not of God, whoever may hold it.

"Well, then," many will say, "If you thus cast to the winds the doctrine of vicarious sacrifice, what theory do you propose to substitute in its place?" In the name of truth: *None.* I will send out no theory of mine to rouse fresh little whirlwinds of dialogistic dust, mixed with dirt and straws and holy words, hiding the Master in talk about him.

OCTOBER 31ST

"Will you then take from me my faith," a man might ask, "and help me to no other?" His faith! God forbid. His theory is not his faith, nor anything like it. His faith is his obedience; his theory I know not what. Yes, I will gladly leave him without any of what he calls faith. Trust in God. Obey the word—every word of the Master. That is faith; and so believing, your opinion will grow out of your true life, and be worthy of it. Peter says the Lord gives the spirit to them that obey him: the spirit of the Master, and that alone, can guide you to any theory that will be of use to you to hold. A theory arrived at any other way is not worth the time spent on it. Jesus is the creating and saving lord of our intellects as well as of our more precious hearts; nothing that he does not think, is worth thinking; no man can think as he thinks, except he be pure like him; no man can be pure like him, except he go with him and learn from him. To put off obeying him till we find a credible theory concerning him, is to set aside the potion we know it our duty to drink, for the study of the various schools of therapy. You know what Christ requires of you is right: *do it.* If you do not do what you know of the truth, I do not wonder that you seek it intellectually, for that kind of search may well be, as Milton represents it, a solace even to the fallen angels. How can you, not caring to be true, judge concerning him whose life was to do for very love the things you confess your duty, yet do them not? Obey the truth, and let theory wait. Theory may spring from life, but never life from theory.

NOVEMBER 1ST

I will tell you what I believe: I believe in Jesus Christ, the eternal Son of God, my elder brother, my lord and master; I believe that he has a right to my absolute obedience whereinsover I know or shall come to know his will; that to obey him is to ascend the pinnacle of my being; that not to obey him would be to deny him. I believe that he died that I might die like him—die to any ruling power in me but the will of God—live ready to be nailed to the cross as he was, if God will it. I believe that he is my Savior from myself, and from all that has come of loving myself, from all that God does not love, and would not have me love—all that is not worth loving; that he died that the justice, the mercy of God, might have its way with me, making me just as God is just, merciful as he is merciful, perfect as my father in heaven is perfect. I believe and pray that he will give me what punishment I need to set me right, or keep me from going wrong. I believe that he died to deliver me from all meanness, pretense, falseness, unfairness, cowardice, fear, anxiety, self-love, all trust or hope in possession; to make me merry as a child, the child of our father in heaven, loving nothing but what is lovely, desiring nothing I should be ashamed to let the universe of God see me desire. I believe that God is just like Jesus, only greater yet, for Jesus said so; that he is absolutely, grandly beautiful, with the beauty that creates beauty, not merely shows it; that he has always done, is always doing his best for every man; that he is not a God to crouch before, but our father, to whom the child-heart cries exultant, "Do with me as thou wilt."

NOVEMBER 2ND

I believe that there is nothing good for me or for any man but God, and more and more of God, and that alone through knowing Christ can we come nigh to him. I believe that no man is ever condemned for any sin except one—that he will not leave his sins and come out of them, and be the child of him who is his father. That justice and mercy are simply one and the same thing; without justice to the full there can be no mercy, and without mercy to the full there can be no justice; that such is the mercy of God that he will hold his children in the consuming fire of his distance until they pay the uttermost farthing, until they drop the purse of selfishness with all the dross that is in it, and rush home to the Father and the Son, and the many brethren—rush inside the center of the life-giving fire whose outer circles burn. I believe that no hell will be lacking which would help the just mercy of God to redeem his children.

To him who obeys, and thus opens the doors of his heart, God gives the spirit of his son, the spirit of himself, to be in him, and lead him to the understanding of all truth; the true disciple shall thus always know what he ought to do, though not necessarily what another ought to do. The spirit enlightens by teaching righteousness. No teacher should strive to make men think as he thinks, but to lead them to the living Truth, the Master himself, who will make them in themselves know what is true by the very seeing of it. To be the disciple of Christ is the end of being; to persuade men to be his disciples is the end of teaching.

NOVEMBER 3RD

I believe in Jesus Christ. Nowhere am I requested to believe in any *thing*, or in any *statement*, but everywhere to believe in God and in Jesus Christ. I do not believe in what many mean by *the atonement*, for it would be to believe a lie, and a lie which is to blame for much non-acceptance of the gospel. But, as the word was used by the very best English writers at the time when the translation of the Bible was made—with all my heart, and soul, and strength, and mind, I believe in the atonement, call it the a-tone-ment, or the at-one-ment, as you please. I believe that Jesus Christ *is* our atonement; that through him we are reconciled to, made one with God. There is not one word in the New Testament about reconciling God to us; it is we that have to be reconciled to God. I am not writing a treatise on the atonement, my business being to persuade men to be atoned to God; but I will go so far to meet the commonly held view as to say that, even in the sense of the atonement being a making-up for the evil done by men toward God, I believe in the atonement. Did not the Lord cast himself into the eternal gulf of evil yawning between the children and the Father? Did he not bring the Father to us, let us look on our eternal Sire in the face of his true son, that we might have that in our hearts which alone could make us love him—a true sight of him? Did he not insist on the one truth of the universe, that God was just what he, Jesus, was? Did he not thus lay down his life persuading us to lay down ours at the feet of the Father? Has not his very life by which he died passed into those who have received him?

NOVEMBER 4TH

D id Jesus Christ not foil and slay evil by letting all the waves and billows of its horrid sea break upon him, spend their rage, fall defeated, and cease? Verily, he made atonement! God sacrificed his own son to us; there was no way else of getting the gift of himself into our hearts. Jesus sacrificed himself to his father and the children to bring them together—all the love on the side of the Father and the Son, all the selfishness on the side of the children. If the joy that alone makes life worth living, the joy that God is such as Christ, be a true thing in my heart, how can I but believe in the atonement of Jesus Christ? I believe it heartily, as God means it. And I believe in it as the power that brings about a making-up for any wrong done by man to man. Who that believes in Jesus does not long to atone to his brother for the injury he has done him? Who is the causer, the creator of the repentance, of the passion that restores fourfold? Jesus, our propitiation, our atonement. He could not do it without us, but he leads us up to the Father's knee: he makes us make atonement. Learning Christ, we are not only sorry for what we have done wrong, we not only turn from it and hate it, we are able to offer our whole being to God to whom by deepest right it belongs. Have I failed in love to my neighbor? Shall I not now love him with an infinitely better love than was possible to me before? That I can and will make atonement, thanks be to him who is my atonement, my life, my joy, my lord, my owner, the perfecter of my being. I dare not say with Paul that I am the slave of Christ; but my highest aspiration is to be the slave of Christ.

NOVEMBER 5TH

It may be asked of me, "Do I believe that the sufferings of Christ, as sufferings, justified the supreme ruler in doing anything which he would not have been at liberty to do but for those sufferings?" I do not. I believe the notion as unworthy of man's belief as it is dishonoring to God. It has its origin doubtless in a salutary sense of sin; but sense of sin is not inspiration, though it may lie not far from the temple door. It is indeed an opener of the eyes, but upon home-defilement, not upon heavenly truth; it is not the revealer of secrets. Also, there is another factor in the theory, and that is unbelief—incapacity to believe that it is God's chosen nature to forgive, that he is bound in his own divinely willed nature to forgive. No atonement is necessary to him but that men should leave their sins and come back to his heart. But men cannot believe in the forgiveness of God. Therefore they need, therefore he has given them a mediator. And yet they will not know him. They think of the father of souls as if he had abdicated his fatherhood for their sins, and assumed the judge. If he put off his fatherhood, which he cannot do, for it is an eternal fact, he puts off with it all relation to us. He cannot repudiate the essential and keep the resultant. Men cannot, or will not, or dare not see that nothing but his being our father gives him any right over us.

NOVEMBER 6TH

Too many regard the father of their spirits as their governor! They yield the idea of the Ancient of Days, "the glad creator," and put in its stead a miserable, puritanical martinet of a God, caring not for righteousness, but for his rights; not for the eternal purities, but the goody proprieties. The prophets of such a God take all the glow, all the hope, all the color, all the worth, out of life on earth, and offer you instead what they call eternal bliss—a pale, tearless hell. Of all things, turn from a mean, poverty-stricken faith. But, if you are straitened in your own mammon-worshipping soul, how shall you believe in a God any greater than can stand up in that prison chamber?

I desire to wake no dispute, will myself dispute with no man, but for the sake of those whom certain *believers* trouble, I have spoken my mind. I love the one God seen in the face of Jesus Christ. From all copies of Jonathan Edwards' portrait of God, however faded by time, however softened by the use of less glaring pigments, I turn with loathing. Not such a God is he concerning whom was the message John heard from Jesus, *that he is light, and in him is no darkness at all.*

LIGHT

"This then is the message which we have heard of him, and declare unto you, that God is light, and in him is no darkness at all."

1 John 1:5.

"And this is the condemnation, that light is come into the world, and men loved darkness rather than light, because their deeds were evil."

John 3:19.

NOVEMBER 7TH

We call the story of Jesus, told so differently, yet to my mind so consistently, by four narrators, *the gospel*. What makes this tale *the good news?* Is it good news that the one only good man was served by his fellow-men as Jesus was served—cast out of the world in torture and shame? What makes it fit to call the tale *good news?* If we asked a theologian, we should, in so far as he was a true man, and answered from his own heart and not merely from tradition, understand what he saw in it that made it good news to him, though it might be anything but good news to some of us. The deliverance it might seem to bring might be founded on such notions of God as to not a few of us contain as little of good as of news. To share in the deliverance which some men find in what they call the gospel—for all do not apply the word to the tale itself, but to certain deductions made from the epistles and their own consciousness of evil—we should have to believe such things of God as would be the opposite of an evangel to us—yea, a message from hell itself; we should have to imagine that whose possibility would be worse than any ill from which their "good news" might offer us deliverance: we must first believe in an unjust God, from whom we have to seek refuge. True, they call him just, but say he does that which seems to the best in me the essence of injustice. They will tell me I judge after the flesh: I answer, is it then to the flesh the Lord appeals when he says, "Why even of yourselves judge ye not what is right?"

NOVEMBER 8TH

Who would not rejoice to hear from Matthew, or Mark, or Luke, what, in a few words, he meant by the word *gospel*—or rather, what in the story of Jesus made him call it *good news!* Each would probably give a different answer to the question, all the answers consistent, and each a germ from which the others might be reasoned; but in the case of John, we have his answer to the question: he gives us in one sentence the gospel according to Jesus Christ himself. What in all of what he wrote did John look upon as the essence of the goodness of its news? In his gospel he gives us all *about* him, the message *concerning* him; now he tells us what in it makes it to himself and to us good news—tells the very goodness of the good news. It is not now his own message about Jesus, but the soul of that message—that which makes it gospel—the news Jesus brought concerning the Father, and gave to the disciples as his message for them to deliver to me. Throughout the story, Jesus, in all he does, and is, and says, is telling the news concerning his father, which he was sent to give to John and his companions, that they might hand it on to their brothers; but here, in so many words, John tells us what he himself has heard from The Word—what in sum he has gathered from Jesus as the message he has to declare. He has received it in no systematic form; it is what a life, *the* life, what a man, *the* man, has taught him. The Word is the Lord; the Lord is the gospel.

NOVEMBER 9TH

very man must read the Word for himself. One may read it in one shape, another in another: all will be right if it be indeed the Word they read, and they read it by the lamp of obedience. He who is willing to do the will of the Father shall know the truth of the teaching of Jesus. The spirit is "given to them that obey him." But let us hear how John read the Word—hear what is John's version of the gospel: *"This then is the message, which we have heard of him, and declare unto you, that God is light, and him him is no darkness at all."* Ah, my heart, this is indeed good news for thee! This is a gospel! If God be light, what more, what else can I seek than God, than God himself! Away with your doctrines! Away with your salvation from the "justice" of a God whom it is a horror to imagine! I am saved—for God is light! My God, I come to thee. That thou shouldst be thyself is enough for time and eternity, for my soul and all its endless need. Whatever seems to me darkness, that I will not believe of my God. If I should mistake, and call that darkness which is light, will he not reveal the matter to me, setting it in the light that lightest every man, showing me that I saw but the husk of the thing, not the kernel? Will he not break open the shell for me, and let the truth of it, his thought, stream out upon me? He will not let it hurt me to mistake the light for darkness, while I take not the darkness for light. The one comes from blindness of the intellect, the other from blindness of heart and will. I love the light, and will not believe at the word of any man, that that which seems to me darkness is in God.

NOVEMBER 10TH

Where would the good news be if John said, "God is light, but you cannot see his light; you cannot tell, you have no notion, what light is; what God means by light, is not what you mean by light; what God calls light may be horrible darkness to you, for you are of another nature from him!" Where would be the good news of that? It is true, the light of God may be so bright that we see nothing; but that is not darkness, it is infinite hope of light. It is true also that to the wicked, "the day of the Lord is darkness, and not light;" but is that because the conscience of the wicked man judges of good and evil oppositely to the conscience of the good man? When he says, "Evil, be thou my good," he means by *evil* what God means by evil, and by *good* he means *pleasure*. He cannot make the meanings change places. To say that what our deepest conscience calls darkness may be light to God, is blasphemy; to say light in God and light in man are of differing kinds, is to speak against the spirit of light. God means us to be jubilant in the fact that he is light—that he is what his children, made in his image, mean when they say *light;* that what in him is dark to them, is dark by excellent glory, by too much cause of jubilation; that, however dark it may be to their eyes, it is light even as they mean it, light for their eyes and souls and hearts to take in the moment they are enough of eyes, enough of souls, enough of hearts, to receive it in its very being.

NOVEMBER 11TH

L iving light, thou wilt not have me believe anything dark of thee! Thou wilt have me so sure of thee as to dare to say that is not of God which I see dark, see unlike the Master! All men will not, in our present imperfection, see the same light; but light is light notwithstanding, and what each does see, is his safety if he obeys it. In proportion as we have the image of Christ mirrored in us, we shall know what is and is not light. But never will anything prove to be light that is not of the same kind with that which we mean by light. The darkness yet left in us makes us sometimes doubt of a thing whether it be light or darkness; but when the eye is single, the whole body will be full of light. To fear the light is to be untrue. No being needs fear the light of God. Nothing can be in light inimical to our nature, which is of God. All fear of the light comes of the darkness still in those of us who do not love the truth with all our hearts; it will vanish as we are more and more interpenetrated with the light. In a word, there is no way of thought or action which we count admirable in man, in which God is not infinitely better. Jesus is our savior because God is our savior. God will comfort and console his children better than any mother her infant. The only thing he will not give them is leave to stay in the dark. He gives what his child needs—often by refusing what he asks. If his child says, "I will not be good; I prefer to die!" God's dealing with that child will be as if he said, "No, I will not give you your own will, but mine, which is your one good. You shall not die; you shall live to thank me that I would not hear your prayer."

NOVEMBER 12TH

Come to God, then, my brother, my sister, with all thy desires and instincts, all thy lofty ideals, all thy longing for purity and unselfishness, all thy yearning to love and be true, all thy aspiration after self-forgetfulness and child-life in the breath of the Father; come to him with all thy weaknesses, all thy shames; with all thy helplessness over thy own thoughts; with all thy failure, yea, with the sick sense of having missed the tide of true affairs; come to him with all thy doubts, fears, dishonesties, meannesses, misjudgments, wearinesses, and disappointments: be sure he will take thee, and all thy miserable brood, whether of draggle-winged angels, or covert-seeking snakes, into his care, the angels for life, the snakes for death, and thee for liberty in his limitless heart! For he is light, and in him is no darkness at all. If he were a king, a governor; if the name that described him were *The Almighty,* thou mightest well doubt whether there could be light enough in him for thee and thy darkness; but he is thy father, and more thy father than the word can mean in any lips but his who said, "my father and your father, my God and your God;" and such a father *is* an infinite, perfect light. If he were any less or any other than he is, and thou couldst yet go on growing, thou must at length come to the point where thou wouldst be dissatisfied with him; but he is light, and in him is no darkness at all. If anything seem to be in him that you cannot be content with, be sure that the ripening of thy love to thy fellows and to him, will make thee at length know that anything else than just what he is would have been to thee an endless loss.

NOVEMBER 13TH

B e not afraid to build upon the rock of Christ, as if thy holy imagination might build too high and heavy for that rock, and it must give way and crumble beneath the weight of thy divine idea. Let no one persuade thee that there is in him a little darkness, because of something he has said which his creature interprets into darkness. The interpretation is the work of the enemy—a handful of tares of darkness sown in the light. Neither let thy cowardly conscience receive any word as light because another calls it light, while it looks to thee dark. Say either the thing is not what it seems, or God never said or did it. But, of all evils, to misinterpret what God does, and then say the thing as interpreted must be right because God does it, is of the devil. Do not try to believe anything that affects thee as darkness. Even if thou mistake and refuse something true thereby, thou wilt do less wrong to Christ by such a refusal than thou wouldst by accepting as his what thou canst see only as darkness. It is impossible thou art seeing a true, a real thing—seeing it as it is, I mean—if it looks to thee darkness. But let thy words be few, lest thou say with thy tongue what thou wilt afterward repent with thy heart. Above all things, believe in the light, that it is what thou callest light, though the darkness in thee may give thee cause at a time to doubt whether thou art verily seeing the light.

NOVEMBER 14TH

Darkness is death, but not death to him that comes out of it. It may sound paradoxical, but no man is condemned for anything he has done; he is condemned for continuing to do wrong. He is condemned for not coming out of the darkness, for not coming to the light, the living God, who sent the light, his son, into the world to guide him home. Let us hear what John says about the darkness. For here we have also the word of the apostle himself: at the 13th verse he begins, I think, to speak in his own person. In the 19th verse he says, "And this is the condemnation,"—not that men are sinners—not that they have done that which, even at the moment, they were ashamed of—not that they have committed murder, not that they have betrayed man or woman,—not for any hideous thing are they condemned, but that they will not leave such doings behind, and do them no more: "This is the condemnation, that light is come into the world, and men" would not come out of the darkness to the light, but "loved darkness rather than light, because their deeds were evil." Clinging to evil, therefore turning their backs on the inbreaking light, how can they but be condemned! Whatever of honesty is in man, whatever of judgment is left in the world, must allow that their condemnation is in the very nature of things, that it must rest on them and abide.

NOVEMBER 15TH

It does not follow, because light has come into the world, that it has fallen upon this or that man. He has his portion of the light that lighteth every man, but the revelation of God in Christ may not yet have reached him. A man might see and pass the Lord in a crowd, yet not be to blame like the Jews of Jerusalem for not knowing him. A man like Nathanael might have started and stopped at the merest glimpse of him, but all growing men are not yet like him without guile. Everyone who has not yet come to the light is not necessarily keeping his face turned away from it. We dare not say that this or that man would not have come to the light had he seen it; we do not know that he will not come to the light the moment he does see it. God gives every man time. There is a light that lightens sage and savage, but the glory of God in the face of Jesus may not have shined on this sage or that savage. The condemnation is of those who, having seen Jesus, refuse to come to him, or pretend to come to him but do not the things he says. They have all sorts of excuses at hand; but as soon as a man begins to make excuse, the time has come when he might be doing that from which he excuses himself. How many are there not who, believing there is something somewhere with the claim of light upon them, go on and on to get more from the darkness! This gives broad ground for the Lord to say, "Ye will not come unto me that ye might have life!"

NOVEMBER 16TH

" All manner of sin and blasphemy," the Lord said, "shall be forgiven unto men; but the blasphemy against the spirit shall not be forgiven." God speaks, as it were, in this manner: "I forgive you everything. Not a word more shall be said about your sins—only come out of them; come out of the darkness of your exile; come into the light of your home, your birthright, and do evil no more. Love your neighbor as I love you; be my good child; trust in your father. I am light, come to me, and you shall see things as I see them, and hate the evil thing. I will make you love the thing which now you call good and love not." And if his child should say, "I prefer staying in the darkness: forgive me that, too," the Lord will reply, "No, that cannot be. The one thing that cannot be forgiven is the sin of choosing to be evil, or refusing deliverance. He who chooses to go on sinning annihilates my forgiveness. If a man refuses to come out of his sin, he must suffer the vengeance of a love that would be no love if it left him there. Shall I allow my creature to be the thing my soul hates?" There is no excuse for this refusal. God passes by and forgets a thousand sins, forgiving them all—only we must begin to be good, to do evil no more. He who refuses must be punished until he gives way, repents, and come to the light, that his deeds may be seen by himself to be what they are, and by himself reproved. Who knows but such sin may need for its cure the continuous punishment of an eon?

NOVEMBER 17TH

There are three kinds of punishment: first, mere retribution, which, since entirely human and not divine, is of evil; second, that which works repentance; and third, that which refines and purifies, working for holiness. But the punishment that falls on whom the Lord loveth because they have repented is a very different thing from the punishment on those who hold fast to their sins. There are also various ways in which the word *forgive* can be used. A man might say to his son, "My boy, I forgive you. You did not know what you were doing." Or he might say, "I forgive you; but I must punish you, for you have done the same thing several times, and I must make you remember." Or again, he might say, "I am seriously angry with you. I cannot forgive you. I must punish you severely, I cannot pass it by." Or, once more, "Except you alter your ways entirely, I shall have nothing more to do with you. Never, never, till I see a greater difference in you than I dare hope to see in this world, will I forgive you. I would die to save you, but I cannot forgive you. There is nothing in you now on which to rest forgiveness. To say, I forgive you, would be to say, Do anything you like; I do not care what you do." So God may forgive and punish; and he may punish and not forgive, that he may rescue. To forgive the sin against the holy spirit would be to damn the universe to the pit of lies, to render it impossible for the man so forgiven ever to be saved. He cannot forgive the man who will not come to the light because his deeds are evil. Against that man his fatherly heart is *moved with indignation.*

THE DISPLEASURE OF JESUS

"When Jesus therefore saw her weeping, and the Jews also weeping which came with her, he groaned in the spirit, and was troubled."

John 11:33

NOVEMBER 18TH

G rimm, in his lexicon to the New Testament, after giving as
the equivalent of the word ἐμβριμάομαι (embrimaomai) in
pagan use, "I am moved with anger," "I roar or growl,"
tells us that in Mark 1:43 and Matthew 9:30, it has a meaning
different from that of the pagans, namely, "I command with severe
admonishment." I believe the statement a blunder. Translators
have in those passages used the word similarly, and in one place,
where a true version is of yet more consequence, have taken
another liberty and rendered the word "groaned." The Revisers, at
the same time, place in the margin what I cannot but believe its
true meaning—"was moved with indignation." Let us look at all
the passages in which the word is used of the Lord, and so, if we
may, learn something concerning him. It is indeed right and
necessary to insist that many a word must differ in moral weight
and color as used of or by persons of different character. The
anger of a good man is a very different thing from the anger of a
bad man; the displeasure of Jesus must be a very different thing
from the displeasure of a tyrant. But they are both anger, both
displeasure, nevertheless. We have no right to change a root-
meaning, and say in one case that a word means *he was indignant*, in
another that it means *he straitly or strictly charged*, and in a third, that it
means *he groaned.* Surely not thus shall we arrive at the truth! If any
statement is made, any word employed, that we feel unworthy of
the Lord, let us refuse it; let us say, "I do not believe that;" or
"There must be something there that I cannot see into; I must
wait; it cannot be what it looks to me, and be true of the Lord!"
But to accept the word as used of the Lord, and say it means
something quite different from what it means when used by the
same writer of someone else, appears to me untruthful.

356

NOVEMBER 19TH

We shall take first the passage, Mark 1:43—in the authorized version, "And he straitly charged him;" in the revised, "And he strictly charged him," with *sternly* in the margin. Literally, as it seems to me, it ought to be read, "And being angry," or "displeased," or "vexed" "with him, he immediately dismissed him." There is even some dissatisfaction implied, I think, in the word I have translated "dismissed." The word in John 9:34, "they cast him out," is the same, only a little intensified. This adds something to the story, and raises the question, Why should Jesus have been angry? If we can find no reason for this anger, we must leave the thing as altogether obscure; for I do not know where to find another meaning for the word, except in the despair of a would-be interpreter. Jesus had cured the leper—not with his word only, which would have been enough for the mere cure, but was not enough without the touch of his hand to satisfy the heart of Jesus—a touch defiling him, in the notion of the Jews, but how cleansing to the sense of the leper! The man, however, seems to have been unworthy of this delicacy of divine tenderness. The Lord, who could read his heart, saw that he made him no true response—that there was not awaked in him the faith he desired to rouse: he had not drawn the soul of the man to his. The leper was jubilant in the removal of his pain and isolating uncleanness, in his deliverance from suffering and scorn; he was probably elated with the pride of having had a miracle wrought for *him*. In a word, he was so full of himself that he did not think truly of his deliverer.

NOVEMBER 20TH

The Lord saw this, or something of this kind, and was not satisfied. He had wanted to give the man something so much better than a pure skin, and had only roused in him an unseemly delight in his own cleanness—*unseemly*, for it was such that he paid no heed to the Lord, but immediately disobeyed his positive command. The moral position the man took was that which displeased the Lord, made him angry. He saw in him positive and rampant self-will and disobedience, an impertinent assurance and self-satisfaction. Filled, not with pure delight, or the child-like merriment that might well burst forth, mingled with tears, at such deliverance; filled, not with gratitude, but gratification, the keener that he had been so long an object of loathing to his people; filled with arrogance because of the favor shown to him, of all men, by the great prophet, and swelling with boast of the same, he left the presence of the healer to thwart his will, and commanded to tell no man, at once "began"—the frothy, volatile, talking soul—"to publish it much, and to blaze abroad the matter, insomuch that Jesus could no more openly enter into a city, but was without in desert places."

NOVEMBER 21ST

I n both the authorized and revised versions of the healing of the two blind men in the ninth chapter of Matthew's gospel, the same phrases are used in the translation of the word in question as in the story of the leper in Mark's gospel: "straitly," "strictly," "sternly charged them." I read the passage thus: "And Jesus was displeased" --or perhaps, "much displeased"—"with them, saying, See that no man know it. But they went forth, and spread abroad his fame in all that land." Surely here we have light on the cause of Jesus' displeasure with the blind men! Like the leper, they showed themselves bent on their own way, and did not care of his. Doubtless they were, in part, moved by the desire to spread abroad his fame; that may even have seemed the best acknowledgment they could render their deliverer. They never suspected that a great man might desire to avoid fame, knowing it for a foolish thing. "What is a prophet without honor?" such ask, nor understand the answer, "A man the more likely to prove a prophet." By them he should have his right—but as they, not he, judged fit! They were too grateful not to trumpet his praises, not grateful enough to obey him. How many are there not who seem capable of anything for the sake of the church, except the one thing its Lord cares about—that they should do what he tells them! He would deliver them from themselves into the liberty of the sons of God, and make them his brothers; they leave him to vaunt their church. His commandments are not grievous; they invent commandments for him, and lay them, burdens grievous to be borne, upon the necks of their brethren.

NOVEMBER 22ND

God would have us sharers in his bliss—in the very truth of existence; they worship from afar, and will not draw nigh. It was not the obstruction, the personal inconvenience, that made the Lord angry, but that they would not be his friends, would not do what he told them, would not be the children of his father, and help him to save their brethren. When Peter, in much the same way, opposed the will of the Father, saying, "That be far from thee, Lord!" he called him Satan, and ordered him behind him. Does it affect anyone to the lowering of his idea of the Master that he should ever be angry? If so, I would ask whether he knows but one kind of anger. There is a good anger and a bad anger. There is a wrath of God, and there is a wrath of man that worketh not the righteousness of God. God's anger is at one with his love, helpful, healing, restoring; yet is it verily and truly what we call anger. How different is the anger of one who loves, from that of one who hates! There is the degraded, human anger, and the grand, noble, eternal anger. It is to me an especially glad thought that the Lord came so near us as to be angry with us. The more we think of Jesus being angry with us, the more we feel that we must get nearer and nearer to him—get within the circle of his wrath, out of the sin that makes him angry, and near to him where sin cannot come. There is no quenching of his love in the anger of Jesus. It is his recognition that we are to blame, that we ought to be better, that we are able to do right if we will. We are able to turn our faces to the light, and come out of the darkness; the Lord will see to our growth.

NOVEMBER 23RD

It is a serious thought that the disobedience of the men he had set free from blindness and leprosy should hamper him in his work for his father. But his best friends did the same. That he should be crucified was a horror to them; they would have made him a king, and ruined his father's work. He preferred the cruelty of his enemies to the kindness of his friends. The former with evil intent wrought his father's will; the latter with good intent would have frustrated it. Let us know that the poverty of our idea of Jesus—how much more our disobedience to him!—thwarts his progress to victory, delays the coming of the kingdom of heaven. Many a man valiant for Christ, but not understanding him, and laying on himself and his fellows burdens against nature, has therein done would-be service for which Christ will give him little thanks, which indeed may now be moving his holy anger. Where we do that we ought not, and could have helped it, be moved to anger against us, O Christ! Do not treat us as if we were not worth being displeased with; let not our faults pass as if they were of no weight. Be angry with us, holy brother, when we are to blame; where we do not understand, have patience with us, open our eyes, and give us strength to obey, until at length we are the children of the Father even as thou. For though thou art lord and master and savior of them that are growing, thou art perfect lord only of the true and the free, who live in the light and are divinely glad. Make us able to be angry and not sin; to be angry nor seek revenge the smallest; to be angry and full of forgiveness. We will not be content till our very anger is love.

NOVEMBER 24TH

The Lord did not call the leprosy to return and seize again upon the man who disobeyed him. He did not wrap the self-confident seeing men in the cloud of their old darkness because they wrapped themselves in the cloud of disobedience. He let them go. Of course they failed of their well-being by it; for to say a man might disobey and be none the worse, would be to say that light might sometimes be darkness, that the will of God is not man's bliss. But the Lord did not directly punish them, any more than he does tens of thousands of wrongs in the world. Many wrongs punish themselves, and it is his will it should be so; but, whether he punish directly or indirectly, he is always working to deliver. I think sometimes his anger is followed, yea, accompanied by an astounding gift, fresh from his heart of grace. He is love when he gives, and love when he withholds; love when he heals, and love when he slays. Lord, if thus thou lookest upon men in thine anger, what must a full gaze be from thine eyes of love!

NOVEMBER 25TH

In John 11:32, the authorized translation has the words, "When Jesus therefore saw her weeping, and the Jews also weeping which came with her, he groaned in the spirit and was troubled;" according to the margin of the revised version, "he was moved with indignation in the spirit, and troubled himself." And in the 38th verse we read, according to the margin, "Jesus therefore again being moved with indignation in himself cometh to the tomb." Indignation—anger at the very tomb, in the presence of hearts torn by the loss of a brother four days dead, whom also he loved! Yes, verily, friends, such indignation as, at such a time, it was eternally right the heart of Jesus should be so moved. I can hardly doubt that he is in like manner moved by what he sees now at the death-beds and graves of not a few who are not his enemies, and yet in the presence of death seem no better than pagans. What have such gained by being the Christians they say they are? They fixe their eyes on a grisly phantasm they call Death, and never lift them to the radiant Christ standing by bed or grave! For them, Christ has not conquered Death; Death is rather their king. They would shudder at the thought of saying so in words, but they say it in the bitterness of their tears, in their eyes of despair. "What," they ask, "would you have us not weep?" Weep freely, friends; but let your tears be those of expectant Christians, not hopeless pagans.

NOVEMBER 26TH

The Lord had all this time been trying to teach his friends about his father, who had sent him that men might look on his very likeness, and all they had gained by it seemed not to amount to an atom of consolation when the touch of death came. The fact that God loves them, and that God has Lazarus, seems nothing to them because *they* have not Lazarus! I do not mean that God would have even his closest presence make us forget or cease to desire that of our friend. God forbid! The love of God is the perfecting of every love. He is not the God of oblivion, but of eternal remembrance. He gave us to each other to belong to each other forever. But is it nothing that he who is the life should be present, assuring the well-being of the life that has vanished, and the well-being of the love that misses it? Why should the Lord have come to the world at all, if these his friends were to take no more good of him than this? All their cry was, "Lord, if thou hadst been here, my brother had not died!" You may say they did not know Christ well enough yet. That is plain—but Christ had expected of them, and was disappointed. Was this the way his best friends treated his father, who was doing everything for them possible for a father to do for his children! He cared so dearly for their hearts that he could not endure to see them weeping so that they shut out his father. His love was vexed with them that they would sit in ashes when they ought to be out in his father's sun and wind. And all for a lie! Remember, it was not their love, but a false notion of loss. To think they should believe in death and the grave, and not in him, the Life!

NOVEMBER 27TH

The Lord said to Martha, "Thy brother shall rise again." "I know that he shall rise again in the resurrection at the last day," she replied, and he told her, "I am the resurrection, and the life; he that believeth in me, shall never die." The sisters must surely have known that he raised up the daughter of Jairus and the son of the widow of Nain. Martha had gone away, for the moment at least, a little comforted; and now came Mary, who knew the Lord better than her sister—alas, with the same bitter tears flowing from her eyes, and the same hopeless words, almost of reproach, falling from her lips! Then it was, at the sight of her and the Jews with her, that the spirit of the Lord was moved with indignation. They wept as those who believe in death, not in life. What was to be done with his brother and sisters who *would* be miserable, who would not believe in his father! How was he to comfort them? They would not be comforted! Was existence, the glorious gift of his father, to be the most terrible of miseries, because some must go home before others? It was all so sad! And all because they would not know his father! Then came the reaction from his indignation, and the laboring heart of the Lord found relief in tears. The Lord saw into two worlds—saw Martha and Mary on the one side weeping, on the other Lazarus waiting for them in peace. It was hard on Lazarus to be called back into the winding-sheet of the body, a sacrifice to their faithlessness, but it should be done! Lazarus should suffer for his sisters! Through him they should be compelled to believe in the Father, and so be delivered from bondage!

NOVEMBER 28TH

The Lord turned, not to Mary and Martha, not to punish them for their unbelief, not even to chide them for their sorrow; he turned to his father to thank him. He thanks him for hearing a prayer he had made—whether a moment before, or ere he left the other side of the Jordan, I cannot tell. Surely he had spoken about bringing Lazarus back, and his father had shown himself of one mind with him. "And I know that thou hearest me always, but because of the multitude which standeth around I said it, that they may believe that thou didst send me." He had said something for the sake of the multitude; what was it? The thanksgiving he had just uttered. He was not in the way of thanking his father in formal words, and now would not naturally have spoken his thanks aloud; he had done the unusual thing for the sake of being heard to do it, and for holy honesty-sake he tells the fact, speaking to his father so as the people about him may hear, and there be no shadow of undisclosed doubleness in the action. "I thank thee, father, and I say it that the people may understand that I am not doing this thing of myself, but as thy messenger. It is thou, father, art going to do it. Lazarus, come forth." The trouble of the Lord was that his friends would not trust his father. He did not want any reception of himself that was not a reception of his father—he who did the works! From this disappointment came, it seems to me, that sorrowful sigh, "Nevertheless, when the son of man cometh, shall he find faith on the earth?"

NOVEMBER 29TH

Lazarus must come and help him with these sisters whom he could not get to believe! Lazarus had tasted of death, and knew what it was; he must come and give his testimony! His sisters fancy he has gone to the nowhere of their unbelief; he must set them at rest. It was hard upon Lazarus, but he must come and bear the Lord company a little longer, and then be left behind with his sisters, that they and millions more might know that God is the God of the living, and not of the dead. Can any Christian believe it was from love to Lazarus that Jesus wept? It was from love to God, and to Martha and Mary. He had not lost Lazarus; but Martha and Mary were astray from their father in heaven. "Come, my brother; witness!" he cried; and Lazarus came forth. Oh, the hearts of Martha and Mary! Surely the Lord had some recompense for his trouble, beholding their joy! Lazarus had to die again, and thanked God, we may be sure, for the glad fact. Did his sisters, supposing them again left behind him in the world, make the same lamentations over him as the former time he went? If they did, would you not say it was most unworthy of them to be no better for such a favor shown them? Would it not be hard to persuade you that they ever did so behave? They must have felt it would be a shame not to be patient when they knew there was nothing to fear. It was all right with him, and would soon be all right with them also! I imagine you agreeing heartily with this.

Why, then, should *you* be so miserable when a loved one is taken from you?

NOVEMBER 30TH

When any have husband, son, father, brother, or lover are taken from them, is it but the cold frost of use and forgetting that makes them less miserable than they were a year ago? Perhaps they say, if they had such as miracle wrought for them as was wrought for Martha and Mary, that would make all the difference! When their loved one, miraculously returned, must go once more, they would not lament, they would not sadden the Lord's heart with hopeless tears! Ah, how little they know themselves! Do they not see that they are now in precisely the position supposed—the position of those sisters after Lazarus was taken from them the second time? They know now all the sisters knew then. Martha and Mary had no more of a revelation by the recall of Lazarus than any of us have today. Many are the Christians who profess to believe the story, though they make that doubtful enough by their disregard of the very soul of it. Is it possible that, so far as they are concerned, Lazarus might as well not have risen? Their friends are gone as Lazarus went twice, and they behave as if they knew nothing of Lazarus. They make a lamentable ado, vexing Jesus that they will not be reasonable and trust his father! When Martha and Mary behaved as they are doing, the sisters had not had Lazarus raised; Christians today have had Lazarus raised, yet they go on as Martha and Mary did then!

DECEMBER 1ST

To those who call themselves Christians, but weep such hopeless tears: do you not believe that God is unchangeable, but think he acts one way one time and another way another time just from caprice? He might give back a brother to sisters who were favorites with him, but no such gift is to be counted upon? Why, then, do you worship such a God? If Lazarus were a mere exceptional case, it is worthless indeed—as worthless as your behavior would make it. But you are dull of heart, as were Martha and Mary. Do you not see that he is as continually restoring as taking away—that every bereavement is a restoration—that when you are weeping, others, who love as well as you, are clasping in ecstasy of reunion? If you have not learned this, you cannot have been doing the will of the Father, or you would not be as you are. If you reply, how little I know your loss, I respond, indeed it is great! It seems to include God! If you knew what he knows about death, you would clap your listless hands. But why should I seek in vain to comfort you? You must be made miserable, that you may wake from your sleep to know that you need God. If you do not find him, endless life with the living whom you bemoan would become and remain to you unendurable. The knowledge of your own heart will teach you this—not the knowledge you have, but the knowledge that is on its way to you through suffering. Then you will feel that existence itself is the prime of evils, without *the righteousness which is of God by faith.*

RIGHTEOUSNESS

"—that I may win Christ, and be found in him, not having mine own righteousness, which is of the law, bt that which is through the faith of Christ, the righteousness which is of God by faith."

Philippians 3:8-9

DECEMBER 2ND

What does the apostle mean by the righteousness that is of God by faith? He means the same righteousness Christ had by his faith in God, the same righteousness God himself has. In his second epistle to the Corinthians, he says, "He hath made him to be sin for us who knew no sin, that we might be made the righteousness of God in him;" "He gave him to be treated like a sinner, killed and cast out of his own vineyard by his husbandmen, that we might in him be made righteous like God." As the antithesis stands, it is rhetorically correct. But if the former half means, "he made him to be treated as if he were a sinner," then the latter half should, in logical precision, mean, "That we might be treated as if we were righteous." And not a few argue that is just what Paul does mean, with our sins being imputed to Jesus, in order that we might be treated as if we were righteous, his righteousness being imputed to us. That is, by a sort of legal fiction, Jesus was treated as what he was not, in order that we might be treated as what we are not. This is the best device, according to the prevailing theology, that the God of truth, the God of mercy, could fall upon for saving his creatures! It seems to me that, seeing much duplicity exists in the body of Christ, every honest member of it should protest against any word tending to imply the existence of falsehood in the indwelling spirit of that body. I now protest against this so-called *doctrine*, counting it the rightful prey of the most foolish wind in the limbo of vanities, whither I would gladly do my best to send it.

DECEMBER 3RD

The doctrine of imputed righteousness is a mean invention, false, and productive of falsehood. Say it is a figure, I answer it is not only a false figure but an embodiment of untruth; say it expresses a reality, and I say it teaches the worst of lies; say there is a shadow of truth in it, and I answer it may be so, but there is no truth touched in it that could not be taught infinitely better without it. It is the meagre misshapen offspring of the legalism of a poverty-stricken mechanical fancy, unlighted by a gleam of divine imagination. No one who knows his New Testament will dare to say that the figure is once used in it. I have dealt already with the source of it. They say first, God must punish the sinner, for justice requires it; then they say he does not punish the sinner, but punishes a perfectly righteous man instead, attributes his righteousness to the sinner, and so continues just. Was there ever such a confusion, such an inversion of right and wrong! Justice *could not* treat a righteous man as an unrighteous; neither, if justice required the punishment of sin, *could* justice let the sinner go unpunished. To lay the pain upon the righteous in the name of justice is simply monstrous. No wonder unbelief is rampant. Believe in Moloch if you will, but call him Moloch, not Justice. Be sure that the thing that God gives, the righteousness that is of God, is a real thing, and not a contemptible legalism. Pray God I have no righteousness imputed to me. Let me be regarded as the sinner I am; for nothing will serve my need but to be made a righteous man, one that will no more sin.

DECEMBER 4TH

We have the word *imputed* just once in the New Testament. Whether the evil doctrine may have sprung from any possible misunderstanding of the passage where it occurs, I hardly care to inquire. The word as Paul uses it, and the whole of the thought whence his use of it springs, appeals to my sense of right and justice as much as the common use of it arouses my abhorrence. The apostle says that a certain thing was imputed to Abraham for righteousness; or, as the revised version has it, "reckoned unto him:" what was it that was thus imputed to Abraham? The righteousness of another? God forbid! It was his own faith that was reckoned to him as righteousness. To impute the righteousness of one to another, is simply to act a falsehood; to call the faith of a man his righteousness is simply to speak the truth. Was it not righteous in Abraham to obey God? Paul says faith in God was counted righteousness before Moses was born. Abraham's was no mere intellectual recognition of the existence of a God, which is consistent with the deepest atheism; it was that faith which is one with action: "He went out, not knowing whither he went." The very act of believing in God after such fashion that, when the time of action comes, the man will obey God, is the highest act, the deepest , loftiest righteousness of which man is capable, is at the root of all other righteousness, and the spirit of it will work till the man is perfect.

DECEMBER 5TH

I f you define righteousness in the common-sense, that is, in the divine fashion—for religion is nothing if it be not the deepest common-sense—as a giving to everyone his due, then certainly the first due is to him who makes us capable of owing, that is, makes us responsible creatures. If anyone were born perfect, then the highest duty would come first into the consciousness. Imperfect as we are born, it is the doing of, or at least the honest trying to do many another duty, that will at length lead a man to see that his duty to God is the first and highest of all, including and requiring the performance of all other duties. A man might live a thousand years in neglect of duty, and never come to see that any obligation was upon him to put faith in God and do what he told him. I grant that if God were such as he thinks him he would indeed owe him little; but he thinks him such in consequence of not doing what he knows he ought to do. He has not come to the light, been a man without guile, true and fair. But though faith in God is the first duty, there is more reason than this why it should be counted for righteousness. It is the one spiritual act which brings the man into contact with the original creative power, able to help him in every endeavor after righteousness, and ensure his progress to perfection. The Bible never deals with impossibilities, never demands of any man at any given moment a righteousness of which he is incapable; neither does it lay upon him any other law than that of perfect righteousness. When he yields that righteousness of which he is capable, content for the moment, it goes on to demand more: the common-sense of the Bible is lovely.

DECEMBER 6TH

To the man who has no faith in God, faith in God cannot look like righteousness; neither can he know that it is the germ of life, creative of all other righteousness. It is not like some single separate act of righteousness; it is the action of the whole man, turning to good from evil—turning his back on all that is opposed to righteousness, and starting on a road on which he cannot stop, in which he must go on growing more and more righteous, discovering more and more what righteousness is, and more and more what is unrighteous in himself. In the one act of believing in God—that is, of giving himself to do what he tells him—he abjures evil, both what he knows and what he does not yet know in himself. A man may indeed have turned to obey God, and yet be capable of many an injustice to his neighbor which he has not yet discovered to be an injustice; but as he goes on obeying, he will go on discovering. Not only will he grow more and more determined to be just, but he will grow more and more sensitive to the idea of injustice—I do not mean in others, but in himself. A man who continues capable of a known injustice to his neighbor cannot be believed to have turned to God. At all events, a man cannot be near God, so as to be learning what is just toward God, and not be near his neighbor, so as to be learning what is unfair to him. If a man is to be blamed for not choosing righteousness, for not turning to the light, then the man who does choose and turn is to be justified in his deed, and declared to be righteous.

DECEMBER 7TH

The man who steps out of the darkness and turns to the light is not yet thoroughly righteous, but is growing in righteousness. He needs creative God, and time for will and effort. Born into the world without righteousness, it would be the deepest injustice to demand of him, with a penalty, at any given moment, more than he knows how to yield; but it is the highest love constantly to demand of him perfect righteousness as what he must attain to. He must keep turning to righteousness and abjuring iniquity, ever aiming at the perfection of God. Such an obedient faith is most justly and fairly, being all that God himself can require of the man, called by God righteousness in the man. It would not be enough for the righteousness of God, or Jesus, or any perfected saint; but it is enough at a given moment for the disciple of the Perfect. The righteousness of Abraham was not to compare with that of Paul; he did not fight with himself for righteousness, as did Paul—not because he was better than Paul and did not need to fight, but because his idea of what was required of him was not within sight of that of Paul. Yet was he righteous in the same way as Paul; he had begun to be righteous. His faith was an act recognizing God as his law, and that is an all-embracing and all-determining action. They were righteous because they gave themselves up to God to make them righteous; and not to call such men righteous, not to impute their faith to them for righteousness, would be unjust. But God is utterly just, and nowise resembles a legal-minded Roman emperor, or bad pope formulating the doctrine of vicarious sacrifice.

DECEMBER 8TH

What , then, is the righteousness which is of God by faith? It is simply the thing that God wants every man to be, wrought out in him by constant obedient contact with God himself. It is not an attribute either of God or man, but a fact of character in God and in man. It is God's righteousness wrought out in us, so that as he is righteous, we too are righteous. It does not consist in obeying this or that law; not even in the keeping of every law. To be righteous is to be of such a heart, soul, mind, and will, as would recoil with horror from the lightest possible breach of any law. It is not the love of righteousness in the abstract that makes anyone righteous, but such a love of fair play toward everyone with whom we come into contact, that anything less than the fulfilling, with a clear joy, of our divine relation to him or her, is impossible. For the righteousness of God goes far beyond mere deeds, and requires of us love and helping mercy as our highest obligation and justice to our fellow men—those of them who have done nothing for us, those even who have done us wrong. Our relations with others, God first and then our neighbor, must one day become the gladness of our being; and nothing then will ever appear good for us, that is not in harmony with those blessed relations. Every thought will not merely be just, but will be just because it is something more, because it is live and true. The light of our life, our sole, eternal joy, is simply God, and all his creatures in him. He is all in all; not to be true to anything he has made is to be untrue to him. To be in God is to know him and need no law.

DECEMBER 9TH

In proportion as we know God, we must desire him, until at length we live in and for him with all our conscious heart. The righteousness which is of God by faith in God is then just the same kind of thing as God's righteousness, differing only as the created differs from the creating. The righteousness of him who does the will of his father in heaven, is the righteousness of Jesus Christ, is God's own righteousness. The man who has this righteousness, thinks about things as God thinks about them, loves the things that God loves, cares for nothing that God does not care about. Even while this righteousness is being born in him, the man will say to himself, "Why should I be troubled about this thing or that? Does God care about it? No. Then why should I? I must not care. I will not care!" The man with God's righteousness does not love a thing merely because it is right, but loves the very rightness in it. He feels joy in himself, but it comes to him from others, not from himself—from God first, and from somebody, anybody, everybody next. The man who really knows God is, and always will be, content with what God, who is the very self of his self, shall choose for him; he is entirely God's, and not at all his own. The *being* of what God has made him, and the contemplation of what God himself is, and what he has made his fellows, is what gives the man joy. He wants nothing, and feels that he has all things, for he is in the bosom of his father, and the thoughts of his father come to him. He knows that if he needs anything, it is his before he asks it; for his father has willed him, in the might and truth of his fatherhood, to be one with himself.

DECEMBER 10TH

The righteousness of God by faith is so far from being a thing built on the rubbish heap of legal fiction called vicarious sacrifice, or its shadow called imputed righteousness, that only the child with the child-heart, so far ahead of and so different from the wise and prudent, can understand it. The wise and prudent interprets God by himself, and does not understand him; the child interprets God by himself, and does understand him. The wise and prudent must make a system and arrange things to his mind before he can say, I believe. The child sees, believes, obeys— and knows he must be perfect as his father in heaven is perfect. If an angel, seeming to come from heaven, told him that God had let him off, did not require so much of him as that, because it was so hard for him to be quite good, and he loved him so dearly, the child of God would at once recognize, woven with the angel's starry brilliance, the flicker of the flames of hell, and would say to the shining one, "Get thee behind me, Satan." Nor would there be the slightest wonder or merit in his doing so, for at the words of the deceiver, if but for briefest moment imagined true, the shadow of a rising hell would gloom over the face of creation; hope would vanish; glory would die out of the face of God—until the groan of a thunderous *no* burst from the caverns of the universe, and the truth, flashing on his child's soul from the heart of the Eternal, withered up the lie of the messenger of darkness.

DECEMBER 11TH

I f a man ask, "How can God bring this righteousness about in me?" I reply, let him do it, and perhaps you will know. Help him to do it; God originates the possibility of your being his son, his daughter: he makes you able to will it, but you must will it. If he is not doing it in you—that is, if you have as yet prevented him from beginning, why should I tell you, even if I knew the process, how he would do what you will not let him do? Indeed, how should you be able to know? For it must deal with deeper and higher things than you *can* know anything of till the work is at least begun. Perhaps if you approved of the plans of the glad creator, you would allow him to make of you something divine! To teach your intellect what has to be learned by your whole being, what it would do you no good to understand save you understood it in your whole being—if this be the province of any man, it is not mine. Let the dead bury their dead, and the dead teach their dead; for me, I will try to wake them. To those who are awake, I cry, "For the sake of your father and the first-born among many brethren, for the sake of those he has given us to love the most dearly, let patience have her perfect work. Clay on the wheel, let the fingers of the divine potter model you at their will. Obey the Father's lightest word; hear the Brother who knows you, and died for you; beat down your sin, and trample it to death."

DECEMBER 12TH

rother, when thou sittest at home in thy house, which is the temple of the Lord, open all thy windows to breathe the air of his approach; and thy hand be on the latch to open the door at his first knock. Shouldst thou open the door and not see him, do not say he did not knock, but understand that he is there, and wants thee to go out to him. It may be he has something for thee to do for him. Go and do it, and perhaps thou wilt return with a new prayer, to find a new window in thy soul. Never wait for fitter time or place to talk to him. To wait till thou go to church, to thy closet, is to make *him* wait. He will listen as thou walkest in the lane or the crowded street. Remember, if indeed thou art able to know it, that not in any church is the service done that he requires. He will say to no man, "You never went to church: depart from me; I do not know you;" but, "Inasmuch as you never helped one of my father's children, you have done nothing for me." Church or chapel is not the place for divine service; it is a place of prayer, a place of praise, a place to learn of God, as what place is not? It is a place to look in the eyes of your neighbor, and love God along with him. But the world, the place of your living and loving and labor, is the place of divine service. Serve your neighbor, and you serve him. Do not heed much if men mock you and speak lies of you, or in goodwill defend you unworthily. Heed not much if even the righteous turn their backs upon you. Only take heed that you turn not from them. Take courage in the fact that *there is nothing covered, that shall not be revealed; and hid, that shall not be known.*

THE FINAL UNMASKING

"For there is nothing covered, that not be revealed; and hid, that shall not be known."

Matthew 10:26; Luke 12:2

DECEMBER 13TH

God is not a God that hides, but a God that reveals. His whole work in relation to the creatures he has made, is revelation—the giving them truth, the showing of himself to them, that they may know him, and come nearer and nearer to him, and so he have his children more and more of companions to him. That we are in the dark about anything is never because he hides it, but because we are not yet such that he is able to reveal that thing to us. That God could not do the thing at once which he takes time to do, we may surely say without irreverence. His will cannot finally be thwarted; where it is thwarted for a time, the very thwarting subserves the working out of a higher part of his will. He gave man the power to thwart his will, that, by means of that same power, he might come at last to do his will in a higher kind and way than would otherwise have been possible to him. God sacrifices his will to man that man may become such as himself, and give all to the truth; he makes man able to do wrong, that he may choose and love righteousness. The fact that all things are slowly coming into the light of the knowledge of men—so far as this may be possible to the created—is used in three different ways by the Lord. In Mark 4:22 and Luke 8:16, he uses it to enforce the duty of those who have received light to let it shine; they must do their part to bring all things out. In Luke 12:2, it is recorded how he brought it to bear on hypocrisy, showing its uselessness; and in the case recorded in Matthew 10:25, he uses the fact to enforce fearlessness as to the misinterpretation of our words and actions.

DECEMBER 14TH

The Lord tells us that all such things as the unrighteous desire to conceal, and such things as it is a pain to the righteous to have concealed, shall come out into the light. "Beware of hypocrisy," the Lord says, "for there is nothing covered, that shall not be revealed, neither hid, that shall not be known." What is hypocrisy? The desire to look better than you are; the hiding of things you do, because you would be ashamed to have them known. The doing of them is foul; the hiding of them, in order to appear better than you are, is fouler still. The man who does not live in his own consciousness as in the open heavens, is a hypocrite—and for most of us the question is, are we growing less or more of such hypocrites? Are we ashamed of not having been open, are we fighting the evil thing which is our temptation to hypocrisy? The Lord has not a thought in him to be ashamed of before God and his universe, and he will not be content until he has us in the same liberty. For our encouragement to fight on, he tells us that those that hunger and and thirst after righteousness shall be filled, that they shall become as righteous as the spirit of the Father and the Son in them can make them desire.

DECEMBER 15TH

The Lord says, "If they have called the master of the house Beelzebub, how much more shall they call them of his household! Fear them not therefore, for there is nothing covered, that shall not be revealed; and hid, that shall not be known." The Lord himself was accused of being a drunkard and a keeper of bad company—and perhaps would in the present day be so regarded by not a few calling themselves by his name, and teaching temperance and virtue. He lived upon a higher spiritual platform than they understand, acted from a height of the virtues they would inculcate, loftier than their eyes can scale. The Lord bore with their evil tongues, and was neither dismayed nor troubled; but from this experience of his own, comforts those who, being his messengers, must fare as he. When men count themselves Christians on any other ground than that they are slaves of Jesus Christ, the children of God, and free from themselves, so long will they use the servants of the Master despitefully. Few who have endeavored to do their duty, have not been annoyed, disappointed, enraged perhaps, by the antagonism, misunderstanding, and false representation to which they have been subjected, issuing mainly from those who have benefited by their efforts to be neighbors to all. "Do not hesitate," says the Lord, "to speak the truth that is in you; never mind what they call you; proclaim from the housetop; fear nobody." He spoke the words to the men to whom he looked first to spread the news of the kingdom of heaven; but they apply to all who obey him.

DECEMBER 16TH

Humanity, without willed effort after righteousness, is mean enough to sink to any depth of disgrace. The judgments also of imagined superiority are hard to bear. The rich man who will pay his workers as little as possible, will read his poor relation a solemn lecture on extravagance, because of some humblest little act of generosity! If, in the endeavor to lead a truer life, a man merely lives otherwise than his neighbors, strange motives will be invented to account for it. To the honest soul, it is a comfort to believe that the truth will one day be known. Still more satisfactory will be the unveiling where a man is misunderstood by those who ought to know him better—who take it for granted that he is about to do the wrong thing while he is crying for courage to heed neither himself nor his friends, but only the Lord. How many hear and accept the words, "Be not conformed to this world," without once perceiving that what they call Society and bow to as supreme, is the World and nothing else, or that those who mind what people think, and what people will say, are conformed to the world. The true man feels he has nothing to do with Society as judge or lawgiver: he is under the law of Jesus Christ, and it sets him free from the law of the World. Let a man do right, nor trouble himself about worthless opinion; the less he heeds tongues, the less difficult will he find it to love men. Let him comfort himself with the thought that the truth must out. He will not have to pass through eternity with the brand of ignorant or malicious judgment upon him. He shall find his peers and be judged of them.

DECEMBER 17TH

You who look for the justification of the light, are you prepared to encounter such exposure as the general unveiling of things must bring? Are you willing for the truth, whatever it be? I nowise mean to ask, have you a conscience so void of offence, have you a heart so pure and clean, that you fear no fullest exposure of what is in you to the gaze of men and angels? As to God, he knows it all now! What I mean to ask is, do you so love the truth and the right that you welcome, or at least submit willingly to the idea of an exposure of what in you is yet unknown to yourself—an exposure that may redound to the glory of the truth by making you ashamed and humble? It may be, for instance, that you were wrong in regard to those who you thought did wrong to you: will you welcome any discovery, even if it work for the excuse of others, that will make you more true, by revealing what in you was false? Are you willing to be made glad that you were wrong when you thought others were wrong? If you can with such submission face the revelation of things hid, then you are of the truth, and need not be afraid; for, whatever comes, it will only make you more true and humble and pure. The glory of the true world is, that there is nothing in it that needs to be covered, while ever and ever there will be things uncovered.

DECEMBER 18TH

Y ou may ask, "Will all my weaknesses, my evil habits, all my pettinesses and wrong thoughts which I cannot help—will all be set out before the universe?" Yes, if they so prevail as to constitute your character; that is, if they are you. But if you have come out of the darkness, if you are fighting it, if you are honestly trying to walk in the light, you may hope in God your father that what he has cured, what he is curing, what he has forgiven, will be heard of no more, not now being a constituent part of you. Or if indeed some of your evil things must yet be seen, the truth of them will be seen—that they are things you are at strife with, not things you are cherishing. God will be fair to you—so fair!—fair with the fairness of a father loving his own, who will have you clean, who will neither spare you any needful shame, nor leave you exposed to any that is not needful. The thing we have risen above is dead and forgotten, or if remembered, there is God to comfort us. It will not hurt us so long as we do not try to hide things, so long as we are ready to bow our heads in hearty shame where it is fit we should be ashamed. For to be ashamed is a holy and blessed thing. Shame is a thing to shame only those who want to appear, not those who want to be. In the name of God let us henceforth have nothing to be ashamed of, and be ready to meet any shame on its way to meet us. For to be humbly ashamed is to be plunged in the cleansing bath of the truth.

DECEMBER 19TH

The most supremely terrible revelation is that of a man to himself. What a horror will it not be to a vile man, a man that knew himself such as men of ordinary morals would turn from with disgust, but who has hitherto had no insight into what he is—what a horror will it not be to him when his eyes are opened to see himself as the pure see him, as God sees him! Imagine such a man waking all at once, not only to see the eyes of the universe fixed upon him with loathing astonishment, but to see himself at the same moment as those eyes see him! What a waking, into the full blaze of fact and consciousness, of truth and violation! Or think what it must be for a man counting himself religious, orthodox, exemplary, to perceive suddenly that there was no religion in him, only love of self; no love of the right, only a great love of being in the right! What a discovery—that he was simply a hypocrite—one who loved to *appear*, and *was* not! The rich seem to be those among whom will occur hereafter the sharpest reverses, if I understand aright the parable of the rich man and Lazarus. Who has not known the insolence of their meanness toward the poor, all the time counting themselves of the very elect! What riches and fancied religion, with the self-sufficiency they generate between them, can make man or woman capable of, is appalling. Mammon, the most contemptible of deities, is the most worshipped, both outside and in the house of God: to many of the religious rich, the great damning revelation will be their behavior to the poor to whom they thought themselves very kind.

DECEMBER 20TH

A man may loathe a thing in the abstract for years, and find at last that all the time he has been guilty of it. To carry a thing under our cloak caressingly, hides from us its identity with something that stands before us on the public pillory. Of all who will one day stand in dismay and sickness of heart, with the consciousness that their very existence is a shame, those will fare the worst who have been consciously false to their fellows; who, pretending friendship, have used their neighbor to their own ends; and especially those who, pretending friendship, have divided friends. To such Dante has given the lowest hell. If there be one thing God hates, it must be treachery. Do not imagine Judas the only man of whom the Lord would say, "Better were it for that man if he had never been born!" Did the Lord speak out of personal indignation, or did he utter a spiritual fact? Did he speak in anger at the treachery of his apostle, or in pity for the man that had better not have been born? Did the word spring from his knowledge of some fearful punishment awaiting Judas, or from his sense of the horror it was to be such a man? Beyond all things pitiful is it that a man should carry about with him the consciousness of being such a person—should know himself that false one! "O God," we think, "how terrible if it were I!" Just so terrible is it that it should be Judas! Have I not done things with the same germ in them, a germ which, brought to it evil perfection, would have shown itself treachery? Except I love my neighbor as myself, I may one day betray him! Let us therefore be compassionate and humble, and hope for every man.

DECEMBER 21ST

A man may sink by such slow degrees that, long after he is a devil, he may go on being a good churchman or a good dissenter, and thinking himself a good Christian. Continuously repeated sin against the poorest consciousness of evil must have a dread rousing. There are men who never wake to know how wicked they are, till, lo, the gaze of the multitude is upon them! The multitude staring with self-righteous eyes, doing like things themselves, but not yet found out; sinning after another pattern, therefore the hardest judges, thinking by condemnation to escape judgment. But there is nothing covered that shall not be revealed. What if the only thing to wake the treacherous, money-loving thief, Judas, to a knowledge of himself, was to let the thing go on to the end, and his kiss betray the Master? Judas did not hate the Master when he kissed him, but not being a true man, his very love betrayed him. The good man, conscious of his own evil, and desiring no refuge but the purifying light, will chiefly rejoice that the exposure of evil makes for the victory of the truth, the kingdom of God and his Christ. The only triumph the truth can ever have is its recognition by the heart of the liar. Its victory is in the man who, not content with saying, "I was blind and now I see" cried out, "Lord God, just and true, thou savest me from the death in myself, the untruth I have nourished in me, and even called righteousness! Hallowed be thy name, for thou only art true, thou only art holy, thou only art humble! Thou only art unselfish; thou only hast never sought thine own, but the things of thy children!"

DECEMBER 22ND

There is no satisfaction of revenge possible to the injured. The severest punishment that can be inflicted upon the wrong-doer is simply to let him know what he is; for his nature is of God, and the deepest in him is the divine. Neither can any other punishment than the sinner's being made to see the enormity of his injury give satisfaction to the injured. While the wronger will admit no wrong, while he mocks at the idea of amends, or rejoices in having done wrong, no suffering could satisfy revenge, far less justice. Both would continually know themselves foiled. Therefore, while a satisfied justice is an unavoidable eternal event, a satisfied revenge is an eternal impossibility. For the moment that the sole adequate punishment, a vision of himself, begins to take true effect upon the sinner, that moment the sinner has begun to grow a righteous man, and the brother human whom he has offended has nothing left him but to take the offender to his bosom—the more tenderly that his brother is repentant, that he was dead and is alive again, that he was lost and is found. Behold the meeting of the divine extremes—the extreme of punishment, the embrace of heaven! They run together; "the wheel is come full circle." For there can be no such agony for created soul, as to see itself vile—vile by its own action and choice. Also I venture to think there can be no delight for created soul—short of being one with the Father—so deep as that of seeing the heaven of forgiveness open, and disclose the shining stair that leads to its own natural home, where the eternal father has been all the time awaiting this return of his child.

DECEMBER 23RD

However indignant we may be, however intensely and justly we may feel our wrongs, there is no revenge possible for us in the universe of the Father. I may say to myself with heartiest vengeance, "I should just like to let that man see what a wretch he is—what all honest men at this moment think of him!" But, the moment come, the man will loathe himself tenfold more than any other man could, and that moment my heart will bury his sin. Its own ocean of pity will rush from the divine depths of its God-origin to overwhelm it. Let us try to forethink our forgiveness. Dare any man suppose that Jesus would have him hate the traitor through whom he came to the cross? Has he been pleased through all these ages with the manner in which those calling themselves by his name have treated, and are still treating his nation? We have not yet sounded the depths of forgiveness that are and will be required of such as would be his disciples! Our friends will know us then: for their joy, will it be, or their sorrow? Will their hearts sink within them when they look on the real likeness of us? Or will they rejoice to find that we were not so much to be blamed as they thought, in this thing or that which gave them trouble? Let us remember, however, that not only evil will be unveiled; that many a masking misconception will uncover a face radiant with the loveliness of the truth. And whatever disappointments may fall, there is consolation for every true heart in the one sufficing joy—that it stands on the border of the kingdom, about to enter into ever fuller, ever-growing possession of *the inheritance of the saints in light*.

THE INHERITANCE

"Giving thanks unto the Father, which hath made us meet to be partakers of the inheritance of the saints in light."

Colossians 1:12

DECEMBER 24TH

To have a share in any earthly inheritance is to diminish the share of the other inheritors. In the inheritance of the saints, that which each has, goes to increase the possession of the rest. Hear what Dante puts in the mouth of his guide, as they pass through Purgatory: *Because you point and fix your longing eyes, On things where sharing lessens every share, The human bellows heave with envious sighs. But if the loftiest love that dwelleth there, Up to the heaven of heavens your longing turn, Then from your heart will pass this fearing care: The oftener there the word* our *they discern, The more of good doth everyone possess, The more of love doth in that cloister burn.* Dante desires to know how it can be that a distributed good should make the receivers the richer the more of them there are; and Virgil answers: *Because thy mind doth stick To earthly things, and on them only brood, From the true light thou dost but darkness pick. That same ineffable and infinite Good, Which dwells up there, to Love doth run as fleet, As sunrays to bright things, for sisterhood. It gives itself proportionate to the heat: So that, wherever Love doth spread its reign, The growing wealth of God makes that its seat. And the more people that up thither strain, The more there are to love, the more they love, And like a mirror each doth give and gain.* In this inheritance, then, a man may desire and endeavor to obtain his share without selfish prejudice to others; nay, to fail of our share in it, would be to deprive others of a portion of theirs.

DECEMBER 25TH

It might perhaps be to commit some small logical violence on the terms of the passage to say that "the inheritance of the saints in light" *must* mean purely and only "the possession of light which is the inheritance of the saints." At the same time, the phrase is literally "the inheritance of the saints *in the light;*" and this perhaps makes it the more likely that Paul had in his mind the light as itself the inheritance of the saints—that he held the very substance of the inheritance to be the light. And if we remember that God is light; also that the highest prayer of the Lord for his friends was that they might be one in him and his father; and recall what the apostle said to the Ephesians, that "in him we live and move and have our being," we may be prepared to agree that, although he may not mean to include all possible phases of the inheritance of the saints in the one word *light,* as I think he does, yet the idea is perfectly consistent with his teaching. For the one only thing to make existence a good, the one thing to make it worth having, is just that there should be no film of separation between our life and the life of which ours is an outcome; that we should not only *know* that God is our life, but be aware, in some grand consciousness beyond anything imagination can present to us, of the presence of the making God, in the very process of continuing us the live things he has made us. This is only another way of saying that the very inheritance upon which , as the twice-born sons of our father, we have a claim—that this inheritance is simply the light, God himself, the Light.

DECEMBER 26TH

I f you think of ten thousand things that are good and worth
having, what is it that makes them so but the God in them?
That the loveliness of the world has its origin in the making
will of God, would not content me; I say, the very loveliness of it is
the loveliness of God, for its loveliness is his own lovely thought,
and must be a revelation of that which dwells and moves in
himself. Nor is this all: my interest in its loveliness would vanish, I
should feel that the soul was out of it, if you could persuade me
that God had ceased to care for the daisy, and now cared for
something else instead. The faces of some flowers lead me back to
the heart of God; and, as his child, I hope I feel, in my lowly
degree, what he felt when, brooding over them, he said, "They are
good;" that is, "They are what I mean." If everything were thus
seen in its derivation from God, then the inheritance of the saints,
whatever the form of their possession, would be seen to be light.
All things are God's, not as being in his power—that of course—
but as coming from him. The darkness itself becomes light around
him when we think that verily he hath created the darkness, for
there could have been no darkness but for the light. Without God
there would not even have been nothing; there would not have
existed the idea of nothing, any more than any reality of nothing,
but that he exists and called *something* into being. There is no word
to represent that which is not God, no word for the *where* without
God in it; for it is not, could not be. So I think we may say that the
inheritance of the saints is the share each has in the Light.

DECEMBER 27TH

The true share, in the heavenly kingdom throughout, is not what you have to keep, but what you have to give away. The thing that is mine is the thing I have with the power to give it. The thing I have no power to give a share in, is nowise mine; the thing I cannot share with everyone, cannot be essentially my own. The cry of the thousand splendors which Dante tells us he saw gliding toward them in the planet Mercury, was *Lo, here comes one who will increase our loves!* All the light is ours. God is all ours. Even that in God which we cannot understand is ours. If there were anything in God that was not ours, then God would not be one God. I do not say we must, or can ever know all in God; not throughout eternity shall we ever comprehend God, but he is our father—he must know us, and that in himself which we cannot know, with the same thought, for he is one. We and that which we do not or cannot know, come together in this thought. And this helps us to see how, claiming all things, we have yet shares. For the infinitude of God can only begin and only go on to be revealed, through his infinitely differing creatures—all capable of wondering at, admiring, and loving each other, and so bound all in one in him, each to the others revealing him. For every human being is like a facet cut in the great diamond to which I may dare liken the father of him who likens his kingdom to a pearl. Every man, woman, and child is a revealer of God.

DECEMBER 28ᵀᴴ

I have my message of my great Lord, you have yours. Your dog, your horse tells you about him who cares for all his creatures. None of them came from his *hands*. Perhaps the precious things of the earth, the coal and diamonds, may be said to have come from his hands; but the live things come from his *heart*. Every one of us is something that the other is not, and therefore knows some thing—it may be without knowing that he knows it—which no one else knows; and that it is everyone's business, as one of the kingdom of light, and inheritor in it all, to give his portion to the rest; for we are one family, with God at the head and the heart of it, and Jesus Christ, our elder brother, teaching us of the Father, whom he only knows.

We may say, then, that whatever is the source of joy or love, whatever is pure and strong, whatever wakes aspiration, whatever lifts us out of selfishness, whatever is beautiful or admirable—in a word, whatever is of the light—must make a part, however small it may then prove to be in its proportion, of the inheritance of the saints in the light; for, as in the epistle of James, "Every good gift, and every perfect gift is from above, and cometh down from the Father of lights, with whom is no variableness, neither shadow of turning."

DECEMBER 29TH

Children fear heaven, because of the dismal notions the unchildlike give them of it. I do not see that one should care to present an agreeable picture of it; for, suppose I could persuade a man that heaven was the perfection of all he could desire, what would the man or the truth gain by it? If he knows the Lord, he will not trouble himself about heaven; if he does not know him, he will not be drawn to *him* by it. But would that none presumed to teach the little ones what they know nothing of themselves! What have not children suffered from strong endeavor to desire the things they could not love! Well do I remember the trouble at not being pleased with the prospect of being made a pillar in the house of God, and going no more out! Those words were not spoken to the little ones. Yet are they, literally taken, a blessed promise compared with the notion of a continuous church-going! What boy, however fain to be a disciple of Christ and a child of God, would prefer a sermon to his glorious kite, with God himself for his playmate! He might be ready to part with kite and wind and sun, and go down to the grave for his brothers—but surely not that they might be admitted to an everlasting prayer-meeting! I rejoice that there will be no churches in the high countries, nothing there called religion; for how should there be religion where every throb of the heart says *God!* What room will there be for law, when everything upon which law could lay a *shalt not* will be too loathsome to think of? What room for honesty, where love fills full the law to overflowing—where a man would rather drop into the abyss, than wrong his neighbor one hair's-breadth?

DECEMBER 30TH

Heaven will be continuous touch with God. The very sense of being will in itself be bliss. To those who care only for things, and not for the souls of them, for the truth, the reality of them, the prospect of inheriting light can have nothing attractive, and for their comfort, they may rest assured there is no danger of their being required to take up their inheritance at present. Perhaps they will be left to go on sucking *things* dry, constantly missing the loveliness of them, until they come at last to loathe the lovely husks, turned to ugliness in their false imaginations. The soul of Truth they have lost, because they never loved her. What may they not have to pass through, what purifying fires, before they can even behold her! The notions of so-called Christians concerning the state into which they suppose their friends to have entered, are such as to justify the bitterness of their lamentation over them, and the heathenish doubt whether they shall know them again. Verily it were a wonder if they did! After a year or two of such a fate, they might well be unrecognizable! The early Christians might now and then plague Paul with a foolish question, but was there ever one of them doubted he was going to find his friends again? It is a mere form of Protean unbelief. They believe, they say, that God is love; but they cannot quite believe that he does not make the love in which we are most like him either a mockery or a torture. Little would any promise of heaven be to me if I might not hope to say, "I am sorry; forgive me; let what I did in anger or in coldness be nothing, in the name of God and Jesus!"

DECEMBER 31ST

The man or woman who is not ready to confess, to pour out a heartful of regrets—can such be an inheritor of the light? It is the joy of a true heart of an heir of light, of a child of that God who loves an open soul—the joy of any man who hates the wrong the more because he has done it, to say, "I was wrong; I am sorry." O, the sweet winds of repentance and reconciliation and atonement, that will blow from garden to garden of God! Whatever the place be like, one thing is certain, that there will be endless, infinite atonement, ever-growing love. Certain too it is that whatever the divinely human heart desires, it shall not desire in vain. The light which is God, and which is our inheritance because we are the children of God, insures these things. For the heart which desires, is made thus to desire. For never, in the midst of the good things of this lovely world, have I felt quite at home in it; it is not all I should like for a place to live in. It matters little whether the cause lie in the world or in myself, both being incomplete: God is, and all is well. All that is needed to set the world right is that I care for God as he cares for me; that I have no thought that springs from myself apart from him; that my will and desires keep time and harmony with his music. What springs from myself, and not from God, is evil; it is a perversion of something of God's. Whatever is not of faith is sin; it is a stream cut off from its source. But light is my inheritance through him whose life is the light of men, to wake in them the life of their father in heaven. Loved be the Lord who in himself generated that life which is the light of men!

About the Author

George MacDonald (1824-1905) was a Scottish minister, novelist, and poet, father of the fantasy story, and one of the most inspiring Christian thinkers of all time. A mentor to Lewis Carroll and friend of Mark Twain, MacDonald's writing was a powerful influence on later authors including J.R.R. Tolkien, Madeleine L'Engle, W.H. Auden, and G.K. Chesterton. C.S. Lewis wrote that "I have never concealed the fact that I regarded him as my master; indeed, I fancy I have never written a book in which I did not quote from him."

A wealth of information about George MacDonald can be found on worksofmacdonald.com and on george-macdonald.com.

About the Editor

Jess Lederman came to Christ through the writings of George MacDonald. In gratitude, he administers a popular website, worksofmacdonald.com, that provides exhaustive information on his works and showcases music, art, and writing inspired by the Scotsman. Jess is also an award-winning author. His musings and meditations and information about his writing can be found at jesslederman.com.

403

Wingfold

Celebrating the works of George MacDonald

Wingfold is a quarterly magazine that restores material by and about George MacDonald, in print since 1993. Each issue features the first reprinted reports of MacDonald's extempore sermons and lectures, obscure MacDonald family letters, period articles written by his friends and relatives, and much more. A few of our back issues include previously undocumented short stories and articles MacDonald wrote, and several issues include poems not used in MacDonald's *Poetical Works*. Our contemporary articles explore social and literary influences upon MacDonald's literature. We have documented over seventy topics on which MacDonald lectured, and have chronicled several important friendships and aspects of his life not referenced in the George MacDonald biographies. Every issue also restores some of the numerous beautiful illustrations designed for his fiction and poetry by a wide diversity of important artists.

For information on ordering subscriptions or back issues, contact Barbara Amerll at b_amell@q.com.

Made in the USA
Monee, IL
30 December 2024

4293f7c6-6e01-4b69-b837-5aa886aa1d97R01